Magazine Editorial Graphics

P·I·E BOOKS

Magazine Editorial Graphics

P·I·E BOOKS
Villa Phoenix Suite 301, 4-14-6 Komagome, Toshima-ku, Tokyo 170 Japan
Tel: 03-3940-8302 Fax: 03-3576-7361
e-mail: piebooks@bekkoame.or.jp

ISBN4-89444-046-6 C3070

First published in Germany 1997 by:
NIPPAN / Nippon Shuppan Hanbai Deutschland GmbH
Krefelder Strasse 85, D-40549
Düsseldorf, Germany
Tel: 0211-5048080/89 Fax: 0211-5049326

ISBN3-931884-03-1
Printed in Singapore

P·I·E Books wishes to extend thanks to the following publishers for allowing us
to use their work on this book jacket.

Detour / Detour Inc.
Premiere (French) / Hachette Filipacchi Presse
Ray Gun / Ray Gun Publishing Inc.
W Magazine / Fairchild Publications

EDITORIAL NOTES
CREDIT FORMAT

雑誌名　MAGAZINE TITLE
発行年月日 / シーズン
ISSUE DATE / SEASON
制作スタッフ PRODUCTION STAFF
出版社 PUBLISHER
国名 COUNTRY

各表紙の横にメインクレジットを表記しま
した。
メインクレジットと異なるクレジットのみ
各作品の下に表記されています。

Main credits are listed beside each cover.
Additional credits appear below other artwork
when different from main credits.

Introduction

In today's computerized world of seemingly unlimited information access, magazines have emerged whose cool, raw sensibilities are influencing creators to be more conceptual.

These seven remarkable men and women, whose unique and innovative ideas continually challenge society's taboos, share their views on magazine-making.

In unserer heutigen computerisierten Welt mit scheinbar grenzenlosem Zugang zu Informationen sind Zeitschriften entstanden, deren coole, rauhe Sensibilität Designer beim konzeptionellen Denken beeinflussen.

Sieben bemerkenswerte Frauen und Männer, deren einzigartige und innovative Ideen kontinuierlich die gesellschaftlichen Tabus herausfordern, vermitteln ihre Ansichten über Zeitschriftengestaltung.

コンピュータリゼーションがもたらした情報氾濫の中で、クールでチープな雑誌の感触は、クリエーター達を、よりコンセプチュアルな物作りへと導いている。

斬新なアイデアでタブーに挑戦し続ける、注目のクリエーター7名に、彼らの雑誌作りについて語ってもらった。

*SURFACE

Riley John-donnell

The 90's are the 'aesthetic decade.' We have witnessed the photographer, the designer and the stylist gain status equal to that of a rock star. Although the imagery of the 90's has toyed with taboo and attempted to challenge established notions of how the printed media communicates, the creative community itself has lost interest in what their imagery communicates. It is stated that communication is a 90% visual process. I find the advertising more intriguing than the editorials in most fashion magazines.

Perhaps this is because photographers and designers have lost interest in concept, whereas advertising agencies must be inherently conceptual in order to sell an idea / product. Fashion magazines have the capacity to convey more than pretty pictures: they can offer more than discussions of hemlines, color forecasts and how thin a woman should or should not be. I believe that fashion editorials are under-exploited venues for social commentary. *Surface is an attempt to balance beautiful imagery with concept, to utilize our pages as a way of conveying our concerns and analyzing the culture we live in.

Richard Klein

I get irritated with all the talk about tangible magazines becoming obsolete in the next 'era' (due to the influential presence of the web). The future, when everyone actually does own a computer, is when I think people will turn solely to the web rather than to magazines for information. Moving into the future, we may see less of an abundance of consumer magazines, but possibly an influx of industry magazines that are presented more like consumer books. This is when magazines will have to offer more than just an abundance of information. Printing will become finer, photography more exquisite and design more original. If consumers are going to spend money on subscriptions, for information they can receive on the web, they will demand a bit more. But as far as magazines be coming obsolete... it will never happen.

Profiles:
Riley John-donnell
Co-Publisher / Art Director, *Surface magazine. Art Activist
Richard Klein
Co-Publisher / Art Director, *Surface magazine

Riley John-donnell

Die 90er Jahre sind ide 'Dekade der Ästhetik'. Wir haben erlebt, daß Photographen, Designer und Stylisten einen Status vergleichbar dem eines Rock Stars erreicht haben. Obgleich die Bilder der 90er Jahre damit spielten, Tabus zu verletzen und etablierte Gefühle zu provozieren, hat die kreative Gemeinde selbst das Interesse daran verloren, was ihre Bilderwelt kommuniziert. Es ist erwiesen, daß Kommunikation zu 90% ein visueller Prozeß ist. Ich finde die Anzeigenwerbung spannender als die Editorials in den meisten Modezeitschriften. Vielleicht ist das deshalb, weil Photographen und Designer das Interesse an Konzepten verloren haben, wohingegen Werbeagenturen prinzipiell konzeptionell arbeiten müssen, um eine Idee oder ein Produkt zu verkaufen. Modezeitschriften haben die Kapazität, mehr als schöne, bunte Bilder zu transportieren: sie können mehr anbieten als nur die Diskussion von Hermelinen, Farbtrends und wie schlank eine Frau sein oder auch nicht sein sollte. Ich glaube, daß Zeitschriftenartikel über Mode ein unbearbeitetes Feld für soziale Kommentare sind. *Surface ist ein Versuch, wunderschöne Bilder und ein Konzept miteinander in Einklang zu bringen, unsere Seiten dafür zu nutzen, unsere Bedeken zu vermitteln und die Kultur, in der wir leben, zu analysieren.

Richard Klein

Mich irritiert all dieses Gerede darüber, daß gegenständliche, anfaßbare Magazine in der nächsten Zukunft verschwinden werden... (wegen der einflußreichen Präsenz des World Wide Web). Schaut man in die Zukunft, wenn jedermann dann tatsächlich einen Computer besitzt, erst dann werden Leute meines Erachtens nach für Informationen ins Web gehen, anstatt dafür in Magazinen zu blättern. Bewegen wir uns in die Zukunft, so werden wir vielleicht nicht mehr diesen Überfluß an Konsum-Zeitschriften sehen, aber vielleicht einen Einbruch von Industriemagazinen, die eher präsentiert werden wie Konsum-Bücher. Dies geschieht, wenn Zeitschriften mehr anzubieten haben als nur eine Masse von Informationen. Der Druck wird anspruchsvoller, Photographien exquisiter und Design origineller. Wenn Konsumenten Geld für Zeitschriften-Abonnements ausgeben, für Informationen, die sie sich kostenlos aus dem Web holen können, werden sie etwas mehr fordem. Aber daß Zeitschriften überflüssig werden... das wird nie passieren.

Profile:
Rilley John-donnell
Mitherausgeber / Art Director, *Surface magazine. kunst-Aktivist
Richard Klein
Mitherausgeber / Art Director, *Surface magazine.

ライリー・ジョン・ドネル

　90年代は美の時代である。われわれはフォトグラファー、グラフィックデザイナー、スタイリストといった人々が、ロックスターにも等しいステイタスを得るのをこの目で見てきた。一方で、90年代はタブーに挑戦し、印刷メディアが伝達手段としてどうあるべきか、という既成概念を壊そうとした時代であったにも関わらず、クリエイティブな人々は、自らの創造物で何かを伝えようとすることに興味を失ってしまったのである。伝達手段は、90%まで視覚のプロセスであるといわれている。ほとんどのファッション誌は、今やエディトリアルよりも広告の方がおもしろい。おそらくこれは、フォトグラファーやデザイナーがコンセプトに興味を失い、広告代理店が本来、アイデアや製品を売るためにコンセプチュアルなものだからではないだろうか。ファッション誌はきれいな写真を見せるためだけにあるのではない。ヘムラインやカラーの予測や、女性がスリムであるべきか否かの論議以上のものを提供できるはずである。私はファッション誌が社会批評となり得ると信じている。*SURFACEは、美しいイメージにコンセプトを取り入れようとする試みである。1ページ1ページにわれわれの考えを表わし、私たちが生きる文化を分析しようとしているのである。

リチャード・クライン

　インターネットの存在で、雑誌は次の「時代」にはすたれていくだろう、といった話を聞くたびにいらいらしてしまう。将来、だれもがコンピューターを1台ずつ持つ時代がきたら、その時こそ雑誌が完全に取って代わられる時だと思う。時代の移行期には、いわゆる消費者向けの一般誌は数少なくなっていくかもしれないが、おそらくより書籍に近い形態の企業・産業誌は増えていくだろう。その時雑誌には、大量の情報提供以上のもの、つまり、より質の高い印刷、より美しい写真、よりオリジナリティのあるデザインといったものが必要とされるのである。人々は、インターネットで簡単に得られるような情報を定期購読するために、お金を使うのではない。雑誌に対する要求はもっと高まってくるだろう。しかし、雑誌がすたれるとは…そんなことは起こり得ない。

プロフィール：
ライリー・ジョン・ドネル
＊SURFACE 共同出版人／アートディレクター。アート・アクティヴィスト
リチャード・クライン
＊SURFACE 共同出版人／アートディレクター

COLORS

Oliviero Toscani

Colors is an idea, a challenge to see if it is possible to create an interesting magazine, distinctive from the many already in existence. First, I took away everything on which other magazines are based, 'News' and 'Celebrities', and tried to produce an extemporary magazine, disconnected from the fashion world but with a particular style, where text and image together create a new, modern language. Each issue of Colors addresses, develops and explores a single theme: Religion, Race, Paradise, Ecology, Aids, Sport, War, etc... Colors is attracted by everything which is different, different from the way we are, knowing that we too are different from the rest of the world. Colors recognizes the great value of diversity. Colors is against monoculture.

Profile:
Born in Milan in 1942, I studied photography at the Kunstgewebschule in Zurich from 1961 to 1965 and then began working with fashion magazines, including Elle, Vogue, Uomo Vogue, Lei Donna, GQ, Mademoiselle and Harper's. I started to create advertising campaigns for the image of United Colors of Benetton in 1982. Fabrica, the center for research in the world of communication, and Colors, are an integral part thereof.

Colors ist eine Idee, eine Herausforderung, um zu sehen, ob es möglich ist, ein interessantes Magazin zu schaffen, anders als die vielen anderen existierenden. Zunächst nahm ich alles, auf dem andere Zeitschriften aufbauen, 'Neuigkeiten' und 'Berühmtheiten', und versuchte ein zeitloses Magazin zu schaffen, abgekoppelt von der Modewelt, aber mit einem speziellen Stil, bei dem Text und Bilder zusammen eine neue, moderne Sprache schaffen. Jede Ausgabe von Colors widmet sich einem bestimmen Thema: Religion, Rasse, Paradies, Ökologie, Aids, Sport, Krieg etc. Colors kümmert sich um alles, das verschieden ist, verschieden davon wie wir Sind, wissend, das auch wir vom Rest der Welt verschieden sind. Colors akzeptiertlen großen Wert von Unterschieden Colors ist gegen Monokulturen.

Profil:
Geboren in Mailand 1942, Studium der Photographie an der Kunstgewerbeschule Zürich von 1961 bis 1965. Dann Arbeit für Modemagazine(Elle, Vogue, Uomo Vogue, Lei Donna, GQ, Mademoiselle und Harper's). Erste Werbekampagne für United Colors of Benetton 1982, Fabrica, Forschungszentrum in der Welt der Kommunikation, und Colors sind integraler Bestandteil des Benetton-Konzepts.

　COLORSは、雑誌そのものがひとつのアイデアです。すでに存在する多くの雑誌とは異なった、おもしろい雑誌を創ろうというチャレンジでもあります。私はまず他の雑誌がベースとするもの、つまり『ニュース』や『有名な人々や物ごと』という要素を取り払うことから始めました。ファッションとは関係なく、けれどもしっかりしたスタイルを持ち、テキストとビジュアルがまったく新しいモダンな言語を奏でるような、超時代的な雑誌をつくろうとしたのです。
　COLORSの1号1号が、宗教、民族、パラダイス、エコロジー、エイズ、スポーツ、戦争などといった単一のテーマを特集し、発展させ、深く掘り下げています。COLORSは、異(い)なるもの、私たちの在り方とは異なるものに興味を向けています。私たちとはあまりにも違った他の世界が存在することを認め、そのうえで、全てのものに大きな価値を置いています。COLORSはモノカルチャーに対抗しているのです。

プロフィール：
1942年ミラノ生まれ。61年から65年にかけてチューリッヒの美術学校 Kunstgewebeschuleで写真を学ぶ。
後、Elle、Vogue、Uomo Vogue、Lei Donna、GQ、Mademoiselle、Harper's などのファッション雑誌を経て、1982年より、United Colors of Benettonの広告キャンペーンをプロデュースしている。ワールド・コミュニケーション・リサーチ・センターである Fabrica、そしてCOLORSはその中枢となるプロジェクトである。

CITIZEN K

Vincent Bergerat

You can't play Doom on a typewriter.

Ideas, jokes, statements are interwoven for the viewer / reader / netsurfer, some are a result of our relationship with the new tools we use, working while listening to a record and trying a new game at the same time -- a new way of thinking about magazines.

Design: Plays with questions like: what is a magazine? what does it look like? is there another way? Using simple, funny things, like titling every story on the second double spread in one issue, and then on the third in the next issue; or making a whole story with one page repeating itself over and over (6 times, actually); or when another magazine has featured a subject before you, reproducing exactly the same layout.

Topic: Binds the whole issue in features, pictures, fashion stories, conceived to match / enlighten / fuck up.

Typography: Played in different ways. The main type, 'classic', quiet, very legible, is mixed with 'samples', exploring the history of typography.

Introducing new type design, to suit specific moods and needs, like designing a perfect type for an imaginary milk brand.

Technology: Play with what you've got: computers. Talk about how a magazine is made today. Play with pixels, computer and software aesthetics, even printing machines.

Profile:
Art Director, *Citizen K / Citizen International*.

Auf einer Schreibmaschine kann man nicht Doom spielen. Ideen, Witze, Aussagen sind für den Betrachter / Leser / Internet-Surfer verwoben. Einige sind das Resultat unserer Beziehung zu den neuen Werkzeugen, die wir benutzen- arbeitend, gleichzeitig Musik hörend und ein neues Spiel probierend, ein neuer Weg des Denkens über Magazine.

Design: Spiel mit Fragen wie 'Was ist ein Magazin?', 'Wie sieht es aus?', 'Gibt's noch andere Wege?'. Einfache, witzige Dinge, wie die Plazierung der Titelstory auf der zweiten Doppelseite einer Ausgabe, dann der dritten Doppelseite in der nächsten usw.; oder Präsentation einer Einseiten- Story 6 mal wiederholt auf den Folgeseiten; oder wenn ein anderes Magazin eine Story schneller gebracht hat, Produzieren dieser Geschichte in exakt dem gleichen Layout.

Thema: Binden der ganzen Ausgabe in Features, Bilder, Modegeschichten, alles um zu erhellen / zu irritieren / zu kopieren.

Typographie: auf verschiedene Weise gespielt. Die Hauptschrift klassisch, leise, sehr gut lesbar, gemischt mit Beispielen, die Geschichte der Schrift erforschend.

Neue Schriftdesigns werden vorgestellt, die spezifischen Stimmungen und Ansprüchen gerecht werden, so zum Beispiel die perfekte Schrift für eine imaginäre Milchmarke.

Technologie: Spiele mit dem, was Du hast: Computer. Sprich darüber, wie ein Magazin heute gemacht wird. Spiele mit Pixeln, Computern und Software-Ästhetik, selbst mit Druckmaschinen.

Profil:
Art Director, *Citizen K / Citizen International*.

タイプライターでは、『DOOM』はできない。

この雑誌には、メディア・ウォッチャー、読書家、そしてネットサーファーといった人々のためのアイデアやジョーク、主張が無尽に織り込まれている。それは、新しいツールを使った結果であったり、レコードを聞きながら、新しいゲーム…新しい雑誌の方向性とは何か、にチャレンジした結果である時もある。

デザイン・コンセプト：雑誌とは何か？どんなかたちのものか？ほかに方法はあるのか？こんな質問と常に戯れる。シンプルでおもしろいことをやってみる。例えば、ある号では2つめの見開きページに目次をもってくるとする。だが次の号では3つめの見開きページにもってくる、といった具合に。または、1つのストーリーをつくるために、同じテキスト、同じ内容の1ページを何度も何度も（6回ということもあった）繰り返してみる。あるいは、別の雑誌がぼくたちより先に何かの特集をした時は、それとまったく同じレイアウトを複製してみる等。

トピック：それぞれが調和し、啓発しあうような『ファックな』話題や特集、写真、ファッションのストーリーで1冊を埋め尽くす。

タイポグラフィー：いろいろなフォントで遊ぶ。メインは静的で、読みやすいクラシックなもの。それに遊びを加えたサンプル的なものを合わせ、タイポグラフィーの歴史を探訪する。特定のムードやニーズに見合うように、新しいデザインを導入することもある。例えば、実際にはないミルクのブランドロゴのために、パーフェクトなフォントをデザインする等。

テクノロジー：現在ぼくたちにあるもの、すなわちコンピューターと遊んでみる。最近の雑誌がどんな風に作られているか論じる。ピクルとコンピューターとソフトウェアの美学と、そして印刷機械とも遊ぶ。

プロフィール：
Citizen K / Citizen International
アート・ディレクター

rana

A Poem of *rana*

Once upon a time, there was an idea for a magic magazine dedicated to both a holistic philosophy of Integrated Strategic Design and a policy of inviting students, global leaders and sometimes even competitors to join with its own staff in forming a new kind of community, a community that could powerfully use its many different visions and voices to incisively focus on ideas that mattered, and this magazine's team, despite numerous challenges to its very existence, believed in honesty, optimism and provocation -- by principle -- and they needed such a foundation, because many people outside the company didn't understand that the magazine was tuned to the antennae of an ascendant creative generation and even fewer realized how big an expense it was for the company that produced it --but then the magic became real, and the magazine was finally completed, and it made people stop, smile and even think -- precisely because it wasn't like all the others, and even though the team members couldn't all live together happily ever after, the fact that we cut through most of the crap made our arduous efforts seeking a new information architecture completely worth doing.

Profile:
There was no single person that made *rana* happen. The team comprised frogdesign staff, outside consultants and friends; designers, thinkers and writers from the United States and the European community enriched its look, feel and content. We hope more contributors from around the world will join us, and we thank you in advance for sending your thoughts to: info@frogdesign.com.

Ein Gedicht für *rana*

Es war einmal, da gab es eine Idee für ein magisches Magazin, gewidmet beidem, einer holistischen Philosophie von integriertem strategischem Design und einer Politik, Studenten einzuladen, globale Führer und manchmal sogar Wettbewerber, um sich mit den eigenen Leuten zusammenzutun und um eine neue Art von Gemeinschaft zu formen, eine Gemeinschaft, die kraftvoll ihre vielen verschiedenen Visionen und Stimmen nutzen kann, um sich scharf auf wichtige Ideen zu konzentrieren; und das Team dieser Zeitschrift, trotz vielfältiger existenzbedrohenden Herausforderungen glaubte an Ehrlichkeit, Optimismus und Provokation- aus Prinzip- und sie brauchten solch ein Fundament, weil viele Leute außerhalb der Firma nicht verstanden, daß das Magazin auf die Antennen einer absteigenden, kreativen Generation, ausgenchtet war, und noch weniger erkannten die Höhe der Ausgaben für die Firma, die es produzierte- aber dann wurde das Magische Wirklichkeit. Und die Zeitschrift wurde schließlich vollendet, Und dies machte die Leute anhalten, lächeln und aucfh denken, präzise weil sie nicht wie alle anderen war, und das obgleich die Team-Mitglieder danach nicht glücklich miteinander leben konnten bis zum Ende ihrer Tage. Der Fakt, daß wir den meisten Mist wegwarfen, rechtfertigte unsere ausdauernden Bemühungen auf der Suche nach einer neuen Informationsarchitektur voll und ganz.

Profil:

Es gab keine Einzelperson, die *rana* machte. Das Team bestand aus Mitarbeitern von frogdesign, firmenfremden Beratern und Freunden; Designer, Denker und Texter aus den USA und der Europäischen Gemeinshcaft trugen zum Erscheinungsbild, Feeling und Inhalt bei. Wir hoffen, daß uns mehr Beiträge aus aller Welt erreichen. Wir danken jetzt schon jedem, der uns seine Gedanken mitteilt: info@frogdesign.com.

rana へささげる詩

　昔々、統合的戦略的デザインという全体論の哲学に基づく、魔法のような雑誌のアイデアがあった。この雑誌は、学生やグローバル・リーダーや、時には競合他社までもがスタッフとして参加し、新しい型のコミュニティをつくって、多くの異なったヴィジョンと声を価値ある考え方に鋭くフォーカスしようとしていた。制作チームは、存在そのものの危機を何度も経験したにも関わらず、『誠実さ』と『楽観主義』と『挑発』とを信奉していた。彼らにはそのような組織が必要だった。なぜなら外部の多くの人々は、その雑誌がクリエイティブな人々にはアンテナのような存在であることを理解していなかったし、さらに多くの人々がその雑誌を制作することが会社にとって多大な出費となっていることをわかっていなかったからだ。雑誌が現実のものとなり、ついに完成を見ると、人々を立ち止まらせ、笑わせ、さらに考えさせる機会を与えた。その理由は正確には、この雑誌がその他多数とは全く違っていたからだ。制作スタッフが 必ずしもその後うまくやっていけなかったとしても、さまざまなくだらないいさかいを切り抜けて、全く新しい情報体系をつくろうと骨の折れる努力をしたことは、価値あることだった。

プロフィール：

rana はだれか１人の人間が生みだしたものではありません。制作チームはフロッグデザインのスタッフ、外部コンサルタント、そして友人たちから成り立っています。合衆国およびヨーロッパのメンバーから成るデザイナー、コンセプター、ライターなどがチームの顔触れを豊かにし、感覚を研ぎ澄まし、内容をより深いものにしています。私たちは、もっともっと世界中の人々に参加してもらいたいと考えています。あなたの考えを送っていただければ幸いです。
info@frogdesign.com

VOGUE

Donald Scheider

For me art directing *Paris Vogue* means pushing 'elegance' to new limits. Every issue is a reinvention, it somehow has to reflect the fun we're having putting it together. I want to take risks, find new talents, new visions, new faces and mix them with the old masters of *Vogue*. This work is completely about teamwork, the combined effort of editors and photographers, stylists and graphic designers, production people and printers.

The actual design should transport this 'elegance' with a very modern edge. I like concepts and layouts which work on different emotional levels, which surprise and have quality. For me the biggest compliment is when a hip young design student likes the newest issue and cover as much as a 75-year-old French coulture client.

I think the future of magazines will be based on daring editing, which completely challenges the readers' eyes and brains.

Profile:
I was born and educated in Switzerland. My first job at a magazine was in 1985, art directing *The East Village Eye* in New York City. It was a magazine with an impossibly low budget but great creativity, lots of artists and enthusiastic young writers. *Fame* magazine followed. Then, in 1991, I moved to *Tempo* in Hamburg, and later to *German Vogue*. For the last three years I have been in Paris at *French Vogue*.

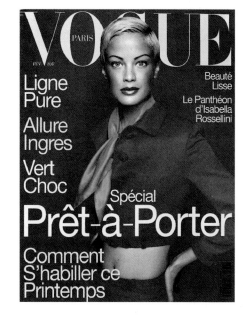

Art Director bei *Vogue* zu sein bedeutet für mich, Eleganz zu neuen Grenzen zu führen. Jede Ausgabe ist eine Neuerfindung. Sie muß irgendwie den Spaß reflektieren, den wir haben, wenn wir sie zusammenstellen. Ich möchte Risiken eingehen, neue Talente finden, neue Visionen, neue Gesichter und diese mischen mit den alten Meistern von *Vogue*. Diese Arbeit ist nichts als Teamwork, die kombinierte Anstrengung von Herausgebern und Photographen, von Stilisten und Graphik-Designern, Produktionern und Druckern.

Das aktuelle Design soll diese 'Eleganz' mit einem modernen Touch transportieren. Ich liebe Konzepte und Layouts, die auf verschiedenen emotionalen Ebenen arbeiten, die überraschen und Qualität haben. Für mich ist das größte Kompliment, wenn die neueste Ausgabe mit ihrem Cover einem jungen Design-Student genauso gefällt wie dem 75jährigen französischen Modedesigner.

Ich denke die Zukunft von Zeitschriften basiert darauf, sich Neues zuzutrauen, das die Augen und das Gehirn des Lesers total herausfordert.

Profil:
Geboren und erzogen in der Schweiz. Erste Arbeit bei einer Zeitschrift 1985 als Art Director der *The East Village Eye* in New York, einer Zeitschrift mit einem unmöglich kleinen Etat, aber großer Kreativität, vielen Künstlern und enthusiastischen jungen Schreibern. Dann folgte das magazin *Fame*. Dann 1991 *Tempo* in Hamburg und später die deutsche *Vogue*. In den letzten drei Jahren bei der französischen *Vogue* in Paris.

私にとってVOGUEフランス版のアートディレクションとは、（そのコンセプトである）「エレガンス」をいかに新しく、極限のところで表現するか、だといえます。毎号毎号が新たな創造であり、それはまた、私たちの感じている雑誌作りの楽しさを、何らかの形で反映したものでなければなりません。そのためにリスクを負っても、新しい才能、新しいヴィジョンを持った人を発掘し、そのニューフェイスをキャリアあるVOGUEの名クリエーターたちと組ませるのです。

この仕事はチームワークが全てです。編集者、フォトグラファー、スタイリスト、グラフィックデザイナー、そしてプロダクションチームに印刷業者、彼らひとりひとりの努力が１つになって作りあげるものなのです。

実際のデザインはこの「エレガンス」を最高に新しく、シャープな方法で伝えるものでなければなりません。私は見る人の異なったレベルの感情を引き出し、しかも新鮮な驚きと質の高さを内包したコンセプトやレイアウトが好きです。私にとって最もうれしい評価は、ヒップな若いデザイン科の学生も、フランス・クチュールの老デザイナーも、共に今回の号は良かったと言ってくれることなのです。

雑誌の将来は、思いきった大胆な編集にかかっていると思います。読者の鍛えられた目や頭に挑戦するものでなければなりません。

プロフィール：
スイス生まれ。スイスで教育を受ける。1985年 *The East Village Eye in New York City* のアートディレクションで雑誌の世界に入る。この雑誌は低予算ではあったが、多くのアーティストや熱心な若いライターが参加し、非常にクリエイティブな雑誌であった。その後、*Fame magazine* に移り、91年にはハンブルグの *Tempo*、そして *German Vogue* とキャリアを重ねる。現在はパリで *French Vogue* をディレクションして3年になる。

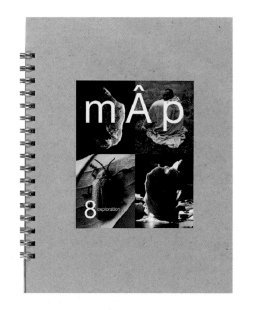

MAP

Robert Bergman-Unger

Originally, *MAP* was just another client for my design and advertising company. They came from Switzerland and asked me to redesign the magazine. It was called *Das Papier* and needed lots of help. The first thing I did was change its name to *MAP*, which is more international and easier to pronounce around the world. Then I brought to it international content, big name talent, and a point of view that really is exciting because it became a totally free expression of creativity. The magazine is almost completely funded by corporate sponsorship and has become a really fun outlet for everyone in the studio to create. It has kind of taken on a life of its own... it flows, evolves, and changes with the moods and interests of the team. It is never the same! When we get overwhelmed with other work, it suffers, but there is always time to create it... because there are no boundaries...... It's about what's cool and what we like.

Profile:
Robert Bergman-Unger works and lives in New York as the owner and creative director of Bergman-Unger Associates, for which he has designed ad campaigns and directed TV commercials for such clients as Aramis, David Byrne, IBM, JVC, Lanvin, Mitsubishi, Moschino, MTV, and Ryuichi Sakamoto.
Bergman-Ungar Associates also creates all the advertising and design for New York's Fashion Collections. Robert Bergman-Ungar was formerly the creative director of *Vogue* magazine, and the founding creative director of *Blindspot* magazine.

Ursprünglich war *MAP* nur ein weiterer Kunde für meine Design- und Werbeagentur. Sie kamen aus der Schweiz und baten um ein Redesign der Zeitschrift. Sie nannte sich *Das Papier* und brauchte viel Hilfe. Zuallererst änderte ich den Namen in *MAP*, was internationaler ist und rund um die Welt leicht auszusprechen. Dann brachte ich internationale Beiträge, große Namen und eine Blickrichtung, die aufregend ist, weil sie eine total freie Entfaltung der Kreativität erlaubte. Das Magazin ist fast gänzlich durch Firmensponsoring finanziert. Es entwickelte sich richtig zur Spaßquelle für jeden im Studio, der daran arbeitet. Es hat eine Art Eigenleben entwickelt... es fließt, wächst und wandelt sich mit den Stimmungen und Interessen des Teams. Es ist nie das gleiche! Wenn wir überschüttet sind mit Arbeit, leidet es, aber es gibt immer Zeit für die Kreation... eben weil es keine Grenzen gibt... Es geht darum, was cool ist und was wir mògen.

Profil:
Robert Bergmann-Unger arbeitet und lebt in New York als Inhaber und Creativ Director von Bergmann-Unger Associates. Er hat Werbekompagnen gestaltet und Regie für TV-Spots geführt. Kunden sind Aramis, David Byrne, IBM, JVC, Lanvin, Mitsubishi, Maschino, MTV und Ryuichi Sakamoto. Bergmann-Unger war vorher Creativ Director der Zeitschrift *Vogue* und Creativ Director bei der Gründung des *Blindspot* magazine.

もともとMAPは、私の経営する広告制作会社のクライアントの1つだった。スイスからやってきた彼らに、この雑誌をリニューアルするよう頼まれたのである。当時はDas Papierという名の雑誌で、かなり手入れを必要とする状態だった。まず最初に、雑誌のタイトルをMAPにした。よりインターナショナルなイメージで、世界中どこでも発音しやすいからである。そして、グローバルな内容と、著名なクリエーターの採用、自由な創造と表現というエキサイティングな視点を確立した。MAPはほぼ１００％スポンサーシップがとれるようになり、スタジオのスタッフにとっても楽しい発表の場になったのである。

チームのムードや興味にあわせて流動的で、進化し、変化していく様子は、まるで雑誌が生命をもっているようでさえある。同じものは二度とできない。私たちが他の仕事で閉口したときなどは苦しいが、必ずそれを作る時間はある。なぜならクリエイティブに限界はないのだから。何がクールで、我々が何を好きなのか、だけである。

プロフィール：
ニューヨークをベースに活動するバーグマン・アンガー・アソシエイツ社のオーナー兼クリエイティブ・ディレクター。主なクライアントにAramis、David Byrne、IBM、JVC、Lanvin、Mitsubishi、Maschino、MTV、坂本龍一など。また、ニューヨーク・ファッション・コレクションではすべての広告とデザインを手がける。元、*Vogue* のクリエイティブ・ディレクター、*Blindspot* magazine の創刊クリエイティブ・ディレクター。

OYSTER

Monica Nakata

Oyster is a synthesis of progressive fashion and lifestyle, generated into a visually and mentally stimulating high-gloss bimonthly -- the most cutting-edge magazine in Australia. Showcasing Australia's foremost talented and creative, *Oyster*'s definitive point of view shines from the myriad of sameness on magazine shelves.

Oyster does not dictate seasonal fashion trends, rather presenting contemporary styles from an array of the most creative non-conformists. We encourage photographers to develop creative concepts with a free rein, therefore producing the highest quality material. *Oyster* is produced by a fresh young team, who are synchronised to the progressionist young adult! I feel that people's lives are so diverse in the 90's, subjected to so much visual communication that their interests have become specialised, and niche-marketed magazines such as *Oyster* bridge the gap successfully. There are no longer men's and women's magazines, they are gender indiscriminate. *Oyster* is an interactive composition, a universal collaborative of ideas, fashion, lifestyle and forefrontness, escalating the aspirations of our market and filling the void in the present Australian market.

Profile:
I was drawn to publishing at the age of 10 years, My earliest memory that conjured up a very significant emotion was the fresh smell of a glossy magazine just released on the newstands. The combination of lollies and magazines sent me to giddy heights. I started working in publishing at the age of 19, in advertising sales. I worked on a free weekly entertainment paper and at the age of 21 I established a free bimonthly fashion paper. When I was 24 years old, I felt that the Australian youth culture needed a more alternative, cutting-edge magazine filled with fashion and lifestyle, hence *Oyster*!

Oyster ist eine Synthese von progressiver Mode und Livestyle, umgesetzt in eine visuell und mental stimulierende glänzende Zweimonatszeitschrift - das herausragende 'Cutting-Edge-Magazin' Australiens. Die kreativen Talente des fünften Kontinents sind hier versammelt, sodaß sich *Oyster* von den vielen Magazin im Zeitschriftenregal abhebt. *Oyster* diktiert keine saisonalen Modetrends, sondern präsentiert zeitgemäße Stile, geschaffen von einem Spektrum kreativer Nonokonformisten. Wir ermutigen Photographen, völlig frei neue Konzepte zu entwickeln, wodurch hochqualitatives Material entsteht. *Oyster* wird von einem frischen, jungen Team von Designern aus der Welt der progressiven jungen Erwachsenen produziert. Wir fühlen, daß das Leben der Leute in den 90er Jahren sehr unterschiedlich ist, ausgesetzt so vielfältiger visueller Ansprache, daß ihre Interessen sehr spezialisiert werden. Nischenmarkt-Magazine wie *Oyster* überbrücken die Kluft erfolgreich. Es gibt nicht mehr Frauen-bzw. Männerzeitschriften, diese sind geschlechtsdiskriminierend. *Oyster* ist eine interaktive Komposition, eine universale Kooperative von Ideen, Mode, Lifestyle und Trendführerschaft, die eine Lücke am Markt füllt und die hohen Ansprüchen gerecht wird.

Profil:
Schon mit 10 Jahren hat mich das Publizieren angezogen. Meine früheste Erinnerung, die eine tiefe Emotion heraufbeschwor, war der frische Geruch von Hochglanzmagazinen, die gerade am Zeitungskiosk ankamen. Die Kombination von Lutschern und Zeitschriften brachte mich auf schwindelnde Höhen. Mit 19 begann ich, im Verlagswesen als Verkäufer für Werbeanzeigen zu arbeiten. Das war ein wöchentliches Unterhaltungsmagazin. Mit 21 gründete ich ein zweimonatlich erscheinendes, kostenloses Modeblatt. Mit 24 dachte ich, daß die australische Jugendkultur eine alternative, hochmoderne Zeitschrift braucht mit Mode und Lifestyle, und daher *Oyster*!

[oyster]
autumn 97
WORLD FASHION
FEB/MARCH AUD $6.95
issue 0:10

The Prodigy
The best rock band in the world?
Kangaroos
Culling a national icon
Extreme Sports
The best high of a lifetime

you have been
tribalised

Science Fiction
Books th
the futu
Samuel L. Jackson
The go
accord

*Oyster*はファッションとライフスタイルのジンテーゼです。刺激的なビジュアルとコンテンツが、上質な光沢感のある誌面に広がり、オーストラリアではいま最も新しい隔月刊マガジンです。オーストラリアでも一流の、才能あふれたクリエイティブな人々をショーケースし、その完成された視点は、書店の棚に無数に並ぶ雑誌の一群からひときわ輝いてみえます。*Oyster*は毎シーズンのファッション・トレンドを押しつけたりせず、最もクリエイティブな「非保守派」デザイナーたちの、現在(いま)のスタイルをプレゼンテーションします。カメラマンには制約をいっさいつけず、彼ら自身のコンセプトで撮らせているため、最もクオリティの高い作品ができ上がるのです。

*Oyster*はプログレッシブなヤング・アダルトの読者と同世代であるフレッシュな若いチームが制作しています。90年代、人々のライフスタイルは多様化し、興味の対象は分化されました。そこでは*Oyster*のようなターゲット性の高い雑誌のみが、彼らの要求を満たすことができるのです。もはや、男性誌、女性誌といった呼称は適当ではありません。雑誌に性の差別はないのです。

*Oyster*はインタラクティヴな構成で、アイデア、ファッション、ライフスタイル、そして『新しさ』を全てコラボレーションしています。そして、マーケット全体の競争力を刺激し、また、現在のオーストラリアのマーケットの隙間を埋めようとしているのです。

プロフィール：
私が出版という仕事に強く魅かれたのは、わずか１０才の時でした。街角のニューススタンドに並んだばかりの、新鮮な匂いのするつやつやした上質の紙に、私の中で何かとても重要な感情が芽生えたことを覚えています。ロリーポップキャンディとそういった雑誌の魅力が一体となって、幼い私を興奮させ、そんな自分をばかげているとさえ感じたほどでした。19才の時出版業界に入り、広告営業の仕事を始めました。週刊のフリーペーパーを経て、21才の時には隔月刊のファッションのフリーペーパーを自ら創刊しました。その後、私はオーストラリアの若い世代のカルチャーが、もっと今までになく新しい、ファッションやライフスタイルの情報にあふれた雑誌を必要としていることを強く感じ、２４才で*Oyster*を創刊したのです。

Interview
1 **Mar. 1997**
2 **Dec. 1996**

EDITOR	Ingrid Sischy
ART DIRECTOR	Christiaan Kuypers
DESIGNER	Christiaan Kuypers
PHOTOGRAPHERS	1 Ellen von Unwerth,
	2 Inez van Lamsweerde,
	2 Vinoodh Matadin
STYLISTS	1 Victoria Bartlett,
	2 Cathy Kasterine
PUBLISHER	Brant Publications, Inc.
	USA

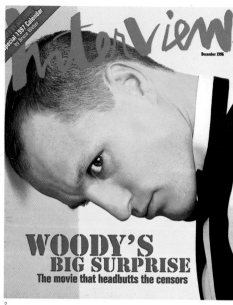

1

2

1-800-TRY-CASH

Country's coolest highwayman, Johnny Cash, once again rides rock's rails
on his transcendent new album, *Unchained*. Here he talks with his daughter Rosanne Cash,
who is herself no stranger to walking the line

Interview by Rosanne Cash Photographs by David Barry

Dec. 1996

PHOTOGRAPHER	Dave Barry
STYLIST	Laura de Leon

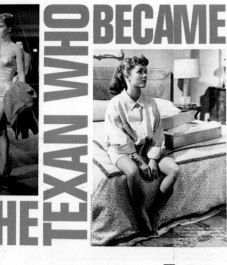

OH! THE TEXAN WHO BECAME DEBBIE REYNOLDS

Once the icon anyone could take home to mother, she now appears in *Mother*

In the fickle world of entertainment, Debbie Reynolds is a survivor. The quintessential girl next door, she sang, danced, and asked her way through such films as *Singin' in the Rain* (1952) and *Tammy and the Bachelor* (1957) until Hollywood tired of her clean looks and naïve demeanor. Now, after more than two decades without a serious film role, she makes a sparkling comeback in Albert Brooks's intimate comedy *Mother*.

Interview by David Furnish

THE ALL-AMERICAN JAZZ OF CLINT EASTWOOD

Talk about staying power!

THE AMERICAN SOUL OF NINA SIMONE

You Al Capone, I'm Nina Simone!

What defines a legend

"[RAPPERS] HAVE RUINED MUSIC AS FAR AS I'M CONCERNED."

Interview by Alison Powell   Photographs by Thierry Le Goués

"I NEVER GOT RICH BEING A MODEL BECAUSE I WAS A KID WHO JUST BLEW MY MONEY"

"I'VE ALWAYS BEEN KIND OF AN ESCAPE ARTIST. I THOUGHT THE DAY-TO-DAY REALITY OF THINGS WAS UNBEARABLY FLAT."

Feb. 1997

PHOTOGRAPHER   Ellen von Unwerth
STYLIST   Victoria Bartlett

Jan. 1997

THE FACE
1 **Mar. 1996**
2 **Apr. 1996**

EDITOR	Richard Benson
ART DIRECTOR	Lee Swillingham
DESIGNER	Stuart Spalding
PHOTOGRAPHERS	1 John Scarisbrick,
	2 Jean Baptiste Mondino
STYLISTS	1 Greg Fay,
	1 Justin Laurie
PUBLISHER	Wagadon Ltd.

UK

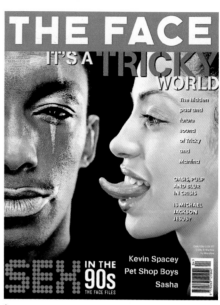

1

2

Jun. 1995

EDITOR	Sheryl Garratt
PHOTOGRAPHER	Andrea Giacobbe
STYLIST	Joanna Thaw

opposite page 1 **May 1995**

EDITOR	Sheryl Garratt
PHOTOGRAPHER	Jean Baptiste Mondino
STYLISTS	Judy Blame,
	Giannie Couji

opposite page 2 **Mar. 1996**

EDITOR	Richard Benson
PHOTOGRAPHER	John Scarisbrick
STYLISTS	Greg Fay,
	Justin Laurie

opposite page 3 **Sep. 1996**

EDITOR	Richard Benson
PHOTOGRAPHER	Saatchi Gallery

SUPER GIRLS

Naomi

Amber

PHOTOGRAPHY
Jean-Baptiste Mondino

STYLING
Judy Blame and Giannie Couji

1

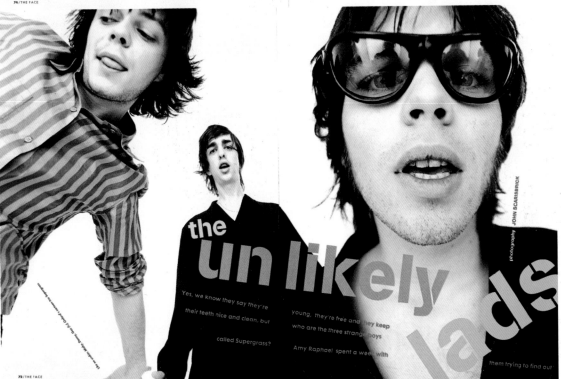

the un likely lads

Yes, we know they say they're
their teeth nice and clean, but
called Supergrass?

young, they're free and they keep
who are the three strange boys
Amy Raphael spent a week with
them trying to find out

photography JOHN SCARISBRICK

2

JOHN ISAACS was once a biology student. He turned to art in order to express his fear of the chaos he saw science causing in the modern world. And, in an age when scientists grow human ears on the backs of mice, and cows have been forced to become cannibals, he is asking if the words "nature" and "progress" now mean anything ▶

weird science

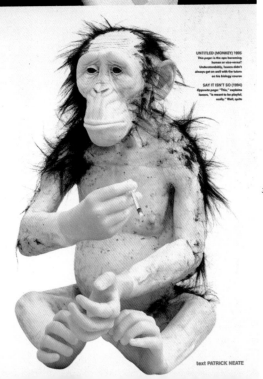

UNTITLED (MONKEY) 1995
This page is the ape becoming
human or vice-versa?
Understandably, Isaacs didn't
always get on well with the tutors
on his biology course

SAY IT ISN'T SO (1994)
Opposite page: "No," explains
Isaacs, "is meant to be playful,
really." Well, quite

3

text PATRICK NEATE

13

TUFFMETAL

Work like a champion
Talk like a champion
Dress like a Queen

Mar. 1996

EDITOR   *Richard Benson*
PHOTOGRAPHER *Peter Robathan*
STYLIST   *Seta Niland*

Aug. 1995

EDITOR   *Sheryl Garratt*
PHOTOGRAPHER *Mark Mattock*

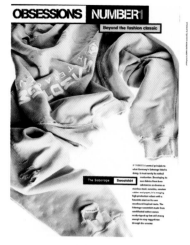

OBSESSIONS NUMBER1
Beyond the fashion classic

The Sabotage   Sweatshirt

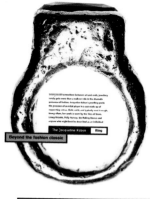

Beyond the fashion classic
The Jacqueline Rabun   Ring

OBSESSIONS NUMBER2

Beyond the fashion classic
The Prada   Belt

OBSESSIONS NUMBER3

The Gucci   Hipsters

OBSESSIONS NUMBER4
Beyond the fashion classic

The Helmut Lang Reflective   Jacket

OBSESSIONS NUMBER5
Beyond the fashion classic

OBSESSIONS NUMBER6
Beyond the fashion classic

The Nike Chris Webber   Sneaker

OBSESSIONS NUMBER7
Beyond the fashion classic

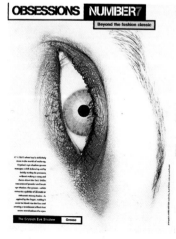

The Crayolan Eye Shadow   Grease

The Sony MDRD 77   Headphones

Beyond the fashion classic

OBSESSIONS NUMBER8

SUPER GRRRL

Strip Tease

PHOTOGRAPHY **David LaChapelle**
STYLING **Arianne Phillips**

Fashion icon, female fantasy, sex symbol... Tank Girl has finally made it from cartoon to the big screen. Andrew Smith asks her creator, Jamie Hewlett: how was it for you?

Jun. 1995

EDITOR   *Sheryl Garratt*
PHOTOGRAPHER   *David Lachapelle*
STYLIST   *Arianne Phillips*

> ❝ If a man had made this movie, the guns would've been bigger, the bullet-holes would've been bigger, and the blood would've been bigger. Instead, we have a lot of humour, plus a lot of sex that isn't boring, garter-belt sex ❞
>
> **LORI PETTY, TANK GIRL**

Wild at heart: a war-battered Tank Girl (Lori Petty) struts her stuff

The creator becomes his creation: Jamie Hewlett as Tank Girl in Santa Monica Boulevard, Los Angeles

They'd cordoned off Hollywood Boulevard with barriers watched over by dozens of shade-wearing, Harley-straddling cops in their best dress uniforms. This was to be the biggest night of Jamie Hewlett's life. For him, the previous year had danced past in a haze of fear, frustration, frantic excitement. Making a movie, it turned out, felt very much like being in a movie. The politics and post-production schisms had been intense and frightening. »

THE FACE / 103

Tank Girl is vastly different to anything I've done before. I mean

It's not your typical coming-of-age film, is it?

> "I like being an action hero. It's fun! I just get to go buck wild every day and have a great time! I don't know about pointless violence, as far as Tank Girl goes. I just think she likes to blow shit up"
>
> LORI PETTY, TANK GIRL, right

Detour
1 **Oct. 1996**
2 **Mar. 1997**

EDITOR *Jim Turner*
CREATIVE DIRECTOR *Luis Barajas*
ART DIRECTOR *James Morris*
DESIGNER *James Morris*
PHOTOGRAPHERS *1 David Lachapelle,*
2 Stephan Sedanoui
PHOTOGRAPHY DIRECTOR *Rose Cefalu*
PUBLISHER *Detour Inc.*

USA

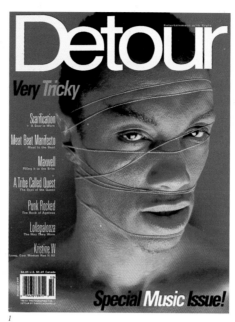

THERE IS SOMETHING MYSTERIOUS ABOUT DANIEL DAY-LEWIS. PERHAPS THAT MYSTERY STEMS FROM HIS APPARENT CONTRADICTIONS: HE IMBUES HIS ROLES WITH A NAKED PASSION BUT OFFSCREEN IS SAID TO BE A DISTANT, IMPENETRABLE FIGURE WHO SHUTS DOWN WHEN A TAPE RECORDER TURNS ON; HE CAN CONVINCINGLY PLAY EVERYTHING FROM A BRITISH PUNK TO A CZECH SURGEON BUT AS A PERSON HE SEEMS INEFFABLE, JUST BEYOND YOUR GRASP

A New Day Dawns

Dec./Jan. 1996-97

ART DIRECTOR *Nelson Anderson*
PHOTOGRAPHER *David Lachapelle*

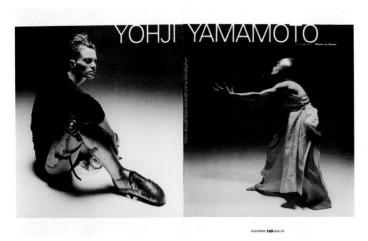

YOHJI YAMAMOTO

REBEL JUST BECAUSE

Mar. 1997

ART DIRECTOR *James Morris*
PHOTOGRAPHER *Thierry Le Gouès*

Nov. 1996

ART DIRECTOR *Luis Barajas*
PHOTOGRAPHER *David Lachapelle*

Do The Hustler

Sep. 1996

ART DIRECTOR *James Morris*
PHOTOGRAPHER *Neil Kirk*

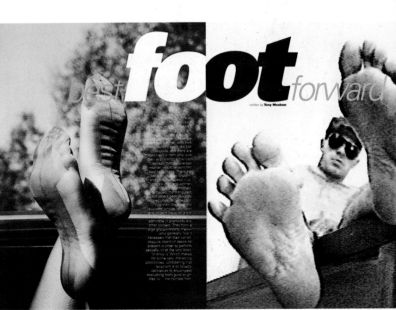

best **foot** forward

Feb. 1997

ART DIRECTOR *James Morris*
PHOTOGRAPHER *Tony Moxham*

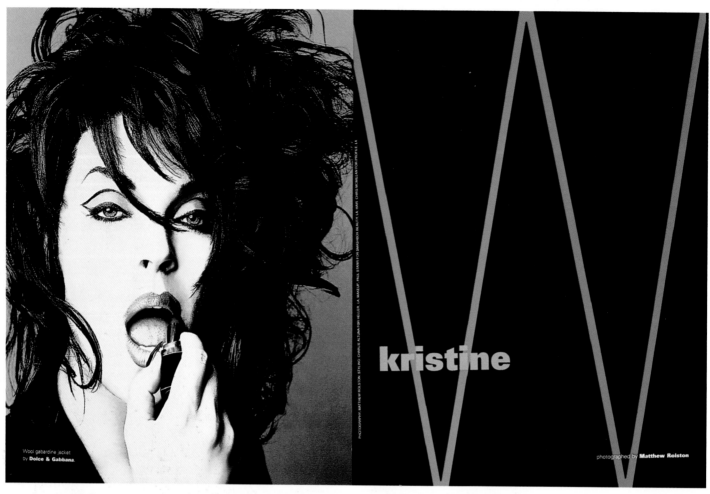

Wool gabardine jacket
by **Dolce & Gabbana**.

kristine

photographed by **Matthew Rolston**

Oct. 1996

ART DIRECTOR *James Morris*
PHOTOGRAPHER *Matthew Rolston*

GUCCI

GUCCI

photographed by **Christian Witkin**

Mar. 1997

ART DIRECTOR   *James Morris*
DESIGNER   *Jennifer Sidel*
PHOTOGRAPHER   *Christian Witkin*

*surface
Vol. 8 1996

ART DIRECTORS Richard M. Klein,
  Riley John-donnell
DESIGNER Riley John-donnell
PHOTOGRAPHER Paco Navarro
RETOUCHING Tom Pitts
DESIGN FIRM *Surface Magazine
PUBLISHER Surface Publishing
USA

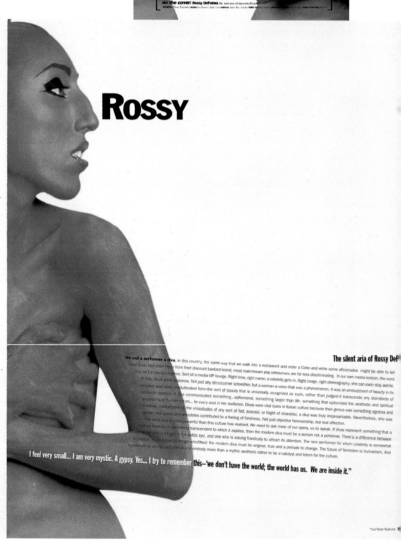

ROSSY

"People in these times should forget organized beliefs... Now, religion is a cheap word. My religion is about being humble. To feel... small...

interview Riley John-donnell **forward** Dina Fayer & Riley John-donnell **images** Paco Navarro

The silent aria of Rossy DeP

We call a performer a diva, in this country, the same way that we walk into a restaurant and order a Coke—and while some aficionados might be able to tell their Coke from their Pepsi from their discount bastard brand, most mainstream pop consumers are far less discriminating. In our own media lexicon, the word diva isn't so far from a prime. Sort of a media VIP lounge. Right time, right name; a celebrity gets in. Right image, right choreography; she can even stay awhile.

I feel very small... I am very mystic. A gypsy. Yes... I try to remember this—'we don't have the world; the world has us. We are inside it."

Vol. 8 1996

EDITOR Derek Peck
ART DIRECTOR Riley John-donnell
PHOTOGRAPHER Paco Navarro
RETOUCHING Nina Alter

"Aspiration

IMAGES KARINA TAIRA

sells

1

2

commodity."

3

Vol. 8 1996

EDITOR 1,2 Gregory Michaels
ART DIRECTOR 3 Riley John-donnell
PHOTOGRAPHERS 1 Karina Taira,
2 Davide Sorrenti,
3 Daniel de Souza

Vol. 8 1996

EDITOR *Derek Peck*
PHOTOGRAPHER *Carter Smith*
RETOUCHING *Nina Alter*

Vol. 8 1996

EDITOR *Dina Fayer*
PHOTOGRAPHER *Robert Trachtenberg*

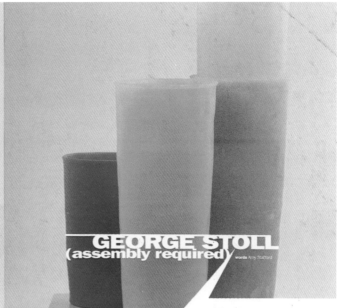

GEORGE STOLL
(assembly required)
words Amy Stafford

With dry humor and obsessive—even perverse—precision, Los Angeles artist George Stoll presents faithful replicas of traditional household objects, from Tupperware to toilet paper rolls. Eliciting an odd, homespun reminiscence, Stoll carefully conjures recollections of an earlier American psyche. In cheerful variations on a practical theme, he challenges the tradition. Throwaway nature of toilet paper by detailing his reproductions with colored pencil and unlikely materials used to create texture and pattern. His beeswax-and-paraffin bowls, storage containers and stacks of semi-translucent drinking cups cry out for cold meatloaf and cherry Kool-Aid. Objects glorified by Stoll's replication outline those elements of American life that are often overlooked, in the perpetual bustle of the everyday.

Stoll's fastidiously handmade rolls of Soft 'N Gentle bath tissue function beyond the simple fond affection for a domestic object. Creating the illusion, in painstaking detail, of squeezable softness—fashioned in semi-precious materials like silk and copper—could easily be considered anal-retentive. A humble token of everyday life has become a fetish; worshipful craftsmanship has turned anal-tickets into tooths.

There was a time when suburban American mothers, the glue holding our domestic front together, considered the preserving of leftovers and the selection of cozy bath tissue to be among the scary challenges of their profession. Housewives cultivated an industry that could and would respond to their demands for improvements in design and technology, complete with a wide range of decorator colors and a Full Lifetime Warranty. Tupperware, seemed to meet countless needs; it could be mixed and matched to enhance the design of the kitchen, increase efficiency and eliminate mess; and provide homemakers with an opportunity to host and/or attend any number of social events, even with toddlers tugging on their apron strings. Now, those dented cups and cereal bowls, nostalgic relics at the neighborhood Goodwill, are steeped in sentimentality—a hermetically-sealed time machine back to America's freshness.

What is it about these objects that is so captivating? Does Stoll offer us a transcendence from banality through his glorification of household objects? Perhaps. His work suggests that our understanding of culture and fine art has already been merged, seductively, with the kitschy icons—kitchen gods—of American mass production. ✳

Vol. 9 1996-97

EDITOR Dina Fayer
ARTIST George Stoll

Vol. 8 1996

EDITOR Derek Peck
PHOTOGRAPHERS Dietmar,
Leigh Beisch,
Karina Taira

★surveillance

KITSCHY COUP
images James Smolka styling Katarina Masterson

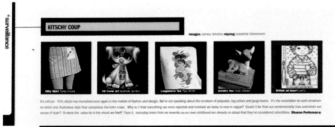

It's official - 70's idiom has triumphed once again in the market of fashion and design. We're not speaking about the revitum of polyester, big collars and go-go boots. It's the resolution to each ornamental detail and illustrative style that completes the retro craze. Why is it that everything we once rejected and mocked as tacky is now in vogue? Could it be that our sentimentality has overtaken our sense of style? Or does the value lie in the shock we feel? Face it, everyday icons from as recently as our own childhood are already so dated that they're considered collectibles. **Sharon Perlowson** ✳

PRESERVATION SOCIETY
images Leigh Beisch

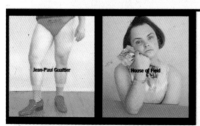

"Kitchissy things" are what 25-year-old Tony Meredith says he was looking for when he found his medium. The San Francisco designer got the idea to use Tupperware at a party where he saw columnists living used as lamp shades. With a history of lighting designs using mostly found objects, Tupperware made some use for right and century. He started by selling them at MAC in San Francisco. There, a rep from New York saw them and ordered cups for five stores, at which Barney's saw them and "had to have them" for their Spring windows. Meredith's lamps lit the window for Vera Wang's gowns.

Because of the smart design and assembly that goes into them, you don't realize at first that they're Tupperware, and when you do you're hit by an amusement that it could look so aesthetic. When asked if he's going to be making Tupperware lamps all his life? No thank you, he explains that this venture just happened to coincide with Tupperware's 50th anniversary, so he decided to make it a tribute to the makers of this uniquely American kitchenware. One thing's for sure, Meredith won't spoil after this year of success. He's been offered other design projects and has plans to follow through with some of them. Although he may never become so household as Earl Tupper, we'll definitely be seeing more from him.

Along the same theory of preservation and recycling check out fine inventor Benjamin Winter's airline luminations (left) and Nathan Meloudon' one-of-a-kind designs, like the Kleenex box lamp (above far left). In San Francisco you can find these innovative objects at I.C.E., in SeaTank by Gautreau. **Clare Gurson** ✳

PANTY RAID
images Dietmar

Jean-Paul Gaultier

House of Field

A few years ago Gaultier, Dolce & Gabbana, Italy led and an onslaught of fashion savvy moguls began "expressing themselves" by having underwear as outerwear. Eyebrows and bustlines were raised as cripples, bustiers and negligees earned their way off the runways and up the aisles of mainstream department stores.

Although the face-top (commonly and irreverently referred to as the "wife beater") has been a staple basic in men's wear for some time, other traditional men's undergarments have stayed nearly tucked away, don't almost. Major trends always have a prelude. Such as hardcore baggy street wear, sagging way below the butt line allowing every one to hum a few musical bars of "I won London, I saw France..." as some skater or hip-hop fanatic's underpants swooshes by. And, of course, ad campaigns promote underwear like sportswear with translation encouragement.

The news here is that those tight little numbers (in the bottom row) have diffused from the women's market and landed in rather on the baskets of the men's market. This season Moschino, Helmut Lang and Gaultier have added a little lace to the the men's brief in bold. So guys, ignore the couch's advice that the boulder holder warm the tightly closes a lower count in the final score. And prepare for the panty raid. **Billy B.** ✳

styling Eric Damon hair Rex Gladone make-up Susan Houser models Mickle & Sam

ANDY LAND

With the release of "I Shot Andy Warhol" in May, director Julian Schnabel's hit-pic on the life of Jean-Michel Basquiat in June, and remembrances of the Godfather of Pop in a dozen magazines, "softer thought to seek out contemporary incarnations of Warhol's art collective, the Factory. We looked for collectives that exhibit a similar approach: those who work together to make a collaborative art lifestyle.

Though the notion of the Factory was the logical starting point, to evaluate artists solely on Andy's terms verges on gross simplification. Things have changed radically since the Factory, In today's climate, rank with hostility engendered by the NEA controversy and the budgetary Restraint of the Republican Congress, artists must learn to exist in a fiercely competitive world.

Their resiliency is evident in the "Factories" of today; artists are previously interconnected, establishing community-based collectives as networks of financial and logistical support. Only rarely did we find groups of flakes and hacks, who'd apparently rather rave and by-in avoid than make the art they talk about making. Today's collectives...

selve in a more democratic and socially-minded paradigm, both in themselves and the communities in which they exist.

San Francisco's SEE-MEN, dedicated to art, to each other, and to you, pose a spontaneous collaborative exploration of the fine issues—with the intent of educating. Sullivan members are encouraged to examine their position in a society increasingly dominated by the intersection of humanity and technology. Her art To elicit response high visceral and cerebral, the See-Men blend robotics, pyrotechnics/theatre, spoken word and music into a molotov cocktail of socio-political critique, and then they throw it in your lap, look for them to explode at Lollapalooza this summer.

CELL, envisioned by founder Jonathan Scott as "a forum for needs to come together, an art community ArcH-funk, and [need] a non-profit organization to help other art collectives." has 32,000 square feet of workspace and 30 members. Cell's collectives encompass the entire spectrum of art practice, from the expanded—sculpture, metalwork, filmvideo, and individual—to the refreshingly unexpected, such as dance, costume design production, and puppeteering.

S.R.L. (Survival Research Laboratories), is legendary in avant-garde art circles. Long known for the precarious juxtaposition of massive pyrotechnics, angry metal monsters and the soft, pliable flesh of spectators, the rewound techno-machine-digital-performance collective offer a wry antique (perhaps unintentionally) of our society's techno-fetishes. Cynically only for the adventure—at US dollars.

Where can you see this type of art? William Vis Sense. That's because he runs to come together, an art community ArcH-funk, and [need] a non-profit organization to help other art collectives.

BLASTHAUS, the pioneering gallery for electronic, digital, and interactive art, located in SOMA. Blasthaus attracts art patrons from around the globe who perks to interface with artwork rather than just look at it.

NEGATIVLAND. Indie boys being sued by U2, these Oakland-based audio-collage artists are notorious for their distribution of celebrity sound bites, obscure samples, and scripted dialogue into a tight, ironic examination of the American cultural landscape. You can buy their tapes at many stores and, when in the Bay Area, hear them weekly live, unbroken, broadcast in realtime, on KPFA 495-something "somethin? Thursday nights from midnight to three a.m.

THE NUYORICAN in New York's old-school yet seminal spoken-word outfit, Brainchild of Bob Holman, Nuyorican is responsible for three infamous and opinionated poetry slams at the Nuyorican Café. If poetry words slated in the Digital Age, Inspellabullrift. These wordslams are concise and high-impact, perfectly attuned to your shattered attention span. "The United States of Poetry," the film documentary of poetry jams across the land, is available on video cassette and also as a CD and a book.

Down in Lower Manhattan, the HOTEL 17 quietly reigns as the residence par excellence for exciting artists and resident bohemians. Rooms range from daily photo-shoots to one-piece designs literally seen to sixteen, three-style real. The atmosphere is playful and conducive to producing lively imagery. Most everyone who wants to be anyone in the arts has stayed, played and, hopefully, created here. If only the walls could talk. **Jack Gwylhine** ✳

THE GAP IS CLOSED
images Karina Taira stylist Susan Pichotte make-up Kristopher Buckle all clothing Susan Concoitti

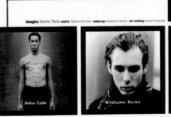

Anton Cobb

Kristopher Buckle

Elena

Mr.

Founded in 1981, A+ was originally an agency for children and has operated as such ever since. But about two years ago, after being approached by production crews for "alternative lifestyle" extras (pronounced: drag queens) in the independent film "Joey's Apartment," they began to recognize a demand for "extreme" people and added a special division to represent them, Nightlife Talent. Since 1990, the Nightlife scouts have been seeking out all manner of striking individuals and the beautifully odd culture: a sampling of the agency's heavily booked talent. "everything from austere to project and avant-garde freaks." says one of the division's managers, Sidney Prawlalmin.

Himself a makeup androgyne, Prawlalmin, 19, says Nightlife's mission is to "fill the gap left by other agencies." "These kids need someone to represent them," he says. Apparently the clients do, too; the exquisitely bizarre are showing up everywhere from television to film to major print ads to magazines. Serving so mass visibility, marketability and acceptance of the strange. Besides materializing on high fashion runways and in mainstream music videos, Nightlife models have appeared in commercials for such traditionally conservative clients as Clothestime, Scott Towels and Blue Cross Blue Shield. Guaranteed visibility insurance for the avant-garde. **Joel Enos** ✳

We build shiny monuments, then tear them down. It's the way of the day. As our cultural screens continue to crumble, we are forced to ask: Who is a pillar of strength? Who can withstand the onslaught of quicktime media & disposable values? Grace claims that "the worst sin is hypocrisy," so get on your knees & pray that your mirror is clean & true. Crank your expectations dial up to 'high' & cast aside your opinions. She inhales through the nose & exhales through the mouth. Grace has not fallen.

interview Billy John-Donnel hair & makeup Chris McMillan / Profile, L.A. styling Heian Meshell / Celestine, L.A.

photography **Greg Gorman**

Grace

"I looked the Devil in the face—& God...now I'm looking at both."

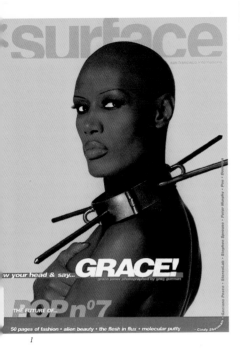

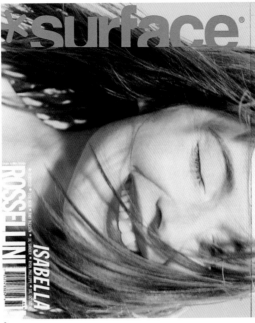

1   **Vol. 7 1996**

PHOTOGRAPHER   Greg Gorman

2   **Vol. 9 1996**

PHOTOGRAPHER
Miles Aldridge
RETOUCHING
Tom Pitts

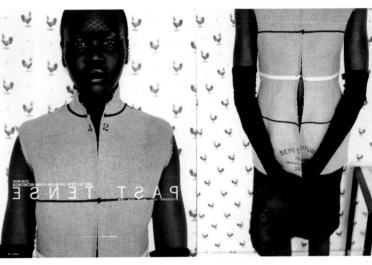

opposite page   **Vol. 7 1996**

EDITOR	Dina Fayer
PHOTOGRAPHER	Greg Gorman
RETOUCHING	Nina Alter

3,4   **Vol. 9 1996**

EDITOR	Dina Fayer
ART DIRECTOR	Riley John-donnell
PHOTOGRAPHER	3 Roger Erickson

5   **Vol. 9 1996**

EDITOR	Riley John-donnell
PHOTOGRAPHER	Michael Williams

Don't Tell It

1 **Vol. 16 Dec./Jan. 1996-97**
2 **Vol. 17 Feb. 1997**

EDITOR	Jiro Ejaife
ART DIRECTORS	1 Little Feet,
	2 Jiro Ejaife
DESIGNER	Christina Obwona
PHOTOGRAPHERS	1 Jiro Ejaife,
	2 Bernhardt von Spreckelsen
PUBLISHER	Don't Tell It Magazine Ltd.

U K

1

2

eat, drink, man, woman

An economic upturn or just people pissed off with the doom and gloom of recession and deciding to get on with life regardless. Ascribe it to whatever you will, but new bars and restaurants springing up by the dozen. Many of them are best described as kennels, but one bar/café worthy of the name is the Retro Café.

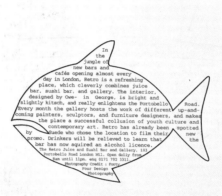

In the jungle of new bars and cafés opening almost every day in London, Retro is a refreshing place, which cleverly combines juice bar, sushi bar, and gallery. The interior, designed by Owe- in George, is bright and slightly kitsch, and really enlightens the Portobello Road. Every month the gallery hosts the work of different up-and-coming painters, sculptors, and furniture designers, and makes the place a successful collusion of youth culture and contemporary art. Retro has already been spotted by Suede who chose the location to film their new promo. Drinkers will be relieved to learn that the bar has now aquired an alcohol licence. The Retro Juice and Sushi Bar and Gallery, 183 Portobello Road London W11. Open daily from 8am until 11pm. enq 0171 792 1311. Photography Credit : Forty Four Design Photography

Vol. 14 Oct. 1996

ART DIRECTOR	Kit Yan Chong
DESIGNER	Silke Roch
PHOTOGRAPHER	Forty Four Design Photography

Kwesi after all these years

Vol. 15 Nov. 1996

ART DIRECTOR	Little Feet
DESIGNER	Evelyn Sobotie
PHOTOGRAPHER	Arid van Straten

jacket and shirt, both by Paul Smith. trousers, by Matsuda by Yukio Kobayashi. trainers, by Airwalk.

Vertigo

Photographer: Eva Mueller, assisted by Gudrun Georgis.
Stylist: Karen Levitt, assisted by Sonya Mayer.
Grooming: Hitomi Kobari.
Model: Analog @ DNA

opposite page, striped jacket and trousers, both by Matsuda by Yukio Kobayashi. Vest, shirt, and tie, all by Paul Smith. trainers, by Airwalk. this page, ribbed top, by D&G by Dolce & Gabbana.

Vol. 14 Oct. 1996

ART DIRECTOR   *Kit Yan Chong*
DESIGNER   *Silke Roch*
PHOTOGRAPHERS   *Eva Mueller,*
Gudrun Georgis

Vol. 16 Dec./Jan. 1996-97

ART DIRECTOR   *Little Feet*
DESIGNER   *Christina Obwona*
PHOTOGRAPHERS   *Patrice Felix-Tchilaya,*
Karin

DAZED & CONFUSED

1   **Vol. 27 1996**
2   **Vol. 28 1996**

EDITOR	*Jefferson Hack*
ART DIRECTOR	*Matt Roach*
PHOTOGRAPHER	*Rankin*
HAIR & MAKEUP	*1 Glen Woods*
GROOMING	*2 Kevin Ford*
STYLIST	*Miranda Robson*
PUBLISHER	*Dazed & Confused*

U K

1

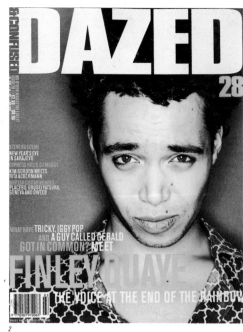

2

FINLEY QUAYE

TEXT RACHEL NEWSOME PHOTOGRAPHY RANKIN ASSISTED BY COURTNEY HAMILTON, RICKIE AND ANNA PORTER STYLING MIRANDA ROBSON GROOMING KEVIN FORD @ CAMILLA ARTHUR

ULTRA STIMULATION
"MAN, I'M JUST SOME
CRAZY POOL SHARK."

Finley Quaye casually glances up from beneath the felt black Kangol cap shading his face and breaks into a broad, mischievous smirk. By some strange twist of family engineering, he's Tricky's uncle, although only 22, and he subverts expectations before he's even opened his mouth.

Finley's just arrived from his current base in Edinburgh, where he's finishing off a track in which he's joined on vocals by Tricky and Iggy Pop. Called "Duppy Umbrella", it staggers under a grinding behemoth of beats and moans: a bizarre, end-of-century tableau comprising the devilish "nearly God", a saturnine '70s anti-hero and, of course, Finley himself.

"It's 13 minutes long, with me on drums and harmonica, me, Tricky and Iggy on vocals, some French friends in this ska band from Lyons on sax. And the sound! Man (voice skips several octaves), it's like Captain Beefheart's 'Tarot' track - big, long and wild as fuck! I like what feels good... what feels right, you know?"

Vol. 28 1996

DESIGNER	*Matt Roach*
PHOTOGRAPHER	*Rankin*
GROOMING	*Kevin Ford*
STYLIST	*Miranda Robson*

FREEDOM

OF SPEECH

These are five representatives of groups of people who have no international legitimacy, no recognition as self-determining nations and no freedom in their homelands. In featuring them, we have found that despite the inconsistencies, injustices and inequalities that exist in this country, the vibrancy and freedom of political debate that exists here is something worth fighting for. We often take our freedoms of expression, movement, and political affiliation for granted: the very possibility of reading this sort of feature is a privilege that could disappear if we allow complacency to slide into regression. Working with Amnesty International, we have not tried to represent "the truth", whatever that might be. We have simply attempted to provoke thought and discussion. This is the only way the truth can be approached...

66 DAZED

NAME: MRS. KESANG Y TAKLA
COUNTRY: TIBET/CHINA
POSITION: REPRESENTATIVE OF HIS HOLINESS THE DALAI LAMA

Agenda: "Our struggle is for the right to statehood for Tibet and the rights of Tibetans in exile. Another important issue for us is the education of Tibetans, so that they can contribute to the government in exile that has been democratically elected since 1949."

The case: "Tibetans are peaceful people, not strong in terms of military might, but very strong in our commitment to non-violent, dedicated protest. The problem is that China has been an extremely violent occupier of our homeland since 1949, and since then the Tibetan people have been treated as second-class citizens in Tibet as well as China. Our people have no economic or religious freedom, no freedom of movement, or of identity as Tibetans. All aspects of life within Tibet are controlled by the Chinese government.

Amnesty's latest report: Widespread human rights violations occurred in the Tibet Autonomous Region. In the first three months of 1995 alone, 123 people were reported to have been detained in connection with peaceful pro-independence activity, or following police raids on monasteries and nunneries. Detention centres and labour camps were reported, as were the use of electric shocks, shackles, sleep deprivation and exposure to extreme heat and cold.

The broader picture: Though the Dalai Lama is an almost universally recognised and respected world leader, and winner of the Nobel Peace Prize, factions within the exiled Tibetan community have recently claimed that the Dalai Lama's failure to recognise certain deities' legitimacy constitutes an infringement of the religious freedom he claims to promote. This splinter group, the Shugden Supporters Community, is made up largely of European Buddhists, and doesn't seem a very credible threat to the Dalai Lama's standing in global politics.

Further information: Free Tibet Campaign 0171-359-7573

"IT IS THE PEOPLE OF BRITAIN AND THE REST OF THE WORLD, RATHER THAN THEIR GOVERNMENTS, THAT HAVE SHOWN THE GREATEST SUPPORT FOR THE TIBETAN PEOPLE."

POLITICAL RESISTANCE LEADERS
WRITTEN AND CO-ORDINATED BY **MICHAEL FORDHAM** PHOTOGRAPHY **PEROU**
THANKS TO **SUSAN KOBRIN** @ AMNESTY INTERNATIONAL 0171-814-6200

DAZED 67

Vol. 25 1996

DESIGNER   *Matt Roach*
PHOTOGRAPHER   *Perou*

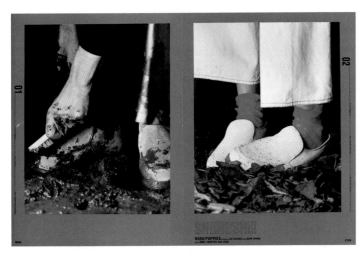

Vol. 28 1996

DESIGNER   *Matt Roach*
PHOTOGRAPHER   *Liz Collins*
STYLIST   *Katie Grand*

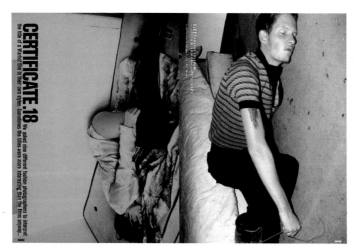

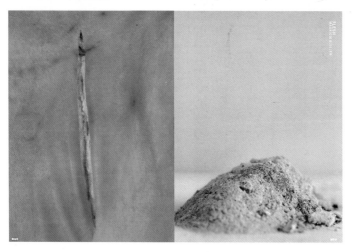

Vol. 27 1996

DESIGNER	*Matt Roach*
PHOTOGRAPHERS	*1 Anders Edstrom,*
	2 Geoffroy de Boismenu,
	3 Mauricio Guillen
STYLIST	*1 Yoshiki Shiojiri*

Vol. 25 1996

ILLUSTRATOR	*Paul Davis*
STYLIST	*Katie Grand*

GET OFF YOUR HORSE AND APPLY YOUR MILK

photographer PHIL POYNTER makeup VAL GARLAND hair ADAM BRYANT stylist KATY ENGLAND words SIMON DINE text CHRIS DORE

Vol. 23 1996

DESIGNER   *Matt Roach*
PHOTOGRAPHER *Phil Poynter*
MAKEUP   *Val Garland*
HAIR   *Adam Bryant*
STYLIST   *Katy England*

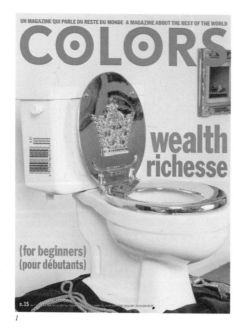

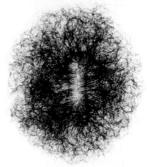

COLORS

1 **Vol. 15 May 1996**
2 **Vol. 18 Dec./Jan. 1996-97**

EDITORIAL DIRECTOR *Oliviero Toscani*
EDITOR IN CHIEF *Alex Marashian*
ART DIRECTORS *1 Paul Ritter,*
 2 Robin King
PHOTOGRAPHERS *1 Shahn Kermani,*
 1 Gamma Liaison,
 2 Marirosa Toscani Ballo
TYPOGRAPHER *De Pedrini*
PUBLISHER *Colors Magazine S.R.I.*

 Italy

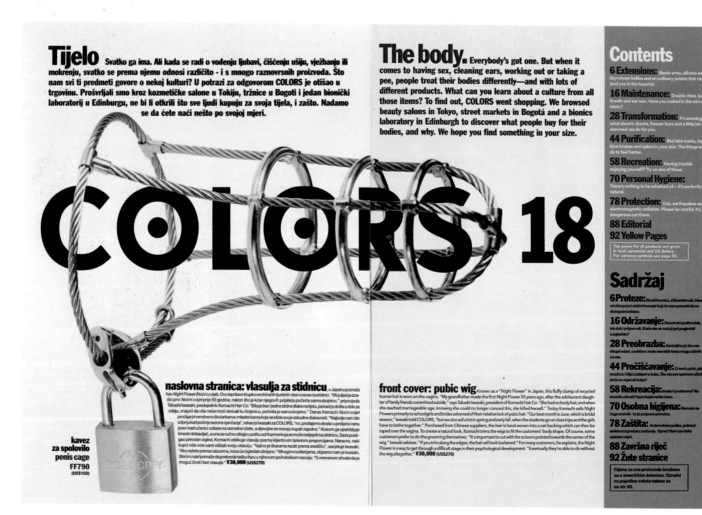

Tijelo

Svatko ga ima. Ali kada se radi o vođenju ljubavi, čišćenju ušiju, vježbanju ili mokrenju, svatko se prema njemu odnosi različito - i s mnogo raznovrsnih proizvoda. Što nam svi ti predmeti govore o nekoj kulturi? U potrazi za odgovorom COLORS je otišao u trgovinu. Prošvrljali smo kroz kozmetičke salone u Tokiju, tržnice u Bogoti i jedan bionički laboratorij u Edinburgu, ne bi li otkrili što sve ljudi kupuju za svoja tijela, i zašto. Nadamo se da ćete naći nešto po svojoj mjeri.

The body.

Everybody's got one. But when it comes to having sex, cleaning ears, working out or taking a pee, people treat their bodies differently—and with lots of different products. What can you learn about a culture from all those items? To find out, COLORS went shopping. We browsed beauty salons in Tokyo, street markets in Bogotá and a bionics laboratory in Edinburgh to discover what people buy for their bodies, and why. We hope you find something in your size.

Contents

Sadržaj

naslovna stranica: vlasulja za stidnicu. u Japanu poznata kao *Night Flower* (Noćni cvijet). Ovo lepršavo klupko recikliranih ljudskih vlasi nosi se na stidnicu. "Moj djed je izradio prvi *Noćni cvijet* prije 50 godina, nakon što je kćer njegovih prijatelja počinila samoubojstvo," pripovijeda Takashi Iwasaki, predsjednik *Komachi Hair Co.* "Bila je bez i jedne stidne dlake na tijelu, pa kad je došla u dob za udaju, znajući da više neće moći skrivati tu činjenicu, počinila je samoubojstvo." Danas Komachi *Noćni cvijet* prodaje prvenstveno školarkama i mladenkama koje se stide svoje oskudne dlakavosti. "Najbolje nam ide u lipnju kad počinje sezona vjenčanja", rekao je Iwasaki za COLORS, "no, prodajemo dosta i u proljeće i ranu jesen kad učenici odlaze na razredne izlete, a djevojke se moraju kupati zajedno." Kosom ga opskrbljuje kineski dobavljač, a ona se nužno utkaje u podlogu od tkanine koja se može naljepiti na stidnicu. Da bi postigao prirodan izgled, Komachi oblikuje vlasulju prema klijentovim proporcijama. Naravno, neki kupci vole vlasi ošišati svoju vlasulju. "Važno je škarama rezati prema središtu," savjetuje Iwasaki. "Ako režete prema rubovima, kosa će izgledati obrijano." Mnogim mušterijama, objasnio nam je Iwasaki, *Noćni cvijet* pomaže da prebrode tešku fazu u njihovom psihološkom razvoju. "S vremenom shvate da je moguć život i bez vlasulje." **¥30,000 (US$270)**

kavez za spolovilo penis cage
FF790
(US$150)

front cover: pubic wig Known as a "Night Flower" in Japan, this fluffy clump of recycled human hair is worn on the vagina. "My grandfather made the first Night Flower 50 years ago, after the adolescent daughter of family friends committed suicide," says Takashi Iwasaki, president of Komachi Hair Co. "She had no body hair, and when she reached marriageable age, knowing she could no longer conceal this, she killed herself." Today Komachi sells Night Flowers primarily to schoolgirls and brides ashamed of their relative lack of pubic hair. "Our best month is June, which is bridal season," Iwasaki told COLORS, "but we also sell a lot in spring and early fall, when the students go on class trips and the girls have to bathe together." Purchased from Chinese suppliers, the hair is hand-woven into a net backing which can then be taped over the vagina. To create a natural look, Komachi trims the wigs to fit the customers' body shape. Of course, some customers prefer to do the grooming themselves. "It's important to cut with the scissors pointed towards the center of the wig," Iwasaki advises. "If you trim along the edges, the hair will look barbered." For many customers, he explains, the Night Flower is a way to get through a difficult stage in their psychological development. "Eventually they're able to do without the wig altogether." **¥30,000 (US$270)**

Vol. 18 Dec./Jan. 1996-97

EDITOR IN CHIEF *Alex Marashian*
ART DIRECTOR *Robin King*
PHOTOGRAPHER *Marirosa Toscani Ballo*

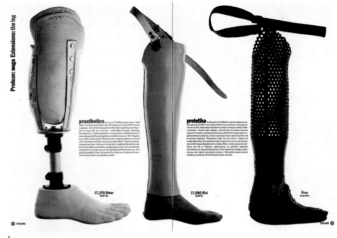

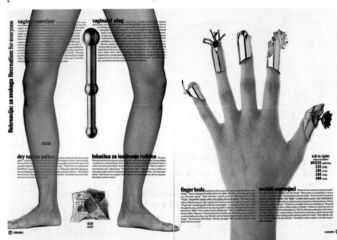

1,3 **Vol. 15 May 1996**

EDITOR IN CHIEF — *Alex Marashian*
ART DIRECTOR — *Paul Ritter*
PHOTOGRAPHER — *Fulvio Maiani*

4,5,6 **Vol. 18 Dec./Jan. 1996-97**

EDITOR IN CHIEF — *Alex Marashian*
ART DIRECTOR — *Robin King*
PHOTOGRAPHERS — *5 Oliviero Toscani (legs),*
4,5,6 Marirosa Toscani Ballo (5 hand)

2 **Vol. 15 May 1996**

EDITOR IN CHIEF — *Alex Marashian*
ART DIRECTOR — *Paul Ritter*
PHOTOGRAPHERS — *Volker Hinz,*
Stern,
Studio X,
Stephan Richter,
Camera Press London,
Grazi Neri,
Bruno Barbey,
Magnum,
Contrasto

Cos'è l'AIDS? WHAT IS AIDS?

Molta gente pensa che per prendere l'AIDS bisogna essere o comportarsi in un certo modo. All'AIDS non gliene importa niente.

Many people think you have to look or act or be a certain way to get AIDS. AIDS doesn't care.

"Solo i froci beccano l'AIDS."
"Only faggots catch AIDS."

MEET THE RAY FAMILY from Florida, USA. The boys, Randy, Robert and Ricky, are hemophiliac and were infected via HIV-tainted blood transfusions. The family had to sue the State of Florida to allow the boys to go to school. There were bomb threats and death threats. Finally their house was burned. Fleeing their home town, they settled in Orlando. Ricky died in December 1992 at 15. Over 47% of hemophiliacs in the USA are HIV positive.
VI PRESENTIAMO LA FAMIGLIA RAY, americani della Florida. I ragazzi, Randy, Robert e Ricky, sono emofiliaci e hanno contratto la malattia con trasfusioni di sangue infettato dall'HIV. La famiglia ha dovuto denunciare lo Stato della Florida per permettere ai propri figli di frequentare la scuola, ricevendo minacce di morte e di attentati. Alla fine la loro casa è stata bruciata. Dopo aver abbandonato la loro città, si sono trasferiti a Orlando. Ricky è morto nel dicembre del 1992 all'età di 15 anni. Più del 47% degli emofiliaci negli USA sono sieropositivi.

Vol. 7 Jun. 1994

EDITOR IN CHIEF — Tibor Kalman
ART DIRECTOR — Scott Stowell

COLORS

Scientists used to say it would take 3 years for symptoms of HIV infection to surface. Then they said it would take 5 years. Then up to 12 years. Now they won't say.

All'inizio gli scienziati dicevano che, dopo il contagio, i sintomi dell'HIV si sarebbero manifestati entro tre anni. Poi hanno detto che ci sarebbero voluti 5 anni. Poi fino a 12. Adesso non si pronunciano.

Last night, Sara and Miguel slept together.

Ieri notte Sara e Miguel hanno fatto l'amore.

COLORS

L'anno scorso, ognuno di loro ha fatto l'amore con altre tre persone.

Last year, they each slept with three other people.

COLORS

Each year before that, those people each slept with three other people.

Ogni anno precedente, ognuno di loro aveva fatto l'amore con altre tre persone.

Over four years, Sara and Miguel will have slept with people who slept with a total of 80 people.

Tra quattro anni Sara e Miguel avranno fatto l'amore con persone che hanno fatto l'amore con un totale di 80 persone.

COLORS

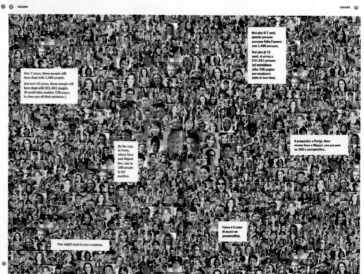

Over 7 years, those people will have slept with 1,460 people.
And over 12 years, those people will have slept with 531,441 people. (It would take another 728 pages to show you all their pictures.)

Nel giro di 7 anni, queste persone avranno fatto l'amore con 1.460 persone.
Nel giro di 12 anni, si arriva a 531.441 persone (ci vorrebbero altre 728 pagine per mostrarvi tutte le loro foto).

By the way, in Paris, where Sara and Miguel live, one in 100 people is HIV positive.

A proposito: a Parigi, dove vivono Sara e Miguel, una persona su 100 è sieropositiva.

You might want to use a condom.

Forse è il caso di usare un preservativo.

BITING Don't be ashamed to let your
lover see your tender side. The gluteal region
is one of the body's erogenous zones. The
skin is delicate, excitable, delicious. Perfect
for a nibble.
MORSI Non ti vergognare di mostrare al/la
partner il tuo lato tenero. I glutei sono una
delle zone erogene del corpo. La pelle è
delicata, eccitabile, deliziosa. Perfetta per
un morsetto.

AIDS has made sex
dangerous.
We have to re-invent it.
Let's get to work.

safe sex

kama sutra

del sesso sicuro

L'AIDS ha reso il sesso
pericoloso.
Dobbiamo riinventarlo.
Mettiamoci al lavoro.

It's a whole new experience. Caressing, fondling
and licking aren't the things we do before we make love:
they are making love. The body is a long, complex field
of pleasure zones. So make a map: lick armpits and
abdomens, suck toes and fingertips, nibble your lover's
inner thighs. Create sensations. Dominate with a tickle.
Soothe with a massage. Just one rule: don't exchange
fluids. The rest is up to you. Sex isn't just one thing. It's
anything you care to try.
There's much to be done.

È un'esperienza completamente nuova.
Accarezzarsi, toccarsi, leccarsi, non sono le cose che
facciamo prima di fare l'amore: è fare l'amore. Il corpo è
un lungo e complesso campo di zone erogene. E allora fai
una mappa: lecca le ascelle e l'addome, succhia gli alluci
e le dita della mano, mordicchia le gambe dietro le
giunture. Crea sensazioni. Domina il/la partner con il
solletico. Rilassa con un massaggio. Una sola regola: non
scambiare liquidi. Il resto sta a te. Il sesso non è solo
quella cosa. È qualsiasi cosa che hai voglia di provare.
C'è tanto da fare.

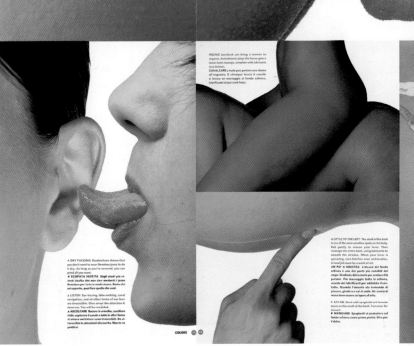

REINE bareback can bring a woman to
orgasm. And whoever plays the horse gets a
lower-back massage, complete with lubricants
(see below).
CAVALCARE a nudo può portare una donna
all'orgasmo. E chiunque faccia la cavalla fa
il fresco un massaggio al fondo schiena,
lubrificanti inclusi (vedi foto).

DRY FUCKING Studies have shown that
you don't need to wear Brooklyn jeans to do
it dry. As long as you're covered, you can
grind all you want.
SCOPATA VESTITA Dagli studi più re-
centi risulta che non devi metterti i jeans
Brooklyn per farlo in modo duro. Basta che
sei coperta, poi fare quello che vuoi.

LISTEN Ear-kissing, lobe-nibbing, nasal
navigation, and all other forms of ear love
are irresistible. Give areas the attention it
deserves. You will be rewarded.
ASCOLTARE Baciare le orecchie, succhiare
i lobi, esplorare il nudo e tutte le altre forme
di amore auricolare sono irresistibili. Da at-
l'orecchio le attenzioni che merita. Non te ne
pentirai.

A LITTLE TO THE LEFT. The small of the back
is one of the most sensitive spots on the body.
Rub gently to arouse your lover. Then
massage the entire back, using lubricants to
smooth the strokes. When your lover is
quivering, turn him/her over and localize.
A hand job must be a work of art.
UN PO' A SINISTRA. L'incavo del fondo
schiena è una dei punti più sensibili del
corpo. Strofinalo delicatamente per eccitare il/la
partner. Poi massaggia tutta la schiena,
usando dei lubrificanti per addolcire il con-
tatto. Quando l'amante sta tremando di
piacere, giralo/a e val di calda. Un lavoro di
mano deve essere un'opera d'arte.

EAT ME. Start with spaghetti and tomato
sauce on the small of the back. Turn over for
dessert.
MANGIAMI. Spaghetti al pomodoro sul
fondo schiena come prima piatto. Gira per
il dolce.

COLORS

Vol. 7 Jun. 1994

EDITOR IN CHIEF   Tibor Kalman
ART DIRECTOR   Scott Stowell
PHOTOGRAPHER   Oliviero Toscani

RAY GUN

1 **Vol. 42 Dec. 1996**
2 **Vol. 44 Mar. 1997**

EDITOR *Marvin Scott Jarrett*
ART DIRECTORS *1 Robert Hales, 2 Chris Ashworth*
DESIGNERS *1 Robert Hales, 2 Chris Ashworth*
PHOTOGRAPHERS *1 John Scarisbrick, 2 Davies and Davies*
DESIGN FIRM *Ray Gun Publishing*
PUBLISHER *Ray Gun Publishing, Inc.*
USA

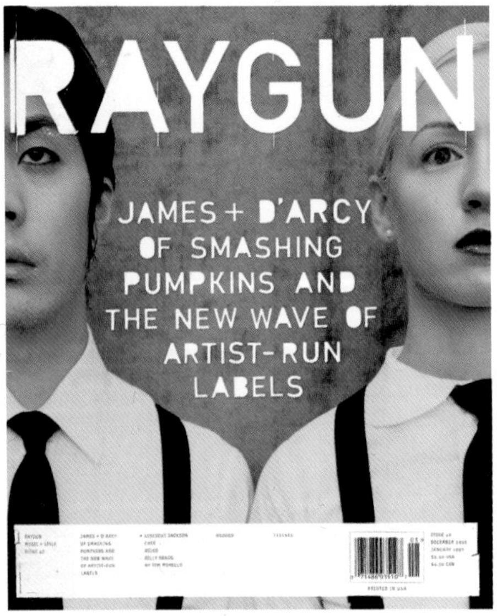

1

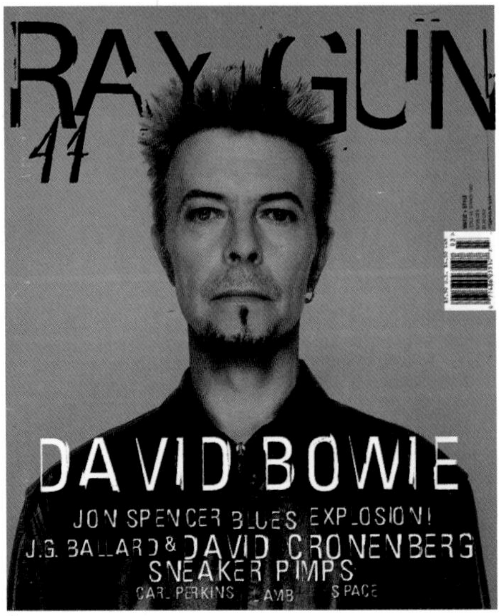

2

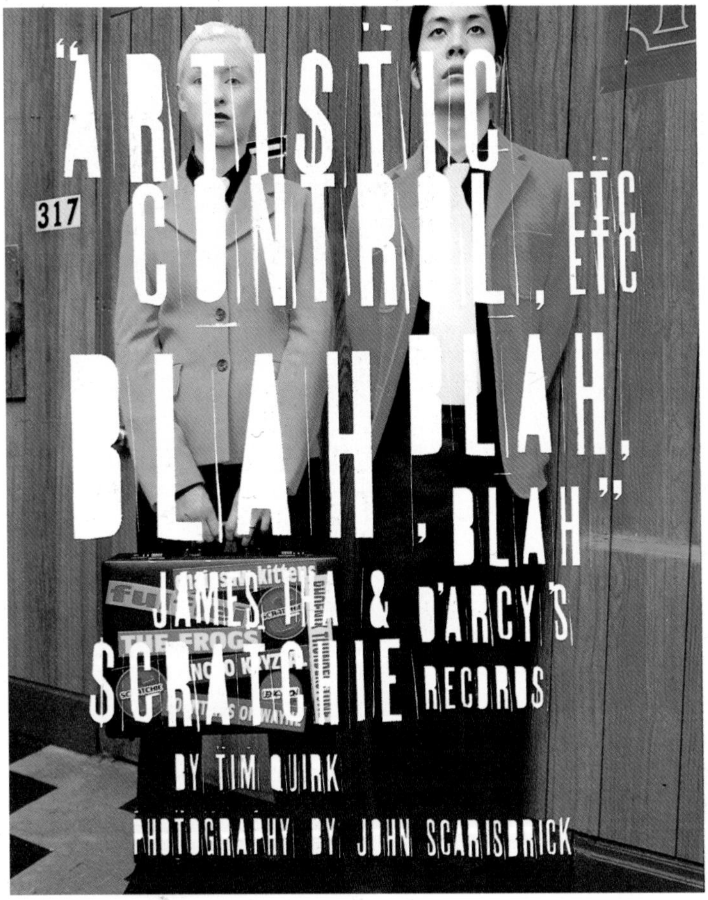

EDITORS' NOTE: We like Joe Ely

Early in 1980, when the Clash came to New York City to play the Palladium, my friend and I joined the majority of the crowd in booing the opening act, Joe Ely. I did this mostly because I was a 15-year-old dunderhead, and hating the opening acts at rock concerts was as much a part of the ritual back then as holding up lighters when our beloved headliners left the stage. Ely's songs were all pretty slow, and his voice was pretty low, so the crowd eventually got louder than he was. It was painful and embarrassing enough that the members of the Clash felt compelled to come out on stage and dance around in trench coats while Ely sang, just so the crowd would start clapping, which, like little robots, we did.

Eight years later, someone gave me a Joe Ely tape: *King of the Highway*. My friend and I were touring with our own band now, and knew what it was like to play for a roomful of people who just wanted us to hurry up and finish so whatever group they actually paid to see could take the stage. Experience and maturity had refined our tastes, so we were ready to listen to the tape with open ears.

We decided he still sucked, and tossed the cassette out the window of our van, figuring, if he was King of the Highway, he'd be pleased.

The point of this little prologue is to explain that I get suspicious when famous acts reach the point where they decide it's not enough that millions of people worship them, now we all have to worship the bands they like, too. So the prospect of artists starting up record companies to inflict their old heroes and new discoveries on not just a captive roomful of fans, but on the whole damn world at once, only turns my dread up a notch or two.

It's like when actors decide that what they really want to do is sing. They might actually be pretty good, but nobody cares. I have a good friend whose band put out an LP for Apple Records in the early '70s, the Beatles' label. No, you never heard of them. You know why? BECAUSE THEY WERE ON APPLE RECORDS!

It's a little *too* easy to resent musicians who extend their tentacles into the business world: if they've been able to amass the requisite levels of cash and clout to start up a bona-fide record company, chances are they've done so by reaching that media-saturation point where even the fans get irritated when their faces pop up on TV or magazine covers, again. The Smashing Pumpkins certainly qualify there.

Of course, it's that infuriating bald guy that does most of the writing, singing, and talking for the Smashing Pumpkins. And it's guitarist James Iha and bassist D'Arcy who've started the label: Scratchie Records. And I have to admit, that's the best name for a record company I've heard in a long time. Anyway, they've just signed a deal with Mercury to distribute and market all their releases, which means somebody thinks they're on to something.

Besides, the Smashing Pumpkins are as proud of their business savvy as they are of their music. To me, they always sounded kind of *grand*, and I mean that precisely how a pretentious seventh-grade girl might: trying to make something small sound really big. But so what? Several million people obviously disagree.

The Smashing Pumpkins have sold an awful lot of records. I have no idea why, so I ask the Pumpkins if they know what made them huge. D'Arcy says, "We believed in the music and we worked our asses off. And we had good business sensibilities. At the time we understood – and wanted, also – that it was important to work our way up slowly, and have a really solid foundation, and fan base. You could almost say, yes, it's been kind of a plan, we pretty much knew a lot more what we were doing than most people. I think we really had a good sense of what was going on in the music industry with the whole alterna-rock thing, and what was necessary to make it work and stick around for a long time. Mostly it comes down to common sense and hard work. And, I think we write really good music."

You'll notice that, while her answer begins and ends with music, the emphasis is on all the work that goes into it. And nowhere in her list, ever, does she mention luck.

That makes sense, if you're in the Smashing Pumpkins. The Pumpkins' devotion to the actual job of being in a band is undeniable. They were probably one of the first groups that, given a choice, decided to release their record on an independent label not because they wanted credibility, but because it was a good business decision. They are the only band I know of who have taken the term "careerist" as a compliment. It doesn't mean they don't have chops, it just means they got them heard.

D'Arcy seems convinced the lessons she's learned as a Pumpkin are all it takes to lead a young band through the obstacle course of the music industry. "You're just going along blind, you're this young band, and you don't know anything. We've been through it already. That's kind of a big part of the reason that we're doing it, in a way. It would be pretty pathetic if we can't make this work."

But understanding how the business works doesn't necessarily make you a businessman – just how much do you think Economics professors get paid, anyway? Pressed for details about the structure of the company, the terms of their deal with Mercury or the division of labor among both the partners, both James and D'Arcy lean toward hopelessly general answers. D'Arcy says, "We help a lot with the business decisions," but isn't too keen on specifying any. When I ask James if there's a legal document somewhere, detailing who put in what and how the money gets divvied up once the company turns a profit, he says, "It's all pretty fluid. I think basically we're all just –Jeremy's the president."

To be fair, I don't get the sense that D'Arcy and Iha are unable to give me specifics, just unwilling; they're very polite, but cautious. Later, on the phone from Scratchie's office in Chicago, label president Jeremy Freeman is perfectly happy to tell me the six partners have a legal agreement, dividing the company into specific shares according to each's contribution. He also explains, patiently and pragmatically, the outlines of Scratchie's arrangement with Mercury, the potential benefits, and some possible dangers.

To hear these two tell it, though, Scratchie Records sounds more like a wacky sitcom pilot than a business. D'Arcy's brother-in-law Jeremy Freeman and his friend Jamie Stewart had been talking about setting up a label to sell Jamaican 7" singles in the US. D'Arcy, her husband Kerry Brown (who plays drums in Catherine) and Iha (who's D'Arcy's ex-boyfriend) had been thinking about starting up a label of their own. The five decided to join forces, and brought in Jeremy's childhood friend Adam Schlesinger, another musician from the band Ivy. "At the beginning," says Iha, "we just threw them money. D'Arcy put in some money, and Adam put in some money. Jeremy couldn't pay his rent and his phone bills."

Can't you just see them holding a board meeting in a suitably urban coffee shop? Iha and Brown trade put-downs. Meanwhile, Jeremy's not talking to D'Arcy due to some unresolved spat with her sister. Jamie just sits there going, "Guys, we have work to do." Someone hits the canned laughter button.

Actually, Scratchie has grown quickly and efficiently. Freeman claims he, D'Arcy, Brown, and Iha first discussed the label in April of '95, and had it officially running three months and $30,000 later. They released mostly dance and alternative 45's, plus a compilation LP of dancehall reggae. It's now just over a year later, they've finalized the deal with Mercury, and have a number of releases slated for the coming months. They've got bands that have been around, like the Chainsaw Kittens and the Frogs (whose concept EP, *Starjob*, was produced by another Smashing Pumpkin, Billy Corgan). They've got brand new bands, like Schlesinger's side-project, Fountains of Wayne, and Fulflej. And they've got what Iha calls "the other side of Scratchie" – dance acts Jeremy dug up, like Pancho Kryztal.

Since D'Arcy and Iha don't pretend to know very much about dancehall reggae, I'm not going to, either. But we can talk about the rock bands. We can state with confidence that not only do none of them suck, most of them fall on the happy side of exciting. That's an amazing feat for any record company. None of them sound like the Pumpkins (that would be *gauche*), but you can hear why a Pumpkin would like them: they're all fond of their guitars (even influence-blending Fulflej), and they all share a musician's love of complex arrangements tempered by a businessman's recognition that ya gotta have singles. Like the Pumpkins, each sounds new in a most familiar way – except for Fountains of Wayne, whose retro tendencies make them sound very familiar, but still leave room for a press flack to say, "There's something really unique about what they do." Listen to three or four Scratchie records in a row, and you can be forgiven for thinking James and D'Arcy started this enterprise just so they could meet some new people to sit around with in hotels talking about obscure '70s bands.

Right now, however, they're sitting around in a hotel talking about their record company. James is just trying to do his job conscientiously. He's very aware of the tape deck. When he says someone's name, he spells it out. He frets that an answer will "read really boring." And he has a frustrating habit of answering the question he expects rather than the one that's asked. D'Arcy is a True Believer. She talks about every band, especially Fulflej, like their mothers were all killed in a plane crash, and she's the concerned aunt who's taking them in.

D'ARCY: I dragged James in kicking and screaming once we had –
JAMES: What do you mean?! You called me one day, "There's this record label...."
D'ARCY: I forced you to sit in my car for like an hour and made you listen to Fulflej.
JAMES: No, I wouldn't sit there for an hour.
D'ARCY: Yeah, because you wouldn't stay, you wouldn't listen. You're like, (puts on a grumpy voice) "It's good. The kids'll buy it."
RAYGUN: Did you say that, James?
JAMES: I didn't understand at first. You pissed me off. I only listened to like two and a half songs.
D'ARCY: I had to seatbelt him and lock the doors.
JAMES: You're over-exaggerating.
D'ARCY: Maybe a little. I had him by the ear. I was in the driver's seat. I'm always in the driver's seat.
JAMES: She thinks so. Could you stop shaking or whatever you're doing?
D'ARCY: No.
JAMES: So what else do you want to know?

There's an intriguing line about Fulflej in some Scratchie press release: "D'Arcy gets this weird look of excitement every time she hears it and repeats: 'This is why I got into music in the first place.'" I read this line over and over when I first saw it because, for all its enthusiasm, it's also got a sad ring to it, as if jumping up and down at Madison Square Garden just wasn't doing it for her anymore. Maybe the whole record company thing is just a way of re-connecting to a musical enthusiasm that the business of being a pop-star beat out of her.

It's a nice theory but I'm about to learn it doesn't fly.

RAYGUN: While we're on the subject of Fulflej –
JAMES: They're a dynamic new band of the '90s, combining hip-hop sensibilities atop epic dramas, with rather fantasy-like lyrics and complex musical arrangements.
RAYGUN: And the kids will buy it.
JAMES: Kids will love it.
D'ARCY: You said: "The kids will buy it."
JAMES: I thought I said the kids will *love* it.
D'ARCY: *Now* you said that.
JAMES: I don't remember.
D'ARCY: No, you didn't. You said, "It'll sell records. And the kids will like it." That's what you said.
RAYGUN: There's a quote from D'Arcy in some press release (I dig the relevant quotation out of my notes). When I first read it, it sounded exciting, like the last thing a record mogul would ever say. At the same time, there's something kind of forlorn about it. You're in the Smashing Pumpkins, but here you are saying *this is why I got into music*.
JAMES: Yeah? So?
D'ARCY: What do you mean?
JAMES: What's your point?
RAYGUN: We're getting to the question that comes after "What is Scratchie?" Which is, "Why are you doing this?" We can assume you're rich enough that it's not a business investment.
D'ARCY: Yeah?
RAYGUN: So why get involved with a record company? Do you think you can do it better than everybody else?
JAMES: I don't think necessarily that we can do it better –
D'ARCY: I think we can. I think we can.
JAMES: I think there are a lot of labels that have done well by bands. And there are a lot of labels that screw bands. Hopefully we're not gonna be one of those labels that screws our bands.
D'ARCY: "Hopefully" James says. What are you, planning some strange transformation into the Evil James?
JAMES: Well, if every record we put out *bombs* –
D'ARCY: He'll do whatever it takes!
JAMES: You're really pissing me off.
D'ARCY: I guess I'm just a romantic. James, he's one of those number-cruncher guys.
JAMES: I'm just speaking realistically. I don't think the record business is like this teen fantasy. I don't expect all of our bands to sell a million records, but I don't want them to sell 100 records just to their friends. I don't sit and think about how many records a band's

Vol. 42 Dec. 1996

EDITOR *Randy Bookasta*
ART DIRECTOR *Robert Hales*
DESIGNER *Scott Denton-Cardew*
PHOTOGRAPHER *John Scarisbrick*

S NEAK PIMPS

SNEAKER PIMPS
by Aidin Vaziri
photography by Stephane Sednaoui

Liam Howe leans forward in his chair and begins to consider the Sneaker Pimps' basic dichotomy. As his eyes search the dark and cluttered conference room of London's One Little Indian office, he eventually articulates the difficult position his band occupies.

"As an artist, you have an obligation to immerse yourself in popular culture and to be a part of the thing you're supposed to be criticizing," the keyboardist says. "If we're going to make music about the confusion of the '80s, the worst thing we could do is stay in an ivory tower and have no connection with the way that popular culture is working. It's really important to be within the system."

Sneaker Pimps' debut album, Becoming X, has been described as both one of the most seductive offerings to roll off the atmospheric-electronic UK assembly line and as one of the most flagrantly derivative byproducts of the trip-hop epidemic. It has also been suggested that the group's sassy first single, "6 Underground," opened the gates for a flood of soundalike bands, ranging from Morcheeba to Baby Fox.

More importantly, perhaps, the Sneaker Pimps — a London-based trio that includes singer Kelli Dayton and guitarist Chris Corner — is not all about appearances. While the group's music may draw from the same claustrophic song structures, eerie movie soundtrack textures and languid hip-hop rhythms that have become cornerstones of the modern urban underground sound, its creators have paid remarkable attention to pursuing a higher purpose.

"We came together in an odd way, and decided early on that we would do whatever we wanted to do," says Dayton. Suffering from a bad hangover, she defends her band's hybrid identity. "It was a very natural thing. We all have really different backgrounds. We have different ideas, and none of us are willing to compromise to the point where our individual musical tastes get pushed away. So we decided to push on and argue musically, and take the best of each of us as far as we can."

"It's always a dilemma, because I've always been excited about how contemporary culture changes," Howe says. "At the same time, I love timeless things. The Sneaker Pimp way is somewhat constrictional, because it's going for timeless songs, but at the same time wanting very fashionable, genre-specific sounds. You'll listen to our album and you'll be able to place it within five years of history, it's definitely about '96 living. If we made it sound totally timeless, then it would lose a lot of its power, it would just be another songwriter harping away on his guitar.

"That was one of the problems," he continues. "If you accept contemporary production of genres or trends, you put yourself up for being cast aside. Sometimes, if you produce things in a contemporary way, you risk losing the song beneath the surface. But it's important for us to be part of what's happening, because you can't really criticize what's happening unless you are a part of it. The first thing we ever thought about before we started the project was that we wanted to make this a songwriter's project. We wanted to be able to listen to the album in 10 years time and go, 'These were great songs.' So the group's sound is basically just a contemporary vessel for songwriters."

Howe began collaborating with Corner in 1992, first under the name F.R.I.S.K. and then later as Line of Flight. Dayton had been in bands around Birmingham since the age of 16. She was discovered singing in a pub by the songwriters, lured into the fold and then shot into the spotlight. The name Sneaker Pimps was adopted from a catch-phrase sputtered out by Beastie Boy Mike D, who used the term to describe a friend he paid to search for hard-to-find gym shoes in the months before Becoming X. "Liam and Chris were the Underground" and the first modern electronic pop icons.

"Liam and Chris are so talented, I couldn't believe it when I first met them," Dayton says. "I used to working with people that just bashed away on three chords. I love that side about them.

"Funnily enough, if we would have done a folk version of our record, we would have got people talking more about what really mattered to us," Howe says. "We've always written songs on an acoustic guitar and everything after that point is pushing it as far as we can, which is important. We understand the excitement of Sneaker Pimps music and DJ culture, so we pushed it that way on purpose. But it's caused a strange backwards effect, because people think it sounds good, therefore the songs can't be that good. The whole point was to make great songs which sounded good, which is not a difficult concept. The purpose was to make the two stand together; to me it represents the bridge between indie music and dance music. It's a game which is really easy to fail at, but the goal is really big. If you succeed, you've really won something."

BOWIE IS THERE LIFE ON EARTH?

Perpetual outsider **David Bowie** talks about mortal sexual, the evolution of the creative urge, and pace of mortality with **Beso Kaquon**.

Photography by **Davies + Davies**

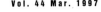

top   **Vol. 44 Mar. 1997**

ART DIRECTOR   Chris Ashworth
DESIGNER   Chris Ashworth
PHOTOGRAPHER   Stephane Sednaoui

bottom   **Vol. 44 Mar. 1997**

ART DIRECTOR   Chris Ashworth
DESIGNER   Chris Ashworth
PHOTOGRAPHER   Davies and Davies

SPEAK

1	Sep. 1996
2	Dec. 1996

EDITOR	Neil Feineman
ART DIRECTOR	Martin Venezky
DESIGNER	Martin Venezky
PHOTOGRAPHER	1 Darin Pappas
PUBLISHER	Speak Magazine

USA

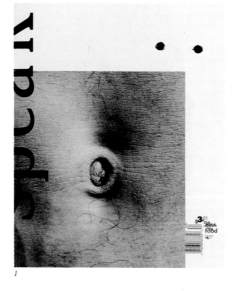

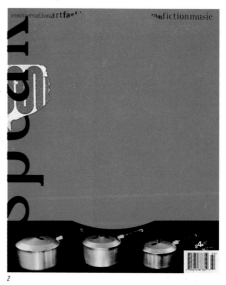

1

2

Apr. 1996

PHOTOGRAPHER
Kanya Niijima

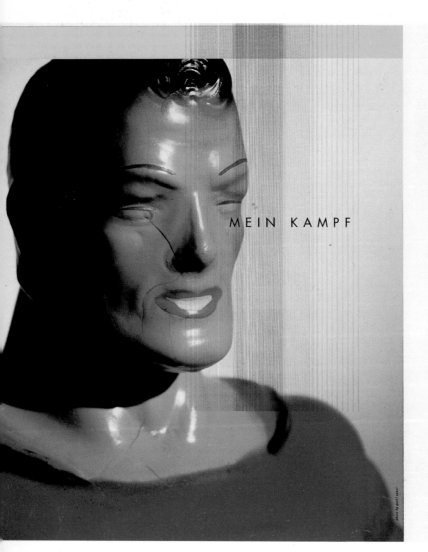

MEIN KAMPF

by J.D. SALINGER

Apr. 1996

ART DIRECTOR	David Carson
DESIGNER	Chip Kidd

582

like being called the world's greatest

penis

camel and woman

by ROBERT RIDDELL
photographs by DAVID PERRY

fast car

SIX HUNDRED MILES

FAST

FormulaShell   SPIRIT OF AMERICA

POWER

Apr. 1996

ART DIRECTOR	David Carson
DESIGNER	David Carson
PHOTOGRAPHER	David Carson
ILLUSTRATOR	Mike Salisbury

Dec. 1996

EDITOR	Neil Feineman
ART DIRECTOR	Martin Venezky
DESIGNER	Martin Venezky
PHOTOGRAPHER	David Perry

creator

Vol. 4 Summer 1996

EDITORS	Nick Crowe, Patrick Collerton
ART DIRECTOR	Adam Shepherd
DESIGNER	Bert Schlechtriem
PHOTOGRAPHER	Tim Kent
METAL LOGO SCULPTURE	Dan Peel
PUBLISHER	Creator Magazine

UK

Good ideas are not difficult to come by, and for a life that wills its own development, acting on a good idea is essential practice. Generally, this means discarding or revising an old idea. Yet loyalty to a particular ideology or doctrine can be so great that to ignore the advantages which a new idea can offer is to act in spite of yourself, in a stubborn gesture of pride. By choosing against your better sense, by choosing insanely, you fail in your duty to yourself, and thus in your duty to those around you. Your duty is not to save face but to change your face, as the world changes around you.

Of course loyalty disguises fear – if you choose an idea whose (perhaps) radical consequences would effect great personal change, then the personality which you've spent so much time cultivating for yourself would probably wilt and die a slow, unsocial death. Your friends and colleagues might eye you differently and their voices might quaver a little. Yet anyone who, in a continuous act of self-renewal, makes a habit of taking on new ideas will tell you that, though his friends may desert him, the confidence, calm, and individuality which he gains will bring him deeper friendships and greater awareness – both of himself and the world. He will have no need of clubs, or the crutch of a social clique, for he will no longer be afraid of himself.

Many believe that someone who assimilates the idea of another is no more than an intellectual thief. Nation states, political parties and religious groups – friends even – view their ideas as they would their property, as a material wealth which must be protected. If then, you decide that one of their ideas might be a useful tool in your own life they instantly demand some kind of pay-back: your undying allegiance, or recognition at least of their superior imagination. To refuse such demands is to risk ridicule and alienation. To accept is to compromise your self. Such power games are of no consequence to a person of ideas, because ridicule, alienation and compromise are the stony cards of membership in the life of little change.

By gathering together ideas, some new some old, some visual some bold, Creator hopes to inspire movement, both in action and in thought. Many you might accept, while others you will reject – with passionate contempt. Whatever the case, the ideas contained in the following pages are free; they belong to no one, and no one should belong to them.

CONTENDERS

CREATOR FOUR

Emperor Penguin
Photo: Jack Daniels ©

06
07
08
15
18
24
27
28
30
34
40
44
47
48
54
55

top **Vol. 4 Summer 1996**
DESIGNERS *James de Ville,*
Adam Shepherd
PHOTOGRAPHER *David Milne Watson*

bottom **Vol. 4 Summer 1996**
DESIGNERS *Adam Shepherd,*
Bert Schlechtriem
PHOTOGRAPHER *Jack Daniels (penguin)*

Vol. 4 Summer 1996

DESIGNERS   1,2,3,4,6 Bert Schlechtriem,
4,5,6 Micosch Holland
ILLUSTRATORS   2,5 Luke Shepherd,
3 Sandra Witkam
PHOTOGRAPHER   4 Anna Rauhala

Best of British Design

What art, if any, exists in commercial design? Creator contacted four of Britain's top graphic design agencies to find out. The brief was as follows:

Creator Magazine
tel & fax
0171 582 1770

To: From:

At: Date:

As you already know in the third issue of Creator, an English design agency, Blue Source, put forward a type of design manifesto. In the next I would like to take this idea further and publish a page of your design, including text, which would sum up the values / ideas (if any) which you may abide by.

Interspersed within the magazine would run similar pieces from other groups, so readers can start to build up a picture of the movement within the business at the moment.

I certainly hope you might find the time to produce something that you would feel happy with. The deadline for the next issue is mid April.

Please find below some suggestions for the writing, but obviously you can do what ever you want, as this is the whole point of our magazine.

Some starting points might be:

a. What moral code or aesthetic principles do you apply in creating a piece?
b. If any values / principles are applied, why so? (And how would these affect the way in which you produce a particular piece of design.)
c. Do you feel any pressure from market forces, and do they effect your approach to work?
d. What do you think of European design at present, and where do you fit in, if at all?
e. As a group of designers, with fresh ideas, where do you see yourselves going?

The dimensions of a single page are 240mm by 297mm with 3mm bleed. I will confirm the spot (which looks like being a type of deep racing green).

16 Crewdson Rd. Oval. London SW9 0LJ.UK
Tel & Fax: ++44 171 582 1770

Best of L.S.D.

My eyes are full of the tears that you should have cried .

this is not England

[if only it could always be like this]. i don't really believe that designers can be true to themselves or be totally creative unless they are able to live in a world of their own making. one in which they have no responsibilities to anyone or anything else, except those to the creation and production of an idea, and the execution of a piece of work. too much information. you're either going to have to create or turn your system off. i find that the radio can be an invaluable friend at times like these. as you know, in order to appreciate good architecture one has to commit murder. if only the same could be said for a designer's aesthetic principles when working on a commissioned piece. [i've often thought about it. but like everyone else, when faced with a similar situation i have declined.] sometimes i get careless and i let my dreams take me for a ride. if only it could still be like that perfect day in London during the long hot Summer of August 1938. it's not going to last for ever you know. all this modern technology. it's only survived this length of time due to the artists & designers in this society. how come sometimes the use of cellotape seems to be the only way out? what's everyone else doing. that's what i'd really like to know. do they feel the same about it as we do? i understand the fact that if you live in the countryside you have to occasionally cut the grass. but what i do find hard to come to terms with is the fact that design is required, but not needed. now why is this. when it has the ability to change our lives? i once saw a film featuring someone that i could have so easily have fallen in love with. surely, the only pressure that we should be giving in to should be in our approach to producing a piece of work. what's happening to us? just what is it about type printed on glass that makes me cry? obviously the way that our new look at things has changed. but has the way he now looks at you changed? driving while the dawn creeps in. wide awake but full of sin. i have a box full of old images. and the prospect of one day being able to look at them is most exciting. i agree that in order to create something new, one has to destroy the old. de-construction. but why should that creatively only relate to 64pt type? we all experience pain at some time. can't you see that it's the fresh ideas that are the problem. it's the traditional ones that are really needed. somehow the past seems to hold more for me now than the future does.

just what is it about a piece of beautiful typography that makes you think of England?

 the gay aesthetic

Adrian Smith interviews Pierre et Gilles

On the corner of a street in the quiet Paris suburb of Le Pré de St Gervais sits a stony grey factory block. The exterior of this drab, council-converted HLM reveals nothing of its inhabitants. Even the gloomy ground-floor corridor is of little help. Only one thing gives any indication: opposite the lift a small splash of colour is posted to a door, a note proclaiming 'Pierre et Gilles'.

One ring of the bell and a short, muscular man called Pierre greets us, rather different to the Pierre of the pictures; an eternal youth with baby-smooth skin and jet black, slick-back hair. This Pierre is more ordinary, an older man with the same skin problems as a million other city dwellers. Gilles, though of solid build, shakes my hand with the polite apprehension usual to anyone inviting inquisitive strangers into his home.

More of a surprise is the large, open-plan kitchen and dining room, which, on first inspection, is reminiscent of a Philippine rickshaw, or a glamourous North African Souk. This is a palace of gold and silver, of sky blues and emerald greens. Giant mosaics of kitsch scream out from the walls, portraits and picture postcards abound (Jesus, Michael Jackson, Marc Almond; Pierre & Gilles dressed as businessmen, as samurai warriors, as a couple of porcelain mermaids). Attached to one wall a three metre high pagoda of shelves, stuffed with more ephemera, rises up in a magnificent act of worship to the TV set. The final touch to this exotic paradise are the birds who not only provide the background music, but are free to fly around, one occasionally stopping on Pierre's shoulder.

Creator 48

---

top	**Vol. 4 Summer 1996**
DESIGNERS	*Adam Shepherd,*
	Bert Schlechtriem
DESIGN FIRM	*Laurence Stevens Design (right)*

bottom	**Vol. 4 Summer 1996**
DESIGNER	*Judith Huinck*
PHOTOGRAPHER	*Pierre et Gilles*

43

Cut

1 **Vol. 51 Jul. 1996**
2 **Vol. 53 Sep. 1996**
3 **Vol. 55 Nov. 1996**

EDITOR · *Ken Sato*
ART DIRECTOR · *Hideki Nakajima*
DESIGNER · *Hideki Nakajima*
PHOTOGRAPHERS · *1 Mark Seliger,*
2 Alexi Tan,
3 Bruce Weber
DESIGN FIRM · *Nakajima Design*
PUBLISHER · *Rockin' On Inc.*

Japan

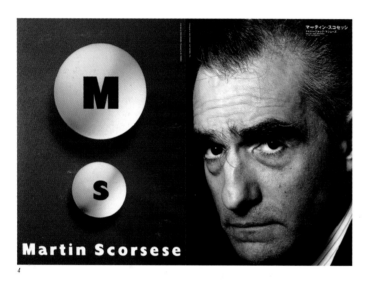

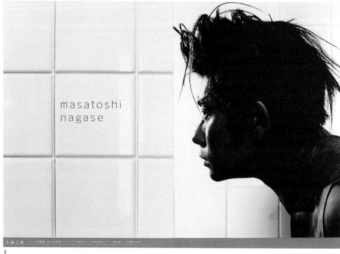

4 **Vol. 48 Mar. 1996**

PHOTOGRAPHERS · *John Stoddart (right),*
Aya Tokunaga (left)
ARTWORK · *Hideki Nakajima (left)*

6 **Vol. 50 May 1996**

PHOTOGRAPHERS · *Diego Uchitel (right),*
Aya Tokunaga (left)
ARTWORK · *Hideki Nakajima (left)*

5 **Vol. 50 May 1996**

PHOTOGRAPHERS · *Akira Matsuo (right),*
Aya Tokunaga (left)
ARTWORK · *Hideki Nakajima (left)*

7 **Vol. 53 Sep. 1996**

PHOTOGRAPHERS · *Alexi Tan,*
Aya Tokunaga (left)
ARTWORK · *Hideki Nakajima (left)*

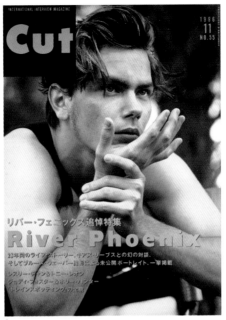

2

3

Larry Clark

8

9

10

11

STUDIO VOICE

1　**Jul. 1996**
2　**Jan. 1997**
EDITOR IN CHIEF　*Shinya Matsuyama*
ART DIRECTOR　*Yasushi Fujimoto (+cap)*
CHIEF DESIGNER　*Yoichi Iwamoto*
DESIGNER　*Yasushi Fujimoto (+cap)*
PHOTOGRAPHY　*2 from "Uchu Suibaku-sen"*
DESIGN FIRM　*Cap*
PUBLISHER　*Infas Co., Ltd.*
Japan

1

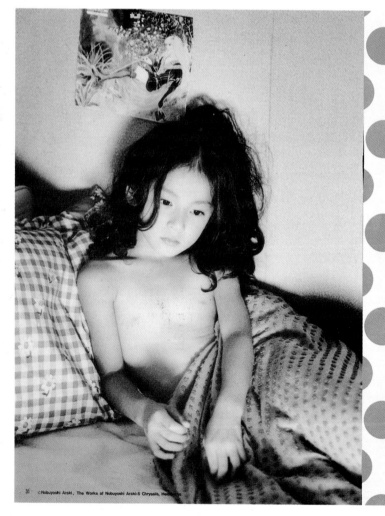

31　©Nobuyoshi Araki, The Works of Nobuyoshi Araki-5 Chrysalis, Heibonsha

ロリコンと少女趣味の相関

文　木村重樹

少女イメージそのものの陳腐化が指摘されてひさしい現在、今なお真性のロリコンを体現している奴は何人ぐらいいるのだろうか？たとえばかをとどめて〈小室哲哉氏など〉、お気に入りの若年女性シンガーをタヱとはべらせ「なんだ面生けしから人ロリコン野郎じゃないか」といった心ない中傷をとばし耳にするが、私見によればほのバラ具合はいかにも「お仕事」くさく、まともに考えるのも阿呆らし、しかしお里が思わぬところで露見してしまう・FNNだ深夜に放送されている所のトーク番組「TK Music Factory」のエンディングを溢きん人はご覧になったことがあるだろうか。歌手でも何でもないこちらの予似ギャロクティーン・モデルを毎週がまえてきては、ろくすっぽ時給もせずプロのバックバンドつきで自分の持ち歌を歌わせるという所向で、これがもう諸説的にどうしよもない歌唱な

少女イメージ ......

Jul. 1996
DESIGNER　*Tomoko Kumagai*
PHOTOGRAPHER　*Nobuyoshi Araki*

Jul. 1996

DESIGNER　Tomoko Kumagai
PHOTOGRAPHY　1 Billy Name,
　　　　　　　2 Art Club 2000

少女の時間　予兆とノスタルジア

文×川崎賢子

2

RANRAN SUZUKI
鈴木蘭々

「自分を信じて行かなくちゃダメです」という無邪気な希望

鈴木蘭々は単なるぶりっ子福耳のCMタレントではなかった、ましてや妙な反発心が西麻布のトレンド女性でもなかった。これが、けっこう90年代に再生した初期アイドルのヴァージョン・アップ「サウンド編」なのである。やや喪失したセブンティーズ・リヴァイヴァルという声も喉まで出かかってはいるんだけど、スピッツやかぐや姫、小沢健二がゴロゴロ、フィッシュマンズやRCサクセションと、どれも日本のコンテクストでは歌謡曲だけがまだまだ「笑

CIBO MATTO
チボ・マット

リカを席捲する
の強靭な胃袋

ヴェルヴェット・アンダーグラウンド以来のニューヨーク・ライトから来た...NYに在住のミキミキとミドリが90年代の最先端...

HANIN ELIAS
ATARI TEENAGE RIOT
ハニン・エライアス

ナチス・ダウン／死んじまえ！／暴動を起こせ！...ロウな歌詞ではない、ARTは当初、英フォノグラムと契約関係にあったグループで...

YUKI
JUDY & MARY
ユキ

カワイくてやかましい
ロリータ・パンクの女王様

経歴は...実はよく知りません（ゴメン）。オルタード・イメージみたいにハッチャキになって歌っているわけではないけど...

KENICKIE

「ポップという言葉はちょっとスポイルされているね」だけど、わたしはポップ・スターになりたい。ポップ・スターと結婚してポップ・スターの赤ちゃんをいっぱい生みたいの」とローレンが言えば...マリーは「世界征服よ」...

トラッシュ・ギャルズは総理大臣を目指す!?

KATIE JANE GARSIDE
ケイティ・ジェーン・ガーサイド

壮絶ホラー・パフォーマンスの不可解さ

コントロールを喪失してしまったビョークのような声か印象的...

CARO-LINE NOVAC
DOOPEES
キャロライン・ノヴァク

若者音楽文化を包囲する
アストロ・エイジ・ガール

ドープ（DOPE）の状態から引き伸ばしてドゥーピーズ（DOOPEES）である。アストロ・エイジ・スティール・オリジンとヤン...

ゴールディもたじたじのジャングル・シスターズ

ディープ・ブルー「ザ・ヘリコプター・チューン」のヒットを機に'94年頃から急速に再浮上してきたジャングル（ドラムンベース）のシーンにおいて...

KEMI-STRY & STORM
ケミストリー&ストーム

22

opposite page top   **Jan. 1997**
DESIGNER   *Tomoko Kumagai*

opposite page bottom   **Jan. 1997**
DESIGNER   *Yoichi Iwamoto*
PHOTOGRAPHER   *Stephane Sednaoui*

Jan. 1997
DESIGNER   *Tomoko Kumagai*

Transistor Radio
For America
50〜60年代アメリカの日本製トランジスタ・ラジオ

特集★
SPACE
BACHELOR
DREAMS

ほしいほしすぎる
感じなメイド・イン・
ジャパンのラジオ

文=伊藤ガビン

SV FASHION PHOTO SELECT
写真=ステファン・セドナウイ

Future is
here
and now

from HK's artificial material collection '96
Stephane Sednaoui

Spirit
Vol. 5 Mar./Apr. 1997

EDITOR   Susan Kamil
ART DIRECTORS   Colin Higgs,
   Jonathan Oppong-Wiafe
PHOTOGRAPHER   William Davis
PUBLISHER   Trojan Horse Publishing
UK

Vol. 5 Mar./Apr. 1997

ART DIRECTOR
Colin Higgs
DESIGNER
Susan Kamil
PHOTOGRAPHER
Michael Chambers

Vol. 5 Mar./Apr. 1997

EDITOR   Susan Kamil
ART DIRECTOR   Colin Higgs
DESIGNERS   Blinkk, Philips, Laurent
PHOTOGRAPHERS   Blinkk, Philips, Laurent

Skin

Vol. 5 Mar./Apr. 1997

EDITOR	Susan Kamil
ART DIRECTOR	Colin Higgs
PHOTOGRAPHER	William Davis

dSIDE

1,3   **Vol. 20 Feb./Mar. 1997**
2   **Vol. 18 Oct./Nov. 1996**

EDITOR   *Melanie Morris*
ART DIRECTOR   *David Smith*
DESIGNER   *David Smith*
PHOTOGRAPHER   *3 Peter Robathan @ Katz*
PUBLISHER   *Wardon Ltd.*

Ireland

FACT FASHION FICTION

dSIDE

LOVE ME TENDER

THE PRODIGY GET PERSONAL

RUAIDHRÍ CONROY • ALEXANDER McQUEEN • REEF • PAVEMENT • PARTY GIRLS

---

www.cdc.net/~drjekyll/negscoobylmain.htm
(Scobby Doo goes leather)

Make-up crisis? Prezzie dilemma? want to buy yourself something funky but cheap? This winter, **WAREHOUSE** launch special make-up sets packed in cute see-through pouches which contain lipstick, two eyeshadows and a nail varnish in metallic blue, purple and green. £8 gets you kitted out in colour-coded chic for sure.

dNOTE

EDITED BY MELANIE MORRIS. CONTRIBUTORS: SUZIE COEN, DONAL SCANNELL, JIM CARROLL, ANGELA McGOLDRICK, JIMMY COSTELLO AND GAVIN LYONS.

IF YOU HAVEN'T MADE IT INTO THE GALLERY OF PHOTOGRAPHY YET, THIS IS YOUR MOMENT. CURRENTLY ON SHOW IS THE **ROBERT MAPPLETHORPE** RETROSPECTIVE, RECEIVED DIRECTLY FROM THE HAYWARD GALLERY ON LONDON'S SOUTH BANK.

THIS IS PROBABLY THE BEST OPPORTUNITY WE WILL GET TO SEE A WIDE CROSS-SECTION OF THE CONTROVERSIAL PHOTOGRAPHER'S WORK. OVER 200 IMAGES ARE ON SHOW IN TWO PARTS, DISPLAYED IN A GOOD SPACE, WITHOUT THE OVER CROWDING SYNONYMOUS WITH ENGLISH GALLERIES.

THE TOTAL GAMMOT OF MAPPLETHORPE'S WORK IS ON EXHIBIT — THE FORMAL SOCIETY PORTRAITS, SEDUCTIVE FLOWER STUDIES, STRUCTURED FIGURE STUDIES ... AND THE RUDIE BITS.

THE EXHIBITION IS PRICED ON TWO TIERS — £3 PER PART OF THE SHOW, OR £4.50 FOR BOTH, SO MAKE ENOUGH TIME TO SEE THE WHOLE THING IN ONE VISIT, AND YOU'LL HAVE MONEY LEFT OVER TO BUY A POSTCARD OF YOUR FAVOURITE IMAGE.

THE GALLERY OF PHOTOGRAPHY IS OPEN SEVEN DAYS A WEEK, FROM 11AM-6PM AND IS SITUATED ON MEETING HOUSE SQUARE, TEMPLE BAR, DUBLIN.

YOU PROBABLY THINK YOU KNOW EVERYTHING THERE IS ABOUT THE DISNEY REAL-LIFE REMAKE OF **101 DALMATIONS**, BUT WHEN YOU SIT THERE BALANCING POPCORN, COKE, HOTDOG AND PICK 'N MIX, THINK OF GLENN CLOSE WHO STARVED HERSELF DOWN TO A 22 INCH WAIST TO BECOME THE TRULY ANGULAR CRUELLA DE VIL. ALSO TAKE A GOOD LOOK AT ANTHONY POWELL'S INCREDIBLE COSTUMES FOR CRUELLA. THE EIGHT OUTFITS WERE STRUCTURED, BUILT, STYLED AND ACCESSORISED DOWN TO THE BLACK GLOVES WITH RAZOR-SHARP NAILS. POWELL WAS GLENN CLOSE'S PERSONAL CHOICE FOR THE JOB AFTER THEY WORKED TOGETHER CREATING NORMA DESMOND IN ANDREW LLOYD WEBBER'S **SUNSET BOULEVARD**. HE WAS ALSO BEHIND THE COSTUMES FOR **SCANDAL**, **HOOK** AND THE INDIANA JONES MOVIES, BUT POWELL'S WORK WITH THE HOUSE OF DE VIL IS THE PROJECT THAT WILL ROCKET HIM INTO AB FAB COUTURE LAND. BEGONE FOUL SWEATSHIRT AND LEGGINGS, IT'S TIME FOR ONE (CRU)ELLAVA MAKE OVER.

GO THE AD CAMPAIGN SUCKS, AND THOSE BIG PINT DRINKING GLOVES ARE PROBABLY THE MOST USELESS LUMPS OF PLASTIC KNOWN TO MAN ... BUT BEFORE YOU COMPLETLY DISREGARD **GUINNESS** SPARE A THOUGHT FOR THE STRESS PINT. THIS LOW KEY PROMOTIONAL GIMMICK HAS WORKED ITS WAY INTO THE STAFF OFFICES. A RUBBER, FOAMY VERSION OF ITS STOUT RELATION WHICH IS BASICALLY AT YOUR DISPOSAL TO BEAT, THROW, SQUEEZ AND TORTURE AS THE MOMENT (OR YOUR MOOD) TAKES YOU.

THOUGH THE STRESS PINT MAY NOT TASTE GREAT WHEN LICKED, THIS LOVABLE LAD NEVER COMPLAINS ABOUT MISTREATMENT, WON'T GIVE YOU A HANGOVER AND IS ALWAYS FULL. AMICABLE FOR THE BLAGGING, WE JUST DON'T KNOW HOW WE SURVIVED BEFORE THIS IMITATION ANTHRAX CAME INTO OUR LIVES.

And you thought the only reason to visit Tralee was to hold up your support cards in the Dome, cheering your favourite at the Rose of Tralee. Little did you know that slap bang in the middle of the tourist shops selling Irish caridgans and useless breakable ornaments lies **SHINDIG**, a veritable haven of cool clothes and accessories.

It was set up over seven years ago by Gary Brosnan who was pissed off with travelling to the capital to find top vintage gear and funky streetwear. Over 1,500 square feet and two floors on Tralee's Russell Street, Shindig is crammed with this season's authentic seventies vibe and a large range of clubwear labels including Hooch, Hippy Chick, Disaster and Stoopid. But it doesn't stop there, Gary is not one to let the grass grow under his Northwaves, and has also opened a second shop called **FRONTIER** which is devoted to menswear and stocks the coolest brands from The States and Europe (Rusty, Mambo, Stussy, Saltrock, Instinct, and Kanna Beach). In its two year existance, Frontier has become a bigger tourist attaction than the Ring of Kerry.

In between buying trips to England and Holland, twenty six-year-old Brosnan can be found behind both counters clothing Tralee's fashion pack and very hip customers. With the success of Shindig and Frontier, Gary is determined that the rest of the county's clued-in kids will soon be battling a path to his door and stamping their firmly on his...

Just when you thought you'd sussed the whole nail varnish thing, along comes another new brand of designer polish. **DELUX** hails from Hollywood's hottest beauty parlour (no surprises there when you look at the forties glamour- style bottles). Delux regular clientele includes Courtney Love, Drew Barrymore, Tim Roth and Winona Rider, so if you want 'in' without having to go transatlantic, the nail varnish is a good place to start. There are ten shades in the range, all of which are named after fifties cocktails and come in opaque, opalescent and stain-tinting finishes. Whether you're after glam gold, bubblegum-babe pink, fashion victim brown or talons-with-attitude moss green, the range has something to appeal to nails and enhance dressing tables. Available from a number of London stockists and through mail order. Delux nailvarnish costs £8.50 per bottle and can be ordered on 00 44 171 636 7911. Look out for their latest shade, **PURRRFECT RED** — a true scarlet which everyone will be gagging for once Evita hits our screens.

IF YOUR VISUAL PERCEPTION OF **BENETTON** IS TOWERS OF JUMPERS FOLDED TO IDENTIKIT PERCISION AND STACKED ON BLAND SHOPPING MALL STORES, THEN IT'S TIME TO HEAD TO NEW YORK. THE BENETTON GROUP HAVE RECENTLY OPENED A MASSIVE MEGASTORE IN THE FAMOUS **FIFTH AVENUE SCRIBNER BOOK STORE**. THIS SUBSTANTIAL BEAUX ARTS BUILDING WAS ORIGINALLY THE OFFICE OF PUBLISHER CHARLES SCRIBNER WHO EDITED THE WORKS OF F. SCOTT FITZGERALD, ERNEST HEMINGWAY, THOMAS WOLDFE AND THEADORE ROOSEVELT AND IS THE EPICENTRE OF TWENTIETH CENTURY AMERICAN LITERARY WORLD. THE METAL, GLASS AND GILT BUILDING WAS ORIGINALLY BUILT IN 1913 AND WAS BOUGHT BY BENETTON IN 1988. SINCE THEN, A MASSIVE $4 MILLION RESTORATION JOB HAS TAKEN PLACE, SO BETWEEN SHOPPING FOR THE FUNKIER BENETTON FASHIONS, SPORTS GEAR, LUGGAGE, LINGERIE AND FRAGRANCES, YOU CAN TAKE IN A BIT OF CULTURE AND SUCK ON AN EXPRESSO IN THEIR BASEMENT CAFÉ. DOES THIS QUALIFY BENETTON FOR THE TITLE OF THE MOST COMPREHENSIVE ONE-STOP-SHOP?

Vol. 19 Dec./Jan. 1996-97

FASHION EDITOR: SONYA LENNON
PHOTOGRAPHER: KHARA PRINGLE AT
CHRIS HILL PHOTOGRAPHIC STUDIO
ASSISTED BY: MARINA MOORE STYLING
ASSISTANTS: SUZIE COEN AND BRONAGH
HEGARTY HAIR: JAMES MOONEY (087
547886) USING KIEHLS MAKE UP:
CARLOS OBREGON AT MORGAN BRAND
MODELS: CLARE AT ASSETS AND BRIAN
PROCESSING: ICL FULL STOCKISTS
DETAILS: FASHION DIRECTORY PAGE 77

ironWORKS

1

2

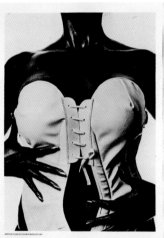

3

Vol. 18 Oct./Nov. 1996

PHOTOGRAPHER   *Shane McCarthy*
FASHION EDITOR   *Sonya Lennon*

Vol. 20 Feb./Mar. 1997

DESIGNERS   *Ronan Davlin,*
                David Smith
PHOTOGRAPHER   *Khara Pringle*
ILLUSTRATORS   *1,3 David Smith,*
                1,3 Ronan Deviln
FASHION EDITOR *2,3 Sonya Lennon*

Blvd.
Mar. 1997

EDITOR	*Frank Bierens*
ART DIRECTORS	*Danny van der Dungen, Marieke Stolk*
DESIGNERS	*Danny van der Dungen, Marieke Stolk*
PHOTOGRAPHER	*Marie-José Jongerius*
PUBLISHER	*Uitgeverij Blvd.*

Netherlands

De godfather van de cyberpunk keert met zijn laatste boek *Idoru*
terug naar de techno-decadente wereld van de 21ste eeuw.
Een reis langs sprekende ijskasten, *cybernetic* popsterren
en vooral door de driedimensionale hallucinatoire matrixruimte,
die William Gibson zelf de naam cyberspace gaf.

cybercowboys verslaan big brother
3.williamgibson

In het voor science-fiction magische jaar 1984 verscheen het boek *Neuromancer*. Deze roman van William Gibson werd de klassieker van een nieuw science-fictiongenre: cyberpunk, waarin cybernetics, cybernauts en computerhacking samengaan met anarchistisch geweld en een zelfkant-mentaliteit.

In *Neuromancer* beschrijft Gibson een nabije toekomst, waarin de mens via een wereldwijd netwerk communiceert, virtueel en interactief, en volledig in de cyberwereld kan bestaan. William Gibsons imaginaire wereld wordt bevolkt door mensen met elektronische hersenimplantaties, gekloonde organen en kunstmatige intelligenties.

In de real-time-wereld speelt het leven zich nog steeds af in grauwe betonnen verpauperde steden. Alles draait om macht, geld en drugs. Dictatoriale regimes, multinationals, religieuze sekten en misdaadsyndicaten maken de dienst uit. Door middel van technologie, zoals informatietechnologie en hersenimplantaties, en drugs houden zij een ijzeren greep op de bevolking.

Gibsons hoofdpersonen leven in de barsten van dit systeem. Het zijn de misfits, het onkruid, mensen die op hun eigen voorwaarden willen leven en weigeren enkel als consument te bestaan. Met dezelfde technologie als wapen voeren Gibsons paria's een anarchistische strijd tegen de onderdrukker.

De held in *Neuromancer* is cybercowboy Case. Hacker Case kraakt databestanden en ontvreemdt bedrijfssoftware, in opdracht van grotere criminelen. Wanneer hij eindelijk eens wat voor zichzelf wil stelen, wordt zijn zenuwstelsel uitgebrand. Case verliest zijn positie op de computernetwerken en daarmee zijn belangrijkste wereld.

'Voor Case, die leefde voor de lichaamsloze verrukking van cyberspace, was dit de ondergang... The body was meat. Case kwam in de gevangenis van zijn eigen vlees'kelijkheid.'

Maar gelukkig: gebruikmakend van zijn contacten in de onderwereld slaagt hij er uiteindelijk toch in zijn vaardigheden en daarmee zijn status op het Net terug te veroveren. Lonesome cowboy Case zegeviert; hij overwint het grotere kwaad en overleeft.

Gibsons sympathie voor de outcast komt niet helemaal uit de lucht vallen. Geboren en getogen in een klein dorpje in Virginia, vertrok hij op zijn negentiende naar Canada om zich aan de dienstplicht voor Vietnam te onttrekken. Maar vooral is Gibson een idealist en strijder voor een ongecensureerd Internet. Niet alleen het Net maar met name de personal computer is voor Gibson een belangrijk wapen tegen Big Brother. 'De uitvinding van de pc is de wraak van de hippies.' In 1970 was de computer nog onbetaalbaar en slechts voorbehouden aan regeringen en grote bedrijven. Het gezag van de overheid werd door de monopolisering van computermacht alleen maar weer versterkt. Maar toen vonden enkele 'acid head' hippies de pc uit. Een guerilla was geboren, aldus Gibson; een subversieve kracht die ongripbaar is voor de sterke arm van de macht en deze langzaam maar zeker ondermijnt.

Naast het veelgeprezen *Neuromancer*, schreef Gibson nog enkele andere bestsellers. *Count Zero* (1986), *Mona Lisa Overdrive* (1988) en *Virtual Light* (1993), waarmee Gibson een nieuw weg insloeg. Aangezien cyberpunk inmiddels al lang weer dood schijnt te zijn, worden *Virtual Light* en opvolger *Idoru*, Gibsons nieuwste boek, ook wel als post-cyberpunk bestempeld. In beide romans is de toekomst menselijker, de technologie minder geavanceerd, en het thema belangrijker dan het plot.

Idoru speelt zich af in het post-millennaire Tokio. Japan is zich nog steeds aan het herstellen van een aardbeving. Nieuwe nanotech gebouwen die in staat zijn zichzelf op te trekken en te herbouwen, veranderen continu het gezicht van de stad. Dit gebeurt met kalme deinende bewegingen 'als de continue beweging van de voelspriten van een weekdier in de zee'. Het maakt de stad dreigend en onvoorspelbaar. Naast dit urbane landschap is er natuurlijk nog de andere wereld, cyberspace. In *Idoru* wordt cyberspace met behulp van een soort oogkleppen binnengetreden en eenmaal binnen reis je door een wereld die real time.

De Idoru is een geavanceerd softwareprogramma, een virtuele verschijning in de vorm van een hologram. De Idoru is een popster, een beeldschone *cybernetic* zangeres

genaamd Rei Toei, ontworpen om een mediahit te zijn. Rez, lid van het legendarisch rockduo Lo/Rez, een popster van vlees en bloed, is vastbesloten met deze Idoru te trouwen. Voor beiden betekent hun verbintenis een essentiële stap in de samensmelting van het virtuele en het lichamelijke.

Een andere hoofdpersoon is Colin Laney. Hij is voor werk in Tokio. Zijn baan is het observeren van informatiepatronen zoals lange lijsten gegevens over de dagelijkse boodschappen, geluisterde muziek en andere banaliteiten, om een verklaring te vinden voor de toch wel lichtelijk bizarre trouwplannen van Rez en Rei Toei. En dan is er nog de Amerikaanse veertienjarige puber Chia Pet McKenzie, die zich om andere redenen in Japan bevindt. Zij is actief in de fanclub van Lo/Rez en tijdens haar reis naar Japan wordt Chia gebruikt om illegale nanoware te smokkelen voor de Russische maffia en ze belandt zodoende ongewild in talloze onverkwikkelijke situaties.

Alles komt gelukkig weer op zijn pootjes terecht. Chia komt veilig thuis, Laney heeft zijn werk gedaan en Rei Toei en Rez leven nog lang en gelukkig.

In snelle zinnen strooit William Gibson een enorme hoeveelheid informatie over je uit. Met zijn verbeeldingskracht schept hij legio fantastische gadgets. Sprekende ijskasten, micropore-pleisters en door middel van uvstralen zelfreinigend wc zijn dan nog vrij voor de hand liggende voorbeelden. Maar zo is er ook bijvoorbeeld in het Tokio van *Idoru* een poeder op de markt om urine in een vaste stof om te zetten. Geurloos en hygiënisch en speciaal bedoeld voor moeders met jonge kinderen of muurschilderingen in kinky-bars.

Ook zijn sociaal-maatschappelijke uitvindingen zijn vreemd genoeg geloofwaardig. Zoals bijvoorbeeld de beschrijving van de sekte 'New logic', die het einde van de wereld voorspelt als het totale gewicht van het menselijk zenuwcelweefsel een bepaald niveau bereikt.

William Gibson is er met *Idoru* weer in geslaagd een fascinerende toekomst te scheppen. Een toekomst die ondanks alle curieuze technologische innovaties niet gelukkig stemt maar eerder aanzet tot revaluatie van culturele, sociale en technologische ontwikkelingen. ■

fenomeen3
tekst margriet kousemaker
beeld nara yoshitomo

yoshitomo nara - 1. *no name* 2. *untitled* 3. *untitled* | galerie d'eendt

Mar. 1997

ILLUSTRATOR   *Yoshitomo Nara*

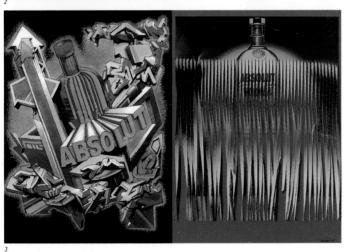

1,3	**Mar. 1997**
PHOTOGRAPHER	*1,3 Gerald van der Kaap (right)*
ILLUSTRATOR	*3 Delta (left)*

2	**Mar. 1997**
ARTIST	*Mischa Klein (left)*
PHOTOGRAPHER	*Edland Man (right)*
STYLIST	*Jennifer Lee (right)*
HAIR	*Alessandro Spuarza (right)*
MAKEUP	*Maurizio Massari (right)*

	Mar. 1997
PHOTOGRAPHER	
Anuschka Blommers	
STYLIST	
Ruud van der Peijl	
STYLING ASSISTANT	
Bas Andrea	
HAIR & MAKEUP	
Dirk Jensma	

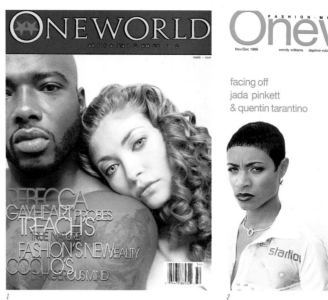

Oneworld

1 **Nov./Dec. 1996**
2 **Winter 1996**

EDITOR *John Pasmore*
ART DIRECTOR *Franc Reyes*
DESIGNER *Franc Reyes*
PHOTOGRAPHER *Christian Witkin*
PUBLISHER *New Image Media Inc.*

USA

1

2

Winter 1996

EDITOR *John Pasmore*
DESIGNER *Franc Reyes*
PHOTOGRAPHER *Katrin Thomas*

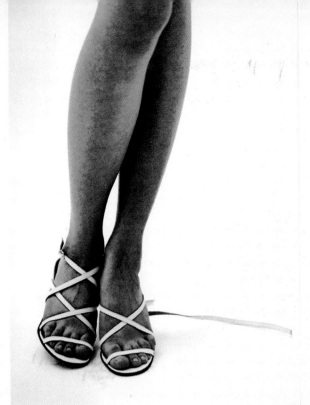

TWO WOMEN
PHOTOGRAPHS by CHRISTIAN WITKIN

Winter 1996

EDITOR   *John Pasmore*
DESIGNER   *Franc Reyes*
PHOTOGRAPHER   *Christian Witkin*

the one @ madonna

russell simmons

I met Madonna in the early eighties when she was just one of the cool girls that hung out at one of New York City's trendiest, coolest, alternative nightclubs, Danceteria. I thought I was her manager for about a week until she came to meet me for lunch. That day she informed me that she had chosen a more experienced manager to handle her career.—Freddy DeMann.

Editor's Note: Madonna's recollection was quite the opposite. She said that it was Russell who turned her down as a client.

At the time, I had no idea that this girl could not only dress the dress, walk the walk, and talk the talk of all that was hot and cool in the underground scene at the time, but more importantly she had the creativity and vision to make countless other cultural statements. In fact, I didn't realize the impact of that lunch until I ran into her a year later at Jellybean's deejay booth at the Funhouse. When she showed me the artwork for her debut album I remember thinking to myself that the clothes she was wearing, the attitude she was expressing and the look in her eyes were exactly what the world needed. She was going to be an absolute star and I had really jerked myself by not giving her the attention she deserved.

Less than eighteen months later, my group, The Beastie Boys, opened her 'Virgin' tour at a small venue in Seattle, Washington. I watched the tour take on momentum from city to city. By the time Madonna and the Beasties hit New York, she had sold out Radio City Music Hall and new dates were being added at Madison Square Garden. She was breaking records across the country. Seeing all the Madonna wanna-be's in the audience, the enormous response from radio, and the love affair that was just beginning to blossom at MTV, confirmed that this woman was predestined to greatness.

This is the first time I have interviewed Madonna. We met at her Maverick office in Los Angeles while she was seven months pregnant. Also present during the interview were: Guy Oseary, A&R director at Maverick, her record company, video director Melodie McDaniels and Caresse Norman, her personal assistant and co-manager. We did experience one problem; within minutes of wrapping up the interview I realized that I had neglected to turn the tape recorder on! However, I was determined to get this interview and in the process, shocked everyone with my nerve as I re-recorded it.

The nature of our relationship is that I have a habit of picking on her when we get together. Now I find myself having to fess up and tell our readers the truth. But let's face it, who am I kidding? I'm sure Madonna knows full well that it pains me that now you do, too) that just like the rest of the world... Russell Simmons is on her dick.

R: You didn't get it?
R: Can you believe it didn't record? That is so fucked up!
R: Oh well, next time
R: I hope we get to do this project together. You didn't waste any time getting a meeting together.
R: I'm not the type to say, 'Let's do lunch.'
M: Is that what you think of me? I don't seem like a 'Let's-do-lunch' type of digger, do I?
R: Well, I always see you at restaurants (laughs).
R: This is going to be a short interview. The last one was incredible.
M: (To her friend, video director Melodie McDaniels): He just interviewed me and it was fierce. Too bad he didn't turn the tape recorder on!
R: Do you wear fur?
R: Yeah, I have a powder blue rabbit fur coat by Dolce and Gabbana that I love.
R: I'm asking you this because my assistant, Simone Reyes, is an animal rights activist and you have another connection too. Her boyfriend Ken used to go out with you.
M: What's his last name? Ken Compton?
R: Yeah, that's it. They've been together forever.
M: She must hate me if she goes out with Ken.
R: No she can forgive you going out with her man but wearing dead animals on your back... never!
R: I think it is really funny seeing you pregnant because it is the first time since I've known you that you look like a woman.
M: This is a really chauvinistic thing to say.
R: Eugene. (Laughs.) But, I meant that you look so different than the way we are used to seeing you as men, you know, chauvinistic men (laughs). Not me necessarily...
Melodie McDaniels: Do you mean she is womanly because she is pregnant?
R: No, it's the fact that Madonna is in some way vulnerable now, with her stomach sticking out like that... (In an Al Pacino *Scarface* voice) Look at you now, I like seeing you like this.
M: Well, I think that is really pathetic that you think that this is the first time in my life that I've been vulnerable.
R: I heard really good things about 'Evita' and I thought you were great in 'Dangerous Game'. It was a big deal to me and I was probably one of the few people to like the movie.
M: You were probably one of the few people to see the movie (laughs).
R: Critics have been so negative about all the movies you have been in, all those happy-ass movies, like the one right after the film with Sean Penn.
M: Huh?
R: The pop movie. The one with the lion in it.
M: "Who's That Girl."
R: Yeah, that was the Madonna we knew. We bought her records, the happy-ass Madonna, that side of you. Most artists get a chance to sell only one side of themselves and audiences won't buy them doing anything else.
M: Can soe substitute the word "sell" with "express", thank you very much. I am not selling different sides of myself, I am expressing different sides of myself.

Nov./Dec. 1996

EDITOR　　*John Pasmore*
DESIGNER　*Franc Reyes*

Nov./Dec. 1996

EDITOR　　　*John Pasmore*
DESIGNER　　*Diddo Ramm*
PHOTOGRAPHER　*Katrin Thomas*

couture geometrique

a location that resembled the abandoned lot of some Crypto-European art film featuring a suitable patina of decay and destruction, the outfits were reading like the costumes for some futuristic movie in which the multi-racial cast was dressed in period costumes for a period yet unseen: a kind of tribal spacewear composed of courtly tonics and ballgowns for both men and women.

The chill in the air triggered a shiver in Rohan, the 5' 11" 117 pound English novelist with bone structure that would have made Garbo spit on the sauerkraut. He stood patiently as the photographer Pablo Ravazzani, restructured the human array featuring Asian model Karen, who stood topless beside Tyson, the rising star from Bethann Management, whose African-Chinese features were stone calm with concentration. The photographer was going about his business with almost fascist precision and Epperson, the designer of all the pieces featured in the unfolding shoot, was deeply unhappy about the surreal interpretation his clothing was being subjected to. It prompted the following exchange between us.

Epperson: I'm sorry but I just don't see this.
W S : Do I look worried? I'm sure we'll find six strong images. We have all the ingredients. Relax.
Epperson: I think that's the problem, I think sometimes you're too relaxed.
W S : (deep breath) Nooo, its more like...I have this line which I never let anyone cross and I'm never worried cause I know since that line is crossed I can always strike out and go home. Y'know what I'm saying? And you should feel free to do the same. Epperson. If you feel like your line is being crossed please feel free to put a stop to all this (Thoughtful pause). Let me ask you something, Cause I'm going to write the whole piece around this question. Do you see your clothes as works of art or as commodities for sale?
Epperson: Both. I see them as both.

Continued on page 63.

Sep. 1994

EDITOR   Wayne Sterling
DESIGNER   Franc Reyes
PHOTOGRAPHER Pablo Ravazzani

Winter 1996

EDITOR   John Pasmore
DESIGNER   Franc Reyes
PHOTOGRAPHER TAR

PROFILE

Tar

M. Franklin Sirmans

"Me speaking my mind is gonna hurt people," Tar says before we can even sit down to talk. Tar is built stocky and he has thin dread locks that fall down on his head. In between him doing a lot of talking and me doing a little, I was there trying to figure out what kind of a photographer the brother was. What I actually found out was that Tar is a race-conscious Black man, a businessman, and then a photographer. And there ain't nothing wrong with that. Tar's photographic work proved competent enough early on to get commercial gigs for recording artists and record companies. "Man, I never have to worry about business, because the artists need me." He makes his point by showing me a poorly taken photograph of a Black woman with blue eyeshadow and pink blush applied to her pretty brown face. "You see this, this is why they need me. As a photographer, I would never let this happen to a sister." And I see what he means. For the past decade, Tar has honed his skills as an independent contractor not as a photographer. "I haven't become a better photographer," he offers, to my surprise. Yet, he is quick to point out that he will never again allow a company to own the negatives from from one of his shoots. That way, he controls which of his images will be seen and which will be edited out by himself. "The one that you dont like is the one they will

part, and I have to keep my integrity." But, if you're not concerned with becoming a better photographer then why such attention to a single advertising image? So it is that our conversation is filled with similar contradictions. He talks of how he gets no respect from magazine publishers but then proceeds with a comment like, "my pictures sell magazines. People like them." Perhaps this is a taste of the arrogance bred by success and longevity. Though, I want to feel ambivalent, Tar impresses me with his pride, direction and seemingly carefree attitude which also stems from a good sense of purpose and self. "I did five years dealing with an almost all white university, (Southern Illinois University)...dont you tell me, I shouldn't be confident."

Along with his sense of business matters, Tar's sense of aesthetics wins out when it comes to his creative work. "I've had to make a lot of photographs that aren't what I'm really about, this project gives me sanity," he says, referring to the stack of photographs he has placed on the desk in front of me. The series is a collection of portraits of Black people above the age of 50. Thus far he has photographed a melange of people including Amiri Baraka, Camille Billops, Ed Clark, David Dinkins, Dr. Jocelyn Elders, Richie Havens, Chester Higgins, Vernon Jordan, Queen Mother Moore, Eleanor Holmes Norton, Odetta, Dr. Muriel Petioni, Percy Sutton, Melvin Van Peebles, and Bruce Wright. The unique facet of these photographs is Tar's use of a small circular mirror to place the face of his subject within the picture which is shot in the intimacy of the subject's home or office. I think of Van Der Zee's portraits and how he would take such pains to decorate the surroundings of his sitters, who would all be photographed in their "Sunday best" outfits. I appreciate the simplicity of these photographs where Tar rolls into somebody's everyday space and just adds that one element, the mirror. It allows for a modest sense of mystery in every portrait unlike a straight on photograph. We get to learn about the sitter beyond their face. The furniture and the surrounding curios of the subject's life speak volumes. A photograph of the poet, writer, and dramatist, Baraka, shows millions of books in a dusty windowsill. Tom Burrell's office highlights a painting by Jacob Lawrence in the background. The lick of clutter or anything for that matter on Dinkins desk could be read as the surroundings of a very neat man or that of a man who is not as busy anymore, an older man. All of the pictures provide a subtle insight into the life of their subjects whose faces are just a part of the staged environments. The people he has chosen to photograph are all people he admires in some way. Here, I've found Tar, the photographer.

It is this sort of project that brings out the things that he likes to talk about: respect for one's elders, respect for self, hard work, independence, and integrity. I ask what the future holds for Tar and he replies, "I have to try and be quiet and do what I'm told." Somehow, I know this ain't happening. And, I'm glad.

SELF SERVICE
Vol. 4 Autumn 1996

ART DIRECTORS   *Ezra Petronio,*
Suzanne Koller
PHOTOGRAPHER   *Mark Borthwick*
DESIGN FIRM   *Work in Progress*
PUBLISHER   *Self Service Magazine*

France

Vol. 4 1996

PHOTOGRAPHER   *Mark Borthwick*

decalé

Nom : MICHEL GONDRY. Occupation : Réalisateur.
Livre préféré : *Manun n'aime pas la Police*, c'était
mon premier livre. **Projets immédiats :** Des pubs
malheureusement, et l'écriture d'un scénario. **Votre
dernier achat important :** Un taps, qui n'a pas été
fait par des petites mains d'enfants.

Michel Gondry est à l'image de ses clips, dis-
cret, décalé et d'une justesse incroyable.
Aussi précis qu'un enfant devant sa maquette,
il enchaîne les réalisations et les coups de
génies défilent en pluie de météorites. Björk,
Lenny Kravitz, IAM, les Stones, tous sont passés dans la salle de jeu du jeune génie expatrié
à Londres. Clip, pub, ciné, tous sollicitent ce
superhéros de l'image. Entre Little Nemo et
Batman, son mix incroyable de la technique et
son univers onirique laissent une trace indélébile
sur les tubes cathodiques. Entretien privilégié avec
le plus fantomatique des réalisateurs.

A quand remontent tes premiers souvenirs
d'images ? Le premier film que j'ai vu c'était *Le voyage en
ballon*, j'ai adoré. D'ailleurs souvent quand on revoit un film
qu'nous a marqué, en est déçu. Les souvenirs le rendent plus
beau. Mais celui-là je l'aime toujours autant. **Certaines personnes résument ton travail à une prouesse technique.
Est-ce que cela te pèse un problème ?** Ça me gêne pas vraiment dans la mesure où les gens ont beaucoup de respect pour les
effets spéciaux. Mais j'ai aussi réalisé beaucoup de choses sans
effets spéciaux. L'essentiel pour moi est de centrer le travail autour de
l'artiste, de ne pas l'utiliser comme un prétexte et de lui plaquer un univers qui n'est pas le sien. Mon travail se compose comme un jeu de cube à
construire. Il y a deux catégories, soit j'arrive avec un cube de départ sur
lequel j'essaie de refléter les envies du groupe, soit j'arrive avec plusieurs cubes,
comme avec Björk, elle aussi et on construit à égalité avec nos éléments. **A ton
avis, l'informatique est-elle une source d'inspiration, ou reste-t-elle simple-
ment un outil supplémentaire ?** J'ai toujours utilisé la technique et l'informatique
comme des outils. Dès le départ, j'ai pris l'habitude d'utiliser les moyens qui m'étaient don-
nés, sans jamais essayer d'imaginer des choses impossibles à maîtriser techniquement. En
général, toutes les techniques au départ surprennent, et au bout d'un moment on voit vite les
défauts. Ma technique c'est de pousser l'effet, de l'utiliser à contre emploi c'est ce que j'ai fait avec
le morphe sur le clip des Stones, ou les rétroprojections dans le premier clip de Björk qui évitait le bleu
incruste traditionnel. **Quelles sont tes références esthétiques et stylistiques ?** L'esthétique n'est
jamais un point de départ dans mon travail. C'est une démarche de plus en plus consciente. Quand une idée
s'impose, l'image tient à distance. **Quelles sont tes relations avec la pub ?** Ce que je n'aime pas dans la pub,
c'est qu'on a tendance à prendre les gens pour des cons, en utilisant des gros stéréotypes pour augmenter l'impact du
message. Ma vision de la publicité c'est qu'il faut que les gens adhèrent, et qu'ils puissent s'y reconnaître dedans. Ce que
je veux, c'est filmer l'essentiel et pas les stéréotypes. **Enormément de réalisateurs de cinéma ont fait leur classe dans la
pub** (Alan Parker, Ridley et Tony Scott...). **Est-ce que le cinéma serait une continuation logique ?** Oui, bien sûr, j'y ai
pensé. J'ai beaucoup d'admiration pour Ridley Scott par exemple. En revanche quand je voyais les films d'Alan Parker, je me disais, ça fait
trop pub. Quand je fais des pubs, je voudrais qu'elles ressemblent à des films avec une vraie recherche personnelle. Je n'aime pas l'esthétique
de la pub surtout celle des années 80. Maintenant, j'ai le cul entre deux chaises, je sais que si je réalise un film un jour on va s'attendre à un truc très
esthétisant. **Ton premier long-métrage serait plus une ambiance onirique à la Tim Burton, ou alors à la Bruce Willis comme dans la pub
Volvo ?** Plutôt la première version quand-même. Suite à la pub de Volvo, j'ai reçu pas mal de scripts. Si c'était *Piège de cristal* n°3, ça ne me déplairait pas. Le film
idéal pour moi serait *Le Jour sans fin*, avec une idée forte, exploitée jusqu'au bout et qui donne des situations géniales. **En France, il y a toujours une mentalité qui
consiste à tout critiquer alors qu'il y a quand-même un énorme potentiel créatif.** En Angleterre, n'importe quel crétin qui va se mettre un potiron sur la tête, ils vont trouver ça génial
et en dix secondes c'est fini. Aux Etats-Unis c'est pire. Par exemple, le chanteur d'Oasis maintenant c'est un sex symbol, je ne comprends pas. Oasis c'est de la merde, du re-sucé des années 60. **Justement, en France,
un magazine va mettre Oasis en couv. On ne manque pourtant pas de chanteur ici...** C'est hélas la manière de procéder en France. On essaye jamais de pousser un truc nouveau, on se contente de regarder ce qui
marche dans les autres charts et on l'intègre ici. Mais c'est difficile de juger. **Deux des meilleurs réalisateurs sont français. Est-ce que tu penses qu'il y a une école française du clip et est-ce grâce à
Mondino ?** Mondino a apporté quelque chose mais c'était à double tranchant. Il fallait comprendre ce qu'il faisait et en tirer les bonnes conclusions. Et ne pas se contenter de prendre le côté visuel qu'il avait développé.
Quand il faisait de sépia, tout le monde en faisait, quand il faisait du bleu, tout le monde en faisait. Mondino a vraiment montré le chemin, magnifier l'artiste avec des moyens pas nécessairement énormes. Avec Sednaoui
on a appliqué ce principe, centrer le clip sur la vedette et en faire un héros. **Tu trouve pas ça paradoxal, qu'il y ait un potentiel de réalisateurs, photographes français qui s'expatrient à l'étranger ?** C'est l'exo-
tisme, ça marche dans tous les pays. En Angleterre ils aiment bien les Négresses Vertes à cause de l'accordéon. Moi j'ai déménagé à une époque où j'étais de plus en plus sollicité en Angleterre. De plus, la pub est plus
créative là-bas. **Est-ce que le vidéo clip est un art ?** Je sais pas ce que c'est l'art. Mon travail se base sur la recherche et ça pourrait s'en rapprocher. Pourtant à la différence de l'art contemporain ça répond à une demande
du public.

Nathalie Canguilhem et Ezra Petronio

SELF SERVICE 20

Nom : MARTIN MARGIELA. Occupation : Créateur. **Créateur préféré :** Ceux qui sont authentiques dans leur démarche. **Qu'est-ce qui vous fait peur ?** The fashion system. **Qu'est-ce qui doit changir**
C'est le début du 18ème arrondissement et déjà le Nord. Une impasse pavée, le plus souvent déserte, avec un bout de course la grève des voies ferrées qui éloignent la pensée de Paris. Une lourde porte e
peinte en noire. Rien ne signale l'activité du couturier, si ce n'est la petite plaque SARL NEUF. Et deux fois par an un improbable ballet de limousines qui valent à l'endroit d'inutiles cambriolages. Martin
aime les vrais lieux, l'anonymat et par dessus tout les vêtements. Cet ancien entrepôt a été préservé dans sa nudité. Parquet disjoint, vieilles peintures, traces des efforts passés, électricité approximative, te
la concentration malgré la tension du travail. C'est la Maison Margiela, non pas au sens de l'artisanat de luxe, mais au sens manuel et intime. Aucune technologie apparente, des machines à écrire et des m
coudre, juste un fax et une photocopieuse Canon, mais pas de logiciel pour la comptabilité : une professionnelle qui s'est réfugiée derrière les vitres de verre. Des rangées de vêtements en attente. Une at
un peu désaffectée et rigoureuse, qui ne contraste qu'en apparence avec la modernité des idées : Margiela puise très loin dans la mémoire de la couture et l'on travaille autour de grandes tab
d'idées en noir et blanc qui attirent des jeunes stylistes de partout, un alphaville dans le 18ème. On se frôle en blouse blanche dans l'escalier bancal sans lumière et l'on travaille autour de grandes tab
toaux jusqu'à tard dans la nuit. Et Martin en pull marin, casquette rivée sur la tête, main chargée de bagues, d'une gentillesse qui vous déboussole, toujours à guetter la solution la plus simple aux probl
vous lui soumettez. Il est déjà 10 heures passées, il vous amène dans un restaurant vietnamien du quartier. *Olin*

PHOTO: ANDERS EDSTROM

neuf

Vol. 4 Autumn 1996

PHOTOGRAPHERS   *Duc Liao (left),*
Anders Edstrom (right)

opposite page   **Vol. 3 Summer 1996**

PHOTOGRAPHER   *Horst Diekgerdes*

SKINDEEP

BIKINI

1 **Vol. 20 Mar. 1997**
2 **Vol. 19 Jan. 1997**

EDITOR **Mark Blackwell**
ART DIRECTOR **Jerôme Curchod**
PHOTOGRAPHER **1 Kevin Kerslake**
DESIGN FIRM **Ray Gun Publishing**
PUBLISHER **Ray Gun Publishing, Inc.**

USA

1

2

NATURAL HIGH

Forget "All the sugar, twice the caffeine." Forget Mugwamp juice. Forget Starbucks. Check out Guarana fortified beverages, the latest buzz in fizz. The Euros have already been guzzling the stuff in mass quantities in drinks named Warp! and Black Booster, and now you can find it here in Sensa iced teas. So what *is* this Guarana stuff, you ask? Well, "Guarana" is basically the same thing as "guano" – i.e. poop. Just kidding! Actually, it starts as a bright red berry grown in the rainforests of Brazil. The berries are boiled down to paste and dried into sticks that are later ground into powder. The Indians used to consume it as a stimulant on long journeys and after a nice Buffalo steak, medium rare. Adherents claim it's also a heart relaxant, a cure for arteriosclerosis, headaches, amnesia...and even a mild aphrodisiac when taken in high doses.

Dan Rogers

CRAPS: THE FINAL FRONTIER

Could Las Vegas ever one-up the monolithic pyramid of the Luxor, the fire breathing volcano of the Mirage, the Jimi Hendrix slot machines of the Hard Rock Casino, or the $1.99 four course steak dinners? The folks at the Las Vegas Hilton think so. They're on deck to hit the next ball straight into outer space with The Spacequest Casino and **Star Trek: The Experience**, scheduled to open this summer.

The new casino will feature huge "space windows," giving broke, bleary-eyed gamblers the illusion they are on a space station orbiting the Earth. But wait! There's more! Plans for the $50 million "Experience" will include a transport to the bridge of the Enterprise followed by a shuttlecraft trip through space (simulated, of course). After the trip, visitors will be able to sample Romulan Ale at a Cardassian restaurant and buy Federation overstock. The creators promise that all sets in the attraction will be exact 1:1 replicas of the sets used in the TV show and feature films. Trekkies better reserve early for opening day!

Mark B. Lasser

NO MORE TIGHTIE-WHITIES

Looking for something to impress your unimpressed girlfriend with? Look no further. The **Boxers Of The Month Club** has the very thing for your dull weekends. For $26 dollars a month you'll receive a custom pair of silk or cotton boxers shipped to your front door and into your bedroom. Each pair of fashionable shorts will be sent with a customized card and a flammable "membership certificate" for your wall. Sexy, exciting, colorful, and personalized, The Boxers Of The Month Club may be the answer to your undergarment wunderlust...or maybe just the thing to drag your woman away from the X-Files for an erotic recess. To sign up call 1-800-SHORTS-5.

Marvell Wynne

HYPED!

At first glance, this documentary by Doug Pray chronicling the topsy-turvy Seattle music scene looks to be just one in a long elephant parade of slick MTV sponsored rockumentaries targeted at 14-year-olds craving a bite of spoon fed pseudo-culture. Surprisingly, *Hype!* is more: Pushing beyond all the angst-driven, 'rock & roll will never die' media pitfalls, this film has a hearty sense of humor (thank God) about itself. Inevitably, this is what makes Pray's efforts distinct and special. But *Hype!* does have all the quality slam dancin'-flannel sportin'-beer guzzlin' you could ever ask for with the entire cast of characters that made it possible: Soundgarden, Nirvana, Mudhoney, and Pearl Jam, plus tons of smaller Northwest bands, various industry types, local record producers and, of course, the fans. *Hype!* is perhaps (hopefully) the last and final word on Seattle until the big rock book is written in 2000. "Grunge" R.I.P.

Jason Black

NEW ADVENTURES IN VIDEO

With so many bands these days putting out CD-ROMs, CD+s, and enhanced CDs, the idea of releasing a home video seems almost retro. But in the case of R.E.M.'s concert film *Road Movie*, it's downright refreshing. Shot at the end of the *Monster* tour, the live *Road Movie* features the same sort of quick-cut/artsy look as their *Green* tour document, *Tourfilm*. Augmented in spots by a violinist, and in others by a set of cajones an elephant would envy, the guys tear through "The One I Love" and "Orange Crush," gently wave by "Losing My Religion" and "Tongue," give out the only version of "Revolution" we might ever get, and road test such tunes as "Wake Up Bomb" and "Binky The Doormat," which have since been released on *New Adventures In Hi-Fi*. As these things go, it's a bit jumpy, and you may (as I did) wish the editor would let a shot last longer than two seconds, but, hey, that's a cool '90s thing, right?

Paul Semel

BIKE TO THE FUTURE

Bulky-thighed cyclists with a spare $36,000 and no plans for the year 2000 may have something to do now: participate in the **Odyssey 2000**, a year-long, multi-national bicycling adventure spanning seven continents and four countries. Departing from L.A. at the dawn of the new millennium, you won't be able to party like it's 1999 the night before (unless you want to leave a trail of vomit from L.A. to Budapest) but you will have the chance to join 250 riders from across the country for a gruelingly unique athletic event. Odyssey 2000 is the step-child of Tim Kneeland, a Vietnam vet and former Air Force survival instructor who has already led nine cross-country treks. Although Kneeland doesn't require health check-ups, he says, "the better your condition, the more discretionary time you'll have to see a museum or check out a ruin or two." If can't make the mileage 'cause you smoked it up in Amsterdam or got a flat in Tunisia, there are 15 support vehicles coming along, including a medi-van and roving bike shop. Sign up before the end of the year and save $4,000 (are you crazy?). For info:1-800 433-0528.

Sue Carpenter

The World Wide Web

www.disinfo.com
A searchable database of all weird, subversive, and "hidden" the Web

www.thx.com
Shhhhhwishhh. Bang. Waw!

www.io.org/-bme/
Body modification, tattoos...

www.teleport.com/ shojo/View/vm.html
Before there was VR there was View-Master (tm).

www.interlog.com/peer/
We may never tell what tea but you can ask on-line Kim Martyn.

http://hisurf.aloha.com. Find.html
This site attempts to translat name into Hawaiian. Never k when it could come in handy Captain Cook had such techt

www.cforce.com
Another cool episodic comic powered with shockwave and

www.tela.bc.ca/hamster,
Hamster love. Mmmm. Ska-w little fuzzy. Hahahaha!

www.greenpeace.org
When the bomb hits, the only left will be the cockroaches, Richards, and these guys. Recy recycle, recycle.

www.lfnetwork.com
Your true on-line entertainm network.

Kelly Sedel

Vol. 19 Jan. 1997

hot on the trail of the navarro boys

Photos By Dave Nagel

We didn't want to do this.

Let us re-phrase that.
We wanted to do this article.
But, when that certain Sunday rolled around, we were trying to find ways to get out of it.
Don't misunderstand.
Dave & Johnny enjoy the outdoors.
Dave & Johnny enjoy physical activity.
But, this particular Sunday, we wanted to enjoy the air-conditioned solitude of a darkened movie theater, or the caffeinated glibness of a coffee house.
The thought of driving 45 minutes to the Santa Monica Mountains to frolic around the hills on Trek mountain bikes during one of the last remaining days of summer...it just wasn't where we were at.

The rough and rugged

brothers **Dave & Johnny Navarro** make a molehill out of a mountain on some new Trek bikes.

Photo by Torres&Barr

The members of Veruca Salt have spent the last few years growing up in public, paying for their early and premature success in innumerable ways. Their debut – the phenomenally successful *American Thighs* – was recorded after the band had only played seven shows. When that album started to break, the quartet was in the midst of a full-fledged, and very public, identity crisis.

"We didn't know what we were doing," admits Nina Gordon, who fronts the band alongside best friend Louise Post. "But we didn't think anyone would ever hear it anyway. This time, our approach is a lot more calculated. We've been around for three or four years now; we've played a million shows, we're a lot more confident." (Though not so confident that Gordon is willing to handle interviews by herself. "Please, talk to Louise too, okay?" she stresses. "If this interview goes wrong, I don't want to be the only one responsible.")

Post and Gordon formed Veruca Salt four years ago when they returned home to Chicago after graduating from Tufts and Barnard, respectively. The two were hooked up by a mutual friend, while bassist Steve Lack answered an ad, and Gordon's brother, Jim Shapiro – who recently left to concentrate on his own band – filled in on drums. "I'll miss him," Gordon says, "but as his sister, I'm really happy that he's going for it."

The band had played only a few dates around town when Jim Powers, head of the local and tiny Minty Fresh label, approached them with a deal. "He came to a few shows, and then asked us if we wanted to make an album," Gordon remembers. "And we got all excited and said yes."

But despite the buzz that rapidly swelled around them – thanks to a much-publicized appearance at the industry conference South By Southwest, and a heightened interest surrounding anything from Chicago – no one expected much from *Thighs*, which was recorded on a shoestring budget. But when the song "Seether" became a left-field hit before the album was even released, the majors came calling.

Veruca Salt wound up signing a reportedly lucrative contract with Geffen, prompting sniping around town that they were betraying an indie aesthetic the band says they never bought into anyway. "The only reason we were on an indie at all is because we signed a deal with the first person that asked us," Gordon says. "We never said, 'Oh no, we don't want to go to a major.' I mean, of course we did. If Geffen had gotten there first, we would have signed with them. All of a sudden, everyone said we were selling out."

As the success of *Thighs* raised the band's profile, to many they came, perhaps unfairly,

to symbolize the under-rehearsed "baby band," hyped unmercifully, thrust into the public consciousness on the strength of one hit single and a marketable image. The band members wound up apologizing to everyone, from disapproving critics to friends in more experienced but less successful bands.

But as Gordon says, "We don't feel apologetic anymore. A lot of bands, they make an album, and they know there's gonna be this major label push, but we didn't have any of that. We weren't prepared, and we didn't feel ready yet, so we wound up apologizing a lot."

Thighs was released at the height of Chicago's 15 minutes; the spotlight directed towards such acts as Liz Phair, Urge Overkill, and Smashing Pumpkins couldn't help but reflect upon Veruca Salt as well. Now that Phair and the Urge have been M.I.A. for a while, and the Pumpkins belong to the world, Veruca Salt are, in many ways, a band without a context. That almost every "post-alternative" act has crashed and burned with their second album doesn't help matters any (though their ambivalence towards success is best typified by the title of an interim EP, *Blow It Out Your Ass It's Veruca Salt*). "I feel sorry for bands that that's happened to," Gordon says, "but it doesn't make me nervous, because we made the album we wanted to make. Finally."

It is that new album, the vigorous and loud *Eight Arms To Hold You* which charts their transition from an inexperienced, slightly thin-voiced baby act to a formidable, almost muscular pop-metal band. Veruca Salt's partnership with uber-metal producer Bob Rock (of Metallica and Cult fame) shouldn't surprise anyone familiar with the band members' love for bad '80s, *Theater Of Pain*-type metal and crunchy '70s rock, (a fondness that led the band to lift *American Thighs*' title from an AC/DC song, and that once prompted Shapiro to tell an interviewer, "Angus Young is our Gazoo").

Gordon says the band had considered, and rejected, an endless list of producers before hearing the Rock-produced "Enter Sandman" played over the loudspeakers before one of their gigs. "It sounded so huge over this huge PA system, and we just kind of looked at each other like, 'Well, what could sound better than this? What sounds better than Bob Rock?' We all just stared at each other and smiled, like, in wonder. It was so perfect, we were wondering why we hadn't thought of it before. We had always seen ourselves as a huge-sounding rock & roll band, anyway. And now we are. For the first time ever, we have no doubts about anything."

Allison Stewart

VERUCA SALT

MUSIC

top **Vol. 19 Jan. 1997**
PHOTOGRAPHER *Dave Nagel*

bottom **Vol. 20 Mar. 1997**
PHOTOGRAPHER *Torres and Barr*

FAD Megazine
Vol. 37 1996

EDITOR	R.J.Garbosky
ART DIRECTOR	Dean Seven
DESIGNER	Richard Stutting
PHOTOGRAPHER	Heather McDonald
PUBLISHER	FAD Megazine

USA

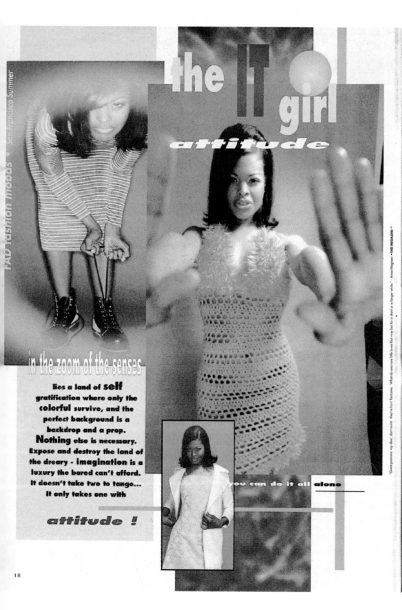

FAD fashion moods • San Francisco Summer

the **IT** girl
attitude

in the zoom of the senses

lies a land of **self**
gratification where only the
colorful survive, and the
perfect background is a
backdrop and a prop.
Nothing else is necessary.
Expose and destroy the land of
the dreary - **imagination** is a
luxury the bored can't afford.
It doesn't take two to tango...
it only takes one with

attitude !

you can do it all alone

let's **hear** it for

insensibility

a
dose
of
brashness,
rashness
and
brio

FOTOS: AMY DAVIS
ASST: JON MORITSUGU
MODEL: DONNA ROSE SIMMONS
HAIR/MAKEUP: LOUIS NGUYEN
CROCHET DRESS: BARBARELLA ·
STRIPED DRESS: IRIE · SPAGHETTI
STRAP DRESS: M.EENA · CROC VINYL
COAT/VINYL'S IN FUR

ALL CLOTHING AVAILABLE AT
ASPHALT
551 HAYES ST. SAN FRANCISCO

Vol. 37 1996

EDITOR	R.J.Garbosky
DESIGNER	Lise Rehanek
PHOTOGRAPHER	Amy Davis

FAD ARTECHNOLOGY

FAD Artechnology in Cyberland
Omnimedia Adventures in Cyberland

GADGET UNIVERSE

by Britt Schoenhoff

Haruhiko Shono's
in the realm of the cd rom

possibilities

When you think of the technological advances Japan has contributed to the world, you generally envision the creators behind the products as being anonymous automatons working for corporate conglomerates like Sony, Toshiba or BMG. But the burgeoning CD-ROM business is changing the face of Japan's technological terrain. Over the past few years young innovators, who dominate the CD-ROM industry, have been challenging the multimedia infrastructure as it exists in Japan by exploring and expanding the interactive possibilities of CD-ROMs.

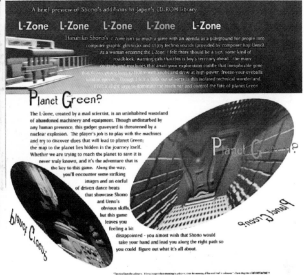

One such innovator is **Haruhiko Shono**, a former graphic design student who began experimenting with multiple media as a graduate student in 1985. While still in school he formed the group Radical TV, whose live performance *TV War* made the Tsukaba '85 Science Exposition. It was with Radical TV that Shono first put his energy into video arts, which later led to computer animation. Shono's true calling was realized when he began to work for Synergy Inc. of Tokyo. With Synergy, Shono has produced 3 award-winning CD-ROMs - **Alice**, **L-Zone** and **Gadget** - that have garnered him critical acclaim as an innovator in cyberspace. Shono's works have also given the CD-ROM industry the much needed buzz to catapult it into the mainstream market.

Though these smaller, independent companies may now swim with the big fish, their breed still stands alone. Because the cost of creating CD-ROMs is much less than that of creating other consumer electronics, artists can concentrate on invention and push creativity to its limits. If appearances aren't deceiving, the CD-ROM's cyberland has no bounds.

A brief preview of Shono's additions to Japan's CD-ROM library

L-Zone L-Zone L-Zone L-Zone L-Zone

Haruhiko Shono's *L-Zone* isn't so much a game with an agenda as a playground for people into computer graphic gimmicks and trippy techno sounds (provided by composer Koji Ueno). As a woman entering the L-Zone, I felt there should be a sign, some kind of roadblock warning girls that this is boy's territory ahead – the many controls and machines that await your exploration coddle that inexplicable gene that drives young boys to tinkle with knobs and drive at high power, freeze-your-eyeballs cruise speeds. Though L-Zone feels out of sorts in this isolated technical wonderland, I feel no deep urge to dominate the machines and control the fate of planet Green.

Planet Green?

The L-Zone, created by a mad scientist, is an uninhabited wasteland of abandoned machinery and equipment. Though undisturbed by any human presence, this gadget graveyard is threatened by a nuclear explosion. The player's job is to play with the machines and try to discover clues that will lead to planet Green; the map to the planet lies hidden in the journey itself. Whether we are trying to reach the planet to save it is never truly known, and it's the adventure that is the key to this game. Along the way, you'll encounter some striking images and an earful of driven dance beats that showcase Shono and Ueno's obvious skills, but this game leaves you feeling a bit disappointed - you almost wish that Shono would take your hand and lead you along the right path so you could figure out what it's all about.

Vol. 37 1996

EDITOR *Lise Rehanek*
DESIGNER *Elissa Cline*

N.Y.C. SOCIOLOGY

CANDY CRAVING NIGHTLIFE
JET DIVAS · DOPE DUDES · NOTABLE NAUGHTIES
OBSERVATIONS AND RUMINATIONS ON THE GORGEOUS
BY ANDYMAN

The 'Lady' Bunny Barbara Eden on Acid

Isabell Van Carter

Mark Cuevas

Superstar Of Food after hours vibe

FAD FASHION NYC

A FIRST FOR OPERALAND
AN AMERICAN OPERA IN MONTE CARLO
LOWELL LIEBERMANN DOES
OSCAR WILDE'S
THE PICTURE OF DORIAN GRAY

Interview · Robert Donford

The consumer should realize that they should support creative people and individualism. Department stores are only interested in the mass market.

Interview · Theodora Hovey

SOHO ZOO WILD AMERICA

photos · Tina Paul

Vol. 37 1996

EDITOR *R.J.Garbosky*
DESIGNER *Dean Seven*
PHOTOGRAPHERS left / Aaron Cobbett, Mr.Chuck,
Barbara Gentile, Barig,
right / Tina Paul

G·Spot

1 **Vol. 24 Oct. 1996**
2 **Vol. 25 Nov. 1996**

EDITOR *Jo Gatt*
ART DIRECTOR *Hard Media*
DESIGNERS *1 Tarren McCallen,*
2 Lance Bellers,
2 Adrian Broadway
PHOTOGRAPHERS *1 Mike Diver,*
2 Pat Pope
PUBLISHER *G·Spot Magazine*

UK

1

2

3

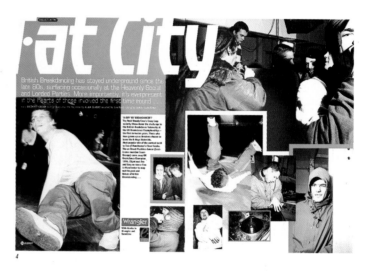

4

5

6

3 **Vol. 25 Nov. 1996**

ART DIRECTOR *Lance Bellers*
DESIGNERS *Lance Bellers,*
Adrian Broadway

5 **Vol. 25 Nov. 1996**

ART DIRECTOR *Lance Bellers*
DESIGNERS *Lance Bellers,*
Adrian Broadway

4 **Vol. 25 Nov. 1996**

ART DIRECTOR *Lance Bellers*
DESIGNERS *Lance Bellers,*
Adrian Broadway

6 **Vol. 24 Oct. 1996**

ART DIRECTOR *Tarren McCallen*
DESIGNER *Tarren McCallen*
PHOTOGRAPHER *Mike Diver*

Joe 90s

Vol. 24 Oct. 1996

ART DIRECTOR   Tarren McCallen
DESIGNER   Tarren McCallen

SPY

1 **Dec. 1996**
2 **Holiday issue 1996**

ART DIRECTOR   *Lisa Marie Giordani*
PHOTOGRAPHERS *1 Ron Davis /*
Shooting Star (Moore Head),
Gabriella Meros /
Rex (Willis Head),
2 Lisa Rose /
Globe (McCarthy Head)
PUBLISHER   *Sussex Publishers*

USA

3 **Jul./Aug. 1996**
PHOTOGRAPHERS   *Globe Photos (Eiffel Tower),*
AP (Crowd),
Outline (Bardot)

5 **Holiday issue 1996**
PHOTOGRAPHER   *Frank Veronsky*

4 **Jul./Aug. 1996**
PHOTOGRAPHER   *Andreas*

6 **Nov./Dec. 1996**
PHOTOGRAPHER   *Chip Simons / FPG*

naked city

The Fine Print
by Roger Ziegler

"Sometimes I Feel Like Killing My Wife"

Could that whole messy O. J. Simpson thing have been avoided? SPY thinks so. It turns out that the Hertz rental car company requires potential employees to undergo, among other tests, a written psychological evaluation. In this "Employee Safety Inventory," each candidate for a position at Hertz must answer 98 scientifically designed questions by checking one of six boxes ranging from "Strongly Agree" to "Strongly Disagree." The test is presumably intended to be a last line of defense against having your rental car delivered by a potential murderer.

What follows is an incomplete list of Hertz's actual questions. Determine for yourself if some rent-a-shrink was fast asleep when Simpson turned in his test, or whether Hertz quite liked the idea of having a wife-beating psycho on the team:
- I have read the instructions and am willing to answer each question as truthfully as posible.
- I enjoy having a good time at all costs.
- I feel full of energy most of the time.
- I sometimes feel resentful

Ataturk, Let's Do Lunch, Babe
Fez Dispensers & Ten Percenters
Ishtar's not Constantinople

The original Young Turks led a bloody revolution and ruled the Ottoman Empire. The enfants terribles of Hollywood's Creative Artists Agency—themselves known as Young Turks!—sit in Mike Ovitz's old office. And there are more similarities between the Aegeans and the Agents!—*Jo Samma*

	Ottoman Empire	CAA Empire
Background	Humble origins. Peasant families.	Humble origins. CAA mailroom.
Education	Commander in chief Enver Bey schooled at apparatchik training ground of Military Staff College in Constantinople.	Talent agent Jay Moloney schooled at apparatchik training ground of USC Film School in South Central Los Angeles.
Group Composition	Tight-knit cadre representing various departments of the Turkish civil service.	Tight-knit cadre representing actors and directors in the Hollywood hierarchy.
Temperament	Ruthless. In a fit of rage, Enver Bey once concluded a meeting by shooting his defense minister dead.	Ruthless. In a fit of rage, agent Doc O'Connor once concluded a tennis match by throwing his racket across the court.
Empire	Young Turks inherited a once all-powerful but badly decaying realm.	Young Turks inherited a once all-powerful but badly decaying agency.
Rise to Power	Displaced aging Sultan Abdülhamid, promising to reinvigorate aging empire.	Succeeded aging überagent Mike Ovitz, promising to reinvigorate aging talent firm.
Marriage	Enver Bey wed to royal Ottoman princess.	Agent Brian Lourd fathered child of *Star Wars*'s Princess Leia.
Dwellings	Built luxurious palaces on the Bosphorus, next to palace of deposed sultan.	Agent Richard Lovett occupied luxurious office of former president, Ron Meyer, who jumped to MCA.
Early Setbacks	Lost colonies of Bulgaria, Salonika, Crete, Aegean Islands, Tripoli, Cyprus, and Egypt, among others.	Lost clients Sylvester Stallone, Alec Baldwin, Steven Seagal, Kevin Costner, and Barbra Streisand, among others.
Foreign Interference	Apprehension with the Young Turks' rule causes Great Britain to cancel battleship building contract.	Apprehension with the Young Turks' rule causes Coca-Cola to pull advertising contract.
Backroom Maneuverings	Enver Bey smuggled German warships *Goeban* and *Breslau* through Dardanelles minefield, thus eluding the British fleet.	Richard Lovett smuggled actor Hugh Grant out of the Four Seasons Hotel following his lewd conduct arrest.
Manneris…	Enver Bey affected Prussian accent and style, often posing before portraits of Frederick the Great.	Agents often affect Party Boy accents and styles. Lovett posed naked for bachelorette-party photo.
Endi…	After being deposed at conclusion of World War I, elite Young Turks died in pauper exile.	Huge Tele-TV deal collapses; Moloney goes to drug rehab for fourth time; agency in disarray.

SPY HOLIDAY ISSUE 1996

Please Don't Feed the Alligators!
Big-House Berlitz
A guide for prisoners-to-be

Hollywood bad boys like Robert Downey, Jr.—who got arrested three times in *one month* last year—seem to greet the prospect of going to jail with about as much reverential terror as they do a trip to a nice restaurant. But if Jr. and Co. are entertaining any illusions that a "blanket party" is where girls do their friends' hair and chew the fat about cellulite, they should probably read on before hitting the exercise yard. As will soon be revealed, Shaquille O'Neal's vaunted ability to "slam" a two-liter bottle of Pepsi is probably not something he wants to brag about.—*Michael D. Naxton*

For the Boyz
Alligators: Apocryphal creatures that keep timid inmates from showering.
A-1 Sauce: Blood.
Bandit: Someone who checks out men's buttocks in the shower.
Blister: An "out" and active homosexual.
Copping a Deuce: Trying to squirm one's way out of trouble.
Feeding the Alligators: Masturbating in the showers.
Feeding the Fish: Masturbating on the toilet.
Gunslingers: Sexually aggressive prisoners made to wear hot-pink uniforms to shame them out of masturbating in front of female guards.
House Mouse: A *blister* who never comes out of his cell.
Killing Alligators: Stomping in the shower to show new inmates it's safe to enter.
Notspitals: Prisoner's medical facilities.
On the Hammer: Sitting in a lockup cell.
Slamming: Storing weapons in one's anal cavity to hide them from authorities. The most popular weapon is a toothbrush that's melted under a lighter and set with two razors.
Tray Monster: Someone who greedily eats from others' trays.
Viking: Someone who has a dirty cell.

And for the Ladies
Blanket Party: Covering a sleeping prisoner with a blanket and pummeling/knifing her.
Cheese Eater: A snitch. The accused will find cheese crumbs in her bunk and should brace herself for a surprise *blanket party*.
Courtesy Knock: Rapping the table twice with the knuckles before leaving the dinner table. Failure to do so is a clear sign of disrespect.
Diana and Lisa: The former is the name of a low-grade shampoo and the latter a similarly low-grade pink soap.
Feeding the Warden: Taking a dump.
Gump: A homosexual male guard, considered harmless by the women.
Having a Hard-On for Someone: Constantly harrassing a prisoner.
Leg Rider: An inmate who kisses up to authorities and powerful prisoners.
Lock-in-a-Sock: A combination lock inside a tube sock, used as a weapon.
Pruno: An effective after-dinner cordial made from apple or grape juice, yeast, sugar, water, rice, and prunes that is allowed to ferment for three days.
Putting Water on It: Flushing the toilet with every new "deposit" as a courtesy to your cellmate.
Shanking: Assaulting someone with a blunt or sharp object. Often used in a *blanket party*.

Cheap Cherokee?
Kathie Lee: Indian Gifford

Actually his [Kathie Lee's father's] grandmother definitely didn't come over on a boat. She was already here, a full-blooded Native American from North Carolina. That's the legend, anyway. But we've never nailed down exactly what tribe she was from. I was told all my life I was part Cherokee. Then it was Crow. The latest is Blackfoot."—*From* I Can't Believe I Said That! *by Kathie Lee Gifford*

HOLIDAY ISSUE 1996 SPY 17

THE FINE PRINT CONTINUED
when I do not get my way.
- I am easily distracted when working.
- Whether I get injured at work or not is a matter of fate, chance, or luck.
- My life and career have been one crisis after another for me.
- I prefer to have an exciting, unpredictable life.
- Thinking about everything that might happen to me at work makes me nervous.
- I prefer to have new and exciting experiences even if they are frightening or dangerous.
- There are too many unfair laws that people must follow.
- I sometimes feel that life is too troublesome.
- On occasion I have taken advantage of someone.
- I enjoy taking risks in life.
- I occasionally like to do my own thing at work instead of always following company rules.
- I probably like to fight more than others.
- When I am angry about something, it usually is not long before I am in a good mood again.
- Experienced workers do not need safety training.
- I have sometimes done dangerous things just for the thrill of it.
- I always stop and think things over before I do something that could get me in trouble with the law.
- I sometimes go weeks where I do not care about anything at work.
- I am always courteous, even to people who are disagreeable.
- I can avoid getting injured at work if I am careful and avoid potential dangers.
- For me, avoiding accidents is a matter of luck.
- I like "wild" parties where people will do anything to have a good time.

1

THE FINE PRINT CONTINUED
- There have been times when I was jealous of the good fortune of others.
- I often cannot sleep because there are too many things on my mind.
- In the past, I have been tempted to break a law I did not really believe in.
- Some jobs are so dangerous that there is no way to avoid accidents and injuries.
- With my luck, I will probably have an accident in the near future.
- I like to do things that scare or shock others.
- If I get really upset, I cannot just forget about the problem and go on with other things like some people.
- People who think they know everything really make me mad.
- I feel unmotivated to work much of the time.
- Maybe I overreact sometimes, but little things at work can really get on my nerves.
- I sometimes enjoy being with fun-loving people who engage in risky activities.
- Lately, my outlook on life has changed for the worse.
- Unfortunately, most things that are enjoyable are also illegal or immoral.
- I guess I have a "short fuse" when other people do something that annoys me.
- I sometimes think of hitting someone who really deserves it.
- I sometimes try to get even, rather than forgive and forget.
- I do not care what happens to me at work or in life.
- The odds are in favor of me having an accident at work in the near future.
- I often get into trouble since I am "in the wrong place at the wrong time."
- Sometimes I wonder what else could go wrong with my life or career.
- I answered all items truthfully.

naked city

P.C. Playthings
Toys "R" Us? Try Toys 'RU-486!
My two moms went to the toystore and all I got was this lousy...

When buying gifts for their offspring, many aging baby-booming breeders look for toys that reflect their hazy Haight-Ashbury political ideals. They may be disappointed, however, by capitalism's offerings. Many manufacturers took a stab at politically correct toys this year but couldn't get quite the right "vibe."—*Todd Svasey*

Honorable sensei Gumby kicks some multi-culti butt.

Toy: G.I. Joe Eco-Soldiers action figures
Concept: These warriors have names like Clean Sweep, Ozone, Sludge Viper, Toxo-Zombie, and Deep Six (latter comes with dolphin!).
P.C. Spin: Enviro-monickers raise children's ecological awareness.
Disillusioning Flaw: Armored vehicles such as Joe's "Septic Tank" offer violence and pollution as problem-solving methods.

Toy: Little African Princess doll
Concept: "Remove her pretty African Princess outfit—and discover the cool contemporary girl underneath!"
P.C. Spin: "Kenya: Growing Up Proud!"
Disillusioning Flaw: "Hip" inner clothing an implicit endorsement of assimilationism.

Toy: Barbie dolls
Concept: Special Kenyan, Indian, Japanese, Ghanaian, Mexican, Norwegian, Dutch, German, Irish, Native American, Chinese, and Polynesian versions of everyone's favorite babe.
P.C. Spin: Varied skin tones and multicultural costumes.
Disillusioning Flaw: No variation in facial structure. No matter where her passport is issued from, her name is still the WASPy "Barbie."

Toy: Tony's Wonder Bone
Concept: "Amazing interactive video learning system" shaped like a dog bone.
P.C. Spin: Gives bourgeois tykes a taste of poorer nations' harsh "toy reality."
Disillusioning Flaw: Spending hours pressing Tony's Wonder Bone may warp sexual development.

Toy: Littlest Pet Shop plastic animals
Concept: Cute characters, such as "Royal Bombay Kitty with Kitty Throne."
P.C. Spin: Some animals hail from distant nations!
Disillusioning Flaw: Kitty is a monarchist.

Toy: Hot Wheels Jungle Ranger
Concept: "Army truck that transforms into an Amazon rain forest!"
P.C. Spin: Youngsters' love of violence converted to budding eco-enthusiasm.
Disillusioning Flaw: Nature harnessed for covert military action.

Toy: Hot Wheels Liberty Base playset
Concept: Statue of Liberty–shaped headquarters, described as "last stronghold of freedom."
P.C. Spin: Symbol of hope to arriving immigrants.
Disillusioning Flaw: "Statue's face unfolds to reveal missile-launching bazooka!"

Toy: Gumby Ninja Playset
Concept: TV's lovable green clay boy becomes culturally diverse assassin.
P.C. Spin: Japanese screens clue kids in to simple beauty of Asian lifestyle.
Disillusioning Flaw: Traditional Japanese *sai* sword wielded to devastating effect by Gumby's mortal enemy, Blockhead.

Toy: VW Combi van
Concept: Scale-model hippie vehicle.
P.C. Spin: Covered with painted butterflies and slogans such as "Flower Powered" and "Peace & Love."
Disillusioning Flaw: Encourages fossil fuel consumption and production of "greenhouse" gases.

Toy: Lava Lick "liquid candy"
Concept: Lava lamp–shaped bottles contain drinkable syrupy snack.
P.C. Spin: Venerates the 1960s.
Disillusioning Flaw: Flashbacks.

Toy: Truffles the Bear
Concept: "Truffles for President: The Only Bearable Candidate."
P.C. Spin: Charming bear underscores inadequacies of human politicians.
Disillusioning Flaw: Truffles will sleep with *anyone*.

18 SPY HOLIDAY ISSUE 1996

2

naked city

Separated at Birth?

Overprincipled loner Charles Bronson...

...and Reds principal owner Marge Schott?

Grand Ole Opry singer Wynonna Judd...

...and grating *Oprah* watcher Katey Sagal?

Federal bill passer Christopher Dodd...

...and former Bills passer Jack Kemp?

IBM-compatible Bill Gates...

...and R.E.M.'s forgettable Mike Mills?

Not-a-dame belle ringer Nathan Lane...

...Notre Dame bell ringer Quasimodo?

Cabbie Genius
Foreign Correspondents Hail Taxis for Quotes
Tired of taciturn despots? Call a cab!

American cabbies are great, but let's face it: if your taxi went flying over a cliff, chances are your driver would *still* end up going round in circles. Ironic, really, because if globe-trotting reporters are to be believed, taxi drivers in *other* countries are perceptive geniuses whose political views are more valuable than those of, say, the country's premier. Why is it unethical to dump $100,000 on Amy Fisher for her life story, when spinning a Burkina Faso feature out of a two-dollar cab ride to the Ouagadougou Hilton gets you a Pulitzer?—*Andrew Wheat*

➤ **On the 1992 South African referendum:** " 'Treurnicht doesn't want freedom for us,' said Patrick Sechibele, 52, a stocky, chain-smoking taxi driver." Christopher Wren, *New York Times*

➤ **On keeping tourists happy in The Gambia:** "As my taxi driver put it, 'After last year's very bad season, everyone is aware that tourists bring in money and must not be harmed.' " Melissa de Villiers, *Daily Mail*

➤ **On Algeria's status quo:** " 'Algerians still go to work and school...and,' said my taxi driver, 'I can still drink beer in Bab el-Oued.' " David Hirst, *The Guardian*

➤ **On skin flicks:** "My taxi driver...is an unhappy man, given to...recounting how much better things were under Nicolae Ceausescu and spitting when he pronounces the word 'democracy.' But he became suddenly animated at the mention of the [pornographic] movie. 'At last,' he exclaimed, 'something about democracy that I can enjoy!' " Thomas Carothers, *International Herald-Tribune*

➤ **On the Final Solution in Poland:** "My taxi driver was extremely jovial....We flew through the hilly countryside in his Mercedes while he talked about what a great car a Mercedes is. 'Yes, the perfect way to go to Auschwitz,' I said. He slammed the dashboard good-humoredly, repeated the joke, and laughed." Mark Kurlansky, *Harpers Magazine*

➤ **On anarchy in Russia:** "In the late 1960s, most things were against the law. But as my driver informed me last week, 'There is no law in Russia today.' To prove it, he steered his rattling Zhiguli over the curb and aimed it down the icy sidewalk." Michael Johnson, *Moscow Times*

➤ **On Nigerian trash:** "Heaps of garbage lay piled along the curb, residue of a month-long sanitation strike. 'This city is hell,' my driver mumbled." Joshua Hammer, *Ottawa Citizen*

➤ **On Kurds vs. Kurds in northern Iraq:** " 'The people are very happy that Barzani is in Erbil,' said Hekmat Hares, a taxi driver and Barzani loyalist. ...'Talabani used to kill the Kurds; we don't kill the Kurds.' " Douglas Jehl, *New York Times*

22 SPY HOLIDAY ISSUE 1996

3

1 **Holiday Issue 1996**

PHOTOGRAPHERS *Neal Peters Collection (top left), Ewing Galloway (bottom left), Archive (top and middle right), Globe Photos (bottom right)*

2 **Holiday Issue 1996**

PHOTOGRAPHY *Courtesy of Trendmasters Inc.*

3 **Holiday Issue 1996**

PHOTOGRAPHERS *Steve Granitz / Retna (Bronson, Sagal, Mills), AP (Schott, Dodd), Eddie Malluk / Retna (Judd), Archive (Kemp), Sygma (Gates, Lane, Hunch Back)*

VILLAGE
1 **Vol. 3 1996**
2 **Vol. 9/10 1996**
EDITOR *Vittorio Corona*
CREATIVE DIRECTOR *Massimo Gentile*
ART DIRECTORS *1,2 Massimo Gentile,*
1 Sergio Sartori
PHOTOGRAPHERS *1 Helmut Newton,*
2 Nick Scott
PUBLISHER *Editoriale Italiana S.P.A.*
Italy

1

2

86 UOMINI NEL CINEMA
Wesley e Woody, nemici per caso

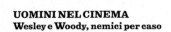

Vol. 9/10 1996
ART DIRECTOR *Massimo Gentile*
PHOTOGRAPHER *Klaus Laubmayer*

opposite page 1 **Vol. 3 1996**
ART DIRECTORS *Massimo Gentile,*
Sergio Sartori
PHOTOGRAPHER *Donna Trope*

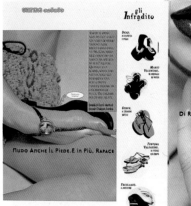

2   **Vol. 3 1996**

ART DIRECTORS   *Massimo Gentile,*
Sergio Sartori

PHOTOGRAPHER   *Antonio Capa*

2

3

4

3   **Vol. 3 1996**

ART DIRECTORS   *Massimo Gentile,*
Sergio Sartori

PHOTOGRAPHER   *Ellen von Unwerth*

4   **Vol. 3 1996**

ART DIRECTORS   *Massimo Gentile,*
Sergio Sartori

PHOTOGRAPHER   *Vincenzo Lo Sasso*

VOGUE PARIS
1 Feb. 1996
2 Nov. 1996
3 Dec./Jan. 1996-97

EDITORS
1 Carine Roitfield,
2 Marcus von Ackermann,
3 Marie-Amélie Sauvé
ART DIRECTOR
Donald Schneider
DESIGNER
Donald Schneider
PHOTOGRAPHERS
1 Mario Testino,
2 Michael Thompson,
3 Jean-Baptiste Mondino
PUBLISHER
Les Publications Condé Nast S. A.
France

1

2

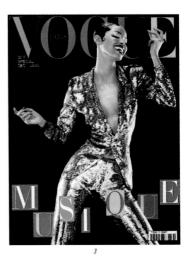

3

les visages des voix

Notre choix est fait. Stars d'aujourd'hui et de demain issues du répertoire rock, rap ou lyrique, venues d'ici ou d'ailleurs, ces artistes sont nos références. A l'unanimité. Neneh, Suzanne, Fiona, Shirley, Laurie, mais aussi Cecilia, Albita et Barbara. Gros plan sur les visages des huit voix qui nous laissent sans voix.

SHIRLEY MANSON
PAR DAVID LACHAPELLE

4

A LA VILLE COMME A LA NEIGE

BARBARA
PAR MATS GUSTAFSON

5

6

4	Dec./Jan. 1996-97	5	Dec./Jan. 1996-97	6	Nov. 1996
EDITOR	John Hullem	EDITOR	Judy Blame (left)	EDITOR	Marie-Amélie Sauvé
DESIGNER	Ezra Petronio	DESIGNER	Ezra Petronio	DESIGNER	Martin Fauquet
PHOTOGRAPHER	David Lachapelle	PHOTOGRAPHER	Jean-Baptiste Mondino (left)	PHOTOGRAPHER	Jean-Baptiste Mondino
		ILLUSTRATOR	Mats Gustafson (right)	PAINTBOX	Janvier
		PAINTBOX	Janvier (left)		

DU POIL DE LA BÊTE

La vraie fourrure fait sa rentrée. Luxueuse, voluptueuse, chaleureuse. Et résolument moderne. De quoi tenter
même ses détracteurs, d'autant qu'on la porte désormais du sport au soir. Photos Jerome Esch.

Nov. 1996

EDITOR	Nathalie Marchal
DESIGNER	Martin Fauquet
PHOTOGRAPHER	Jerome Esch

Fev. 1996

EDITOR	Jenny Capitain
DESIGNER	Martin Fauquet
PHOTOGRAPHER	Jean-Baptiste Mondino
PAINTBOX	Janvier

marie claire

1 **Mar. 1997**
2 **Feb. 1997**

EDITOR *Jackie Frank*
ART DIRECTOR *Sara Beaney*
PHOTOGRAPHERS *1 Patrick Demarchelier,*
2 Christophe Jouany
STYLIST *2 Jane Campsie*
PUBLISHER *Murdoch Magazines*

Australia

1

2

beauty

nineteen ninety seven
nineteen ninety eight
nineteen ninety nine
two thousand

2001:
a beauty odyssey

fasten your seatbelts and get set
for a journey into the future.
Jane Campsie looks at how beauty
is shaping up for the new millennium

beauty

10 steps in 10 minutes

the fast track to perfect make-up. by jane campsie

C TRUS

oranges and lemons with a dash of lime to taste

Sep. 1996

PHOTOGRAPHER Luis Sanchis
STYLIST Gabriele Mihajlovski

Jan. 1997

PHOTOGRAPHER Greg Delves
STYLIST Jane Campsie

opposite page **Feb. 1997**

PHOTOGRAPHERS Guy Aroch,
3 Christophe Jounay,
3 Andrew Lehmann

horoscope special

horoscope 97

by tanya obreza

photographs by delves

aries
march 21 to april 20

taurus
april 21 to may 20

overview

Your problems can be realised, but only with patience and stamina. As gruelling as the past 12 months have been, the pace remains hectic. Stay on course and by early 1998 you'll have made a significant and lasting impression where it matters. For now, finances need controlling.

love

At present, there is conflict between obligation and pleasure, and your best interests are being caught in the crossfire. Tactful planning should keep the tension between personal and professional responsibilities, although putting old demons to rest may not be quite so easy.

career

Despite feeling overworked and under pressure, real breakthroughs are likely this year — some of them totally unexpected. Be prepared for a switch in direction, if necessary. You may have to travel in connection with your work or perhaps even relocate. The main requires real commitment.

leo
july 23 to august 22

virgo
august 23 to september 22

overview

Personal growth and emotional freedom become the primary motives this year. Don't be afraid to make mistakes — the spirit can only grow when challenged and inspired. With each move that's made, you can reinforce your own identity, your talents and your creative potential.

love

Circumstances force you to confront emotional issues and create new ground rules within relationships. In addressing each new conflict, new strengths are revealed. For singles, romantic prospects are splendid, with new partnerships possibly discovered through family connections.

career

New opportunities should open up, with little resistance placed in your path. Work satisfaction rises, either through a new job or better conditions in your present employment. You may be required to travel or commit to further training. Health improves, which can only help your performance.

gemini
may 21 to june 21

cancer
june 22 to july 22

overview

This is your year of emotional and spiritual awakening. Now, more than ever, you will be called upon to demonstrate your individuality, creativity and tenacity. Financially, 1997 will be a positive one, but even so you should bank on some wealth rather than rely on credit.

love

The question means that hang over your romantic life may bring a change in attitude. As family-focused as you are, selfless dedication just won't seem as fulfilling anymore. Confronting your limitations will increase your confidence ... and a more independent Cancer is likely to emerge.

career

This year promises prosperity and professional recognition. But the road to success isn't without disruption; red tape may delay new projects or make it difficult to complete old ones. By now, though, you're used to complication and you've learnt to view obstacles as challenges.

W Magazine

1	**Jan. 1997**
2	**Mar. 1997**

EDITOR	*Patrick McCarthy*
CREATIVE DIRECTOR	*Dennis Freedman*
DESIGN DIRECTOR	*Edward Leida*
ART DIRECTOR	*Kirby Rodriguez*
DESIGNERS	*1 Edward Leida,*
	2 Kirby Rodriguez
PHOTOGRAPHERS	*1 Michael Thompson,*
	2 Mario Testino
PUBLISHER	*Fairchild Publications*
	USA

1

2

Viva la
Frances

Fargo star Frances McDormand suddenly goes from character actress to Oscar favorite.

Six months ago, Frances McDormand was a quirky, working character actress with occasional flashes of brilliance in movies like *Mississippi Burning*—when she registered on the Hollywood radar screen at all. Next thing you know, she does a little movie called *Fargo*, winds up the Oscar front-runner, and everyone in Hollywood says they always loved her.

Anybody other than McDormand would be amazed. Because this year she just did what she's always done throughout her 17-year stage-and-screen acting career: played the hell out of a great character. Only this character was the lead in a movie aimed at arthouse Siberia that instead landed in critics' heaven. "The Coen Brothers [who wrote and directed *Fargo*] just tell great stories, from some weird place inside their heads," is how McDormand sums up *Fargo*'s success—seven Oscar nominations. "And they've always had artistic control of their projects."

There's no underestimating the power of the Coen cult. Their fan base has grown throughout making *Blood Simple* (1983), *Raising Arizona* (1987), *Miller's Crossing* (1990), *Barton Fink* (1991) and *The Hudsucker Proxy* (1994). The Coens wisely keep their budgets low, their box-office expectations modest, but take a lot of chances in terms of plot and style. And they've got great taste in actors: Nicolas Cage, Holly Hunter, Gabriel Byrne, John Goodman and John Turturro all excelled in the Coen's murky offbeat film noirs, on their way to certified Hollywood stardom.

But none fared so well from one particular pic as McDormand, who sat back and watched, bemused, as the L.A. Film Critics, the National Board of Review, the Broadcast Film Critics Association, and countless other critics' associations pile awards (plus Golden Globe and SAG nominations) on her. All for her portrayal of one of the movies' plainest and sanest women: Marge Gunderson, a pregnant small-town cop in Brainerd, Minnesota, who singlehandedly solves a kidnap caper that leads to mass murder—without ever once losing the odd demeanor McDormand calls "Minnesota Nice" and her heavy hayseed accent.

And Marge never takes off her clothes, commits adultery, becomes a serial killer, does a courtroom scene, gets a terminal illness or has a nervous breakdown. How many female Oscar nominees can say that?

The 39-year-old McDormand did not have to kill for the part other actresses are now calling the best female role of the year, and one of the most unique ever for a leading actress. That's because she's married to Joel Coen. "Yeah, Joel and Ethan pretty much wrote Marge for me," she admitted the day after The Golden Globes—one of the few awards she didn't win (Madonna did.) But you can't accuse McDormand of nepotism. She and her writer/director husband met when he gave her her first movie role in his first movie, *Blood Simple*, and after they meandered into becoming a couple, didn't work together again 'til now.

"During *Blood Simple*, we felt it was very unprofessional for two people who were working together to get involved," she says, over a coke with lemon in the Four Seasons Hotel in Beverly Hills ("it breaks up the nicotine"). "So we admitted our attraction, but didn't really act on it 'til the movie was finished. And then, after we got involved, we made a conscious effort to work separately, to try to establish our identities independently of each other. Anyway, I couldn't expect Joel to cast me in every single one of his female parts," she says, understandingly. "Although they're all such great parts, I kinda wish he had."

She didn't ask, but McDormand couldn't resist hinting. Eventually, when they were finished writing *Fargo*, Joel and Ethan handed it to her without prefacing it in any way. She had no idea what to expect. And she wasn't exactly flattered.

"But when I first read *Fargo*," she says, "I laughed, but I was a little miffed. 'Ha, ha, ha, OK you guys, you want *me* to play Marge?' There's a certain amount of my background that's a lot like Marge. I grew up in the corn belt, in Illinois, and of course, they're very aware of that. They grew up as fish out of water, as Jewish kids in Minnesota. The movie is sort of their homage to their childhood. But as an actor, you're looking for something that's far away: give me a good psychokiller, a good prostitute. It wasn't until I started working on Marge that I realized that it was about *truly* transforming yourself into another person. And that was a bigger stretch than anything I'd done before."

But McDormand can't explain or articulate *Fargo* that much better than anybody else. At several public appearances, the Coen Brothers uttered few and nearly unfathomable monosyllabic responses to questions about *Fargo*'s meaning—and the brouhaha that it was based on a real event that turned out, as the *New York Post* concluded, not to be so real. No one in Minnesota could find anything on the books about a small-town bloodbath related to a kidnapping that had occurred in the last 30 years.

PHOTO BY MARY ELLEN MARK

"When I first read *Fargo*," says McDormand, "I laughed, but I was a little miffed."

Mar. 1997

DESIGNER	*Kirby Rodriguez*
PHOTOGRAPHER	*Mary Ellen Mark*

Mississippi Yearning

PHOTOGRAPHED BY BRUCE WEBER

Mar. 1997

DESIGNER　*Edward Leida*
PHOTOGRAPHER　*Bruce Weber*

Elements of Style

PHOTOGRAPHED BY RICHARD BURBRIDGE

Mar. 1997

DESIGNER　*Edward Leida*
PHOTOGRAPHER　*Richard Burbridge*

What a Feeling

It's *Flashdance* revisited with tighter-than-tight tops, skirts and leggings, set off by bright enamel jewelry.

PHOTOGRAPHED BY MICHAEL THOMPSON

Dec. 1996

PHOTOGRAPHER	Michael Thompson
HAIR	Neil Moodie
MAKEUP	Dick Page
STYLIST	Joe Zee
FASHION ASSISTANT	Geriada Kefford

White Lightning

Time to sparkle! White metal watches with diamonds are the winning combination for holiday.

There's no better time to splurge than the holiday season and no better way than with white-gold and platinum watches that can carry you gleaming well into the night.

"White gold is becoming very fashionable again," says Gerry Grinberg, president of Concord and Piaget. "Many years ago, one would only wear yellow gold during the day and white gold at night. It's more formal; there's no question about that. People are now returning to these types of formalities because it's time for a change. Just like anything in fashion, whatever looks freshest to the eye, looks prettiest." According to Valerie Lichtman, vice-president of Harry Winston, "To me, platinum is the ultimate in luxury. People say it's cold, but I say it's only as cold as the shiver that goes up your spine when you see it."

—ANNE SLOWEY

From the top: Tiffany & Co.'s stainless steel watch at Tiffany & Co., $650; Baume & Mercier's 18k-white-gold watch with 500 diamonds, $52,000; Concord's 18k-white-gold watch at Tourneau, New York, $7,250; Piaget's 18k-white-gold watch with diamonds at Piaget, New York, $19,900; Harry Winston's platinum and 16-carat diamond watch at Harry Winston; Breguet's 18k-white-gold watch with diamonds and emeralds, at Cellini, New York, $73,250; Patek Philippe's 18k-white-gold watch with diamonds at Tiffany & Co., $22,300; Van Cleef & Arpels' 18k-white-gold and diamond watch at Van Cleef & Arpels, $27,500.

106 W DECEMBER 1996

Dec. 1996

PHOTOGRAPHER *Stephen Lewis*
STYLIST *Anne Slowey*

High Color

Say so long to pasty hues. When it comes to jewelry, it's rich shades or nothing at all.

Not since the Southwestern craze of the Eighties have these two clashing colors coalesced in quite so fetching a way. But coral and turquoise, near-opposites on the color chart, are in league for resort. And they're saturating some of the best baubles around.

Angela Pintaldi, who likes them both, says, "I love rich colors in nature. When I work with coral or turquoise, I try to keep each piece as close to its original form as possible. Sometimes I smooth it in order to enhance its color and beauty."

Think bold, though, not earthy. "Turquoise has a primal, ethnic reputation," says designer Michelle Savitt. "But there has been a progression toward elegance than is very far from that piled-on look. It's polished and exquisite inside and out."

And it works with the feminine clothes of the season.

"A lot of things you can live without," says Savitt, "but good turquoise is as wonderful as a great strand of pearls."

—KIMBERLY FORREST

From the top: Angela Pintaldi's turquoise ring; M & J Savitt's triple-strand turquoise necklace and Ken's coral necklaces.

100 W DECEMBER 1996

Dec. 1996

PHOTOGRAPHER *Kenji Toma*
STYLIST *Kimberly Forrest*

1

2

SPORTSWEAR International

1 **Vol. 118 Feb. 1997**
2 **Vol. 119 Mar./Apr. 1997**

EDITOR	*Michael Belluomo*
ART DIRECTOR	*Robert Cristofaro*
DESIGNERS	*1 Robert Cristofaro, 1,2 Henry Lee*
PHOTOGRAPHERS	*1 Simko, 2 Eva Mueller*
STYLISTS	*1 Melissa Berry, 2 Edina Suitanik*
ASSISTANTS	*2 Nina Flores, 2 Megan Dillon*
PUBLISHER	*Opal Publishing Co.*

USA

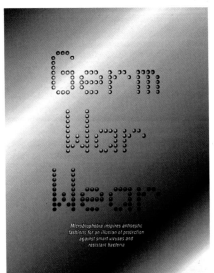

Germ War Wear

*Microbiophobia inspires antiseptic
fashions for an illusion of protection
against smart viruses and
resistant bacteria*

unseen by the naked eye

Photography by Eva Mueller. Styling by Edina Suitanik. Assisted by Megan Dillon and Nina Flores. Set
Design by Kena Dakota. Hair by Robert de Knose for Loli. Make-up by Hirami for Gebler Naaman.
Models: Liskula/Karin, Yann Keesing/RPM, Rhea Henderson/Company, Jeff Shoebin, Lukas.

**Technicians
evaluate the
evidence**

This page: She wears a
white mini-style dress
by PURR. Boots, BELLÒ.
Necklace, BIENE.
Opposite page: from left
to right: She wears a
clear plastic jacket
with holographic trim by
LINDTHAI, over a corset
by FIXER ENTRE, with
white shirt by AMY CHAN.
Boots, BELLÒ. Plastic
chokers, GREEN. She
wears a sheer zip t-
shirt by C-MENT, over
white "spat-rool" pants
by MECE. Platform san-
dals, BB NR. He wears
a plastic jacket by
MERCERON, over U.S.
military tights from
THE SPORTSMAN'S GUIDE
CATALOG. Sneakers,
BB NR.

**RX:
Microcontamination
control**

This page: He wears
a long-sleeved lycra
top by RXE CLOTHING,
over white pants
with reflective trim
by E-PUFF.
Opposite page: She
wears a silver lycra
long-sleeved shirt
by MECER USA, with
silver lycra pants by
DREAM LAB. Boots,
FREELANCE. He wears
a black vinyl top by
DIANA GOODMAN FOR
TRIPP NYC, with
black vinyl pants by
LIP SERVICE. Boots,
BELLÒ.

defensive hygiene

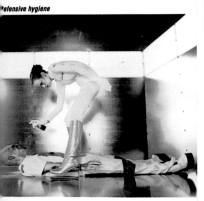

Viral host isolation

**High-density barrier
shield required**

Sterilization...complete

This page: She wears a hypodermic dress by SERBS AND ROBOT. Shoes, ELSÉ MITTA.
The victim wears white pants by MARTINE & FRANCOIS GIRBAUD. Shoes, BELLÒ.
Opposite page: She wears a white bodysuit by WU WEAR. Boots, FREELANCE. Gloves, SHANNAN.
He wears a white T-shirt by PÖSCH; over white synthetic pants by PEPE. Shoes, BELLÒ.

This page: She wears a stone trooper jacket by ARMOUR, to wears a white zip jacket with black taping
by PROTECTIVE CLOTHING. The Victim on the left wears satin textured pants by PURR. Boots, BELLÒ. The vi...
on the right wears nylon grey pants by CYBERTEX. Platform shoes, BB NR.
Opposite page: He wears a cleanroom garment constructed of Integrity 2000, a static
dissipative barrier fabric, by MICRON-CLEAN UNIFORM.

NO PLACE LIKE HOME

...d the scenes, models live fabulously. Right? Go inside the apartments and lives of New York's Beautiful People.

...htswitch broken, mattress like a porcupine;

...the toilet chain is broken,...

...'s darker than hell and twice as expensive.

...and the phot... ...cells down

the hall light, the front ...and the light has burned out—
light, the back light, the inner light;

Vol. 118 Feb. 1997

DESIGNER   Robert Cristofaro
PHOTOGRAPHER   Marc Andrew
STYLISTS   Melissa Berry,
                Nina Flores

opposite page   **Vol. 119 Mar./Apr. 1997**

DESIGNER   Henry Lee
PHOTOGRAPHER Eva Mueller
STYLIST   Edina Suitanik
ASSISTANTS   Nina Flores,
              Megan Dillon

Dutch

1 **Vol. 8 Autumn 1996**
2 **Vol. 9 Winter 1996**

ART DIRECTOR *Sandor Lubbe*
PHOTOGRAPHER *Cometti*
STYLIST *Matthias Vriens*
DESIGN FIRM *Proforma*
PUBLISHER *Art View BV*

Netherlands

1

2

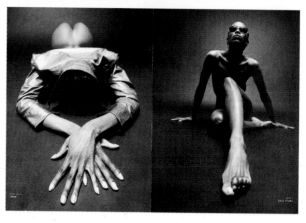

Vol. 7 Summer 1996

ART DIRECTOR *Sandor Lubbe*
PHOTOGRAPHER *Carli Hermès*
STYLIST *Marlou Hage*

CITY ANGELS

Red Hot

Vol. 7 Summer 1996

ART DIRECTOR *Sandor Lubbe*
PHOTOGRAPHER *Norman Watson*
STYLIST *Alistair Green*

Vol. 9 Winter 1996

ART DIRECTOR
Sandor Lubbe
PHOTOGRAPHER
Carli Hermès
STYLIST
Maarten Spruyt

Zonden jegens de Heer hebben ons kennelijk niet met voldoende schuldgevoelens opgezadeld. Er is immers een nieuwe god opgestaan: onze Gezondheid, met Zijn profeet Postbus 51 en een gevolg van talloze discipelen en predikanten. Hun toorn geldt de kleine geneugten des levens, zoals een glas wijn en een sigaret. Wie zich eraan bezondigt, zal ervoor boeten. Onzin, vindt psychonoom en 'plezierwetenschapper' Jan Snel van de Universiteit van Amsterdam. Genotmiddelen verminderen negatieve stress – met andere woorden, de schadelijke variant van stress. Want ook stress is niet altijd ongezond. Het kan de gezondheid zelfs goed doen, zegt stress-onderzoeker professor Orlebeke. En daarmee rijst de vraag: hoe 'fout' zijn de Bourgondiërs en andere levensgenieters onder ons nu eigenlijk bezig?

DOOR David de Leeuw | ILLUSTRATIE Vaiyaz Jafri

DROOM OF NACHTMERRIE? ACHT UUR. DE wekker gaat. Monter springt X uit bed, wast zich en ontbijt: twee volkorencrackers met magere kaas. Plus een kop magere melk. Dan fietst hij naar zijn werk, luncht daar 's middags met twee bruine boterhammen en een appel. 's Avonds dineert X uiteraard met maximaal vijftig gram vlees, twee ons groente en twee stuks fruit. Hij brengt nog een bezoekje aan de sportschool. Thuisgekomen is er tijd voor de dagelijkse uitspatting: een grapefruit. Tevreden gaat X vervolgens onder zeil. Fijn, weer zo'n gezonde dag achter de rug. En morgen weer een. Jippie! Zó moet het, verzekert men mij herhaaldelijk van alle kanten: vrienden, vriendinnen, de dokter, de tv, de bladen. Zó werkt het niet, weet ik uit eigen ervaring. Althans niet voor mij. Het levenspatroon van X zou me horendol maken. Niet dat ik geen pogingen heb gedaan. Lekker de koffie, de snacks en de zoetigheid laten staan. En een lusteloos stuk chagrijn worden. Tegenwoordig bezondig ik mij regelmatig aan allerlei fouts. Kan ik me lekker schuldig voelen over mijn zwakke vlees.
«U zich schuldig voelen? Waarom?», wil psychofysioloog dr. Jan Snel van de Universiteit van Amsterdam weten. Hij is een van de woordvoerders van de internationale beweging van geleerden ARISE (Association for Research Into the Science of Enjoyment). ARISE bestaat uit onder meer filosofen, psychologen, sociologen, farmacologen, artsen en biologen. Een prominent lid is directeur dr. Cornelis van der Heijden van de VN-World Health Organization (WHO). Snel: «Gezondheidsgoeroes praten u en vele anderen een schuldcomplex aan. Maar het is echt klinkklare onzin te denken dat uw leven er per definitie drastisch op achteruitgaat als u bijvoorbeeld regelmatig frites of chocolade consumeert. Niet alle slechte gewoonten zijn zo schadelijk als men zou denken. Er zijn er zelfs bij die de gezondheid ronduit bevorderen. Dat is ook de achtergrond van de 'Franse paradox': Fransen, die relatief veel wijn en vette kaas tot zich nemen, blijken niet zelden lang te leven. Terwijl ze volgens wetenschappers allang het loodje hadden moeten leggen vanwege hun 'ongezonde' leefgewoonten. Die zijn dan toch kennelijk niet zó ongezond. Wijn verwijdt de bloedvaten, wat het vaatsysteem flexibeler maakt. Het raakt gewend snel te reageren op fysieke of mentale stress en weer snel terug te keren naar de basistoestand. Eenzelfde effect als met sport bereikt wordt. U kunt dus eigenlijk net zo goed wijn drinken.»
Wijn heeft trouwens nog een voordeel: het zorgt ervoor dat vet minder snel neerslaat op de wanden van bloedvaten. Zo'n drie glazen wijn per dag is optimaal gunstig voor het cardiovasculaire systeem, adviseert de Amsterdamse psychofysioloog. Risico's op hartinfarcten en dergelijke nemen dan behoorlijk af, blijkt uit een in mei '95 in het British Medical Journal gepubliceerd onderzoek. Drie tot vijf glazen bier per dag sorteert – in mindere mate – eenzelfde effect, gedestilleerd vrijwel niet.

Koffie: stimulerend en kalmerend
Snel wordt in de wandelgangen wel 'Coffee Boy' genoemd omdat hij gespecialiseerd is in onderzoek naar de werking van dit zwarte nat. Ook koffie is prima, stelt hij. «Grotere hoeveelheden cafeïne hebben een stimulerend effect op de neurotransmitter noradrenaline. Daarom verbetert koffie meestal iemands waarneming: hij wordt alerter. Reageert lichamelijk en geestelijk sneller. Cafeïne verhoogt de concentratie, want het verbetert de 'selectieve aandacht': uit de brij van informatie die de zintuigen moeten verwerken, pikt men er sneller de op dat moment belangrijke dingen uit. Bovendien versterkt cafeïne het lange-termijngeheugen.» Uit EEG-hersenonderzoeken blijkt dat koffie niet alleen de hersenen stimuleert, maar ook kalmerend werkt op het gemoed. Snel noemt dat het 'paradoxale koffie-effect'. Bij redelijk actieve mensen gebruikt het lichaam koffie, normaal gesproken een opwekkend middel, op de een of andere manier om het tempo wat te vertragen. In de praktijk is dat ook een veelgezien fenomeen: mensen die 's ochtends koffie drinken om wakker te worden en dat op hun werk en 's avonds doen om te ontspannen. Koffie werkt bij de meeste mensen optimaal (opwekkend dan wel kalmerend) na ongeveer twee kopjes.
Volgens dr. David Warburton, oprichter van ARISE en professor in de psychofarmacologie aan de Universiteit van Reading, is de werking van chocola te vergelijken met die van koffie, waarschijnlijk omdat het ook cafeïne bevat. «Niet voor niets eten vrouwen meer chocola tegen de tijd dat ze ongesteld moeten worden. En eet men het meer in de donkere winterdagen dan 's zomers: chocola als strijdmiddel tegen de 'winter blues'.» Zelfs sigaretten deugen volgens hem een beetje. «Net zoals cafeïne kalmeert nicotine èn kan het als opwekkend middel dienen. Nicotine is ook goed voor het geheugen.»

Stressverminderend stappen
Uitgaan tot in de kleine uurtjes (of later) is een gewoonte die bij consensus tot 'ongezond' is bestempeld. Ook dat is maar betrekkelijk, vindt psychofysioloog Jan Snel. «Men denkt dat acht uur slaap het minimum nodige is. Dat hoeft niet per se. U kunt heel flexibel zijn in uw slaapgewoonten. De kernslaap bestaat maar uit vier tot vijf uur, de rest is optioneel. Mensen met drukke levens kunnen erop worden getraind hun totale slaap terug te brengen tot zesenenhalf tot zeven uur. Er bestaan zelfs mensen die jarenlang toe kunnen met drie uur slaap per nacht. Voor de meesten van ons is dit natuurlijk overdreven kort. Wel geldt het principe: iets heel leuks doen geeft óók energie. De volgende dag gaat u extra gemotiveerd weer aan de slag. Partygangers zien de volgende werkdag vaak met angst en beven tegemoet, vrezen een totaal verlies aan productiviteit, maar dat valt vaak reuze mee.» Het is, zegt Snel, alleen wel belangrijk dat we na een lange nacht toch op het gebruikelijke tijdstip opstaan – om ons bioritme niet in de war te schoppen. Dus zelfs al eindigt het feest pas om vijf uur 's ochtends, toch hard zijn en drie uur later weer opstaan. Maar niemand moet zich volgens de psychofysioloog laten weerhouden van een wilde nacht op z'n tijd: «Ook uitgaan bestrijdt de negatieve gevolgen van stress, vermindert de weerstand en slaapproblemen. Het ontspant en maakt minder snel ziek. Het stimuleert en motiveert. En dat hangt weer samen met een betere concentratie en prestatie de dag erop.»

LEKKER DE KOFFIE, DE SNACKS EN DE ZOETIGHEID LATEN STAAN. EN EEN LUSTELOOS STUK CHAGRIJN WORDEN.

Natuurlijk is te veel van het goede ongezond, weet ook Jan Snel. Maar hoe gezond of ongezond uitgaan, koffie, gebak, enzovoorts zijn is voor elke persoon verschillend en hangt af van diens psychische en fysieke constitutie. Een introvert iemand heeft bijvoorbeeld meer alcohol nodig om los te komen. De één verdraagt tien glazen wijn goed, de ander heeft na drie glazen genoeg gehad. «Men zou in theorie van iedereen een 'plezier-/effect-rapportage' kunnen maken en precies bepalen in hoeverre 'foute' gewoon-

111

TEKST & FOTOGRAFIE Willem Baars

LANG, WAT VETTIG HAAR, EEN FLANELLEN houthakkershemd en zwarte, *baggy trousers*. Verdomd, ja: Bryan Ferry is *grunge!* De man die zo lang te boek stond als de meest stijlvolle en best geklede popartiest, draagt nog net geen geitesikje. Even denken. Een optreden tijdens het jaarlijkse samenzijn van de bond voor ingedutte popsterren, twee verschillende verzamel-CD's met oud Roxy Music-materiaal en verder niets nieuws. Zijn uiterlijke transformatie naar een wandelend anachronisme maakt de verwarring compleet. Wat is er in godsnaam aan de hand?

1st Scene. How men are
«*What about the Baja Beach Club?*», vraagt Ferry plotseling, nadat hij even daarvoor heeft geklaagd over het feit dat Rotterdam de saaiste stad is die hij ooit heeft bezocht. «*Any beautiful girls there?*». Je zou het, net zomin als zijn outfit, nooit achter de gentleman aller gentlemen zoeken, maar toch: schijn bedriegt. Ook Bryan Ferry is niet (meer) de man die we kennen uit onze gedachten en uit de verhalen. Eenmaal van huis, de Britse *countryside* en vrouw en kinderen verwijderd, is Ferry er ook zo een die de bloemetjes maar wat graag buiten zet. Of heeft hij last van een midlife-crisisje? «Ik moet zeggen dat ik me in het verleden nooit echt druk heb kunnen maken over onjuistheden die over Roxy Music of mijzelf in de media zijn verschenen. Het enige wat we me wel irriteert, is dat mij nu al bijna vijftien jaar lang een soort van stereotiep *country-life*-image wordt aangemeten. In de tijd van Roxy vielen de woorden *art-school* en glamour in elk stuk dat over mij geschreven werd. Daar kon je gewoon gif op innemen. Maar sinds ik getrouwd ben, is dat het sjieke Engelse country-leven, inclusief openhaardvuur, Jack Russell-terriërs en *plusfours*. Geloof me, ik ben niet zo saai als ik eruitzie. Doordeweeks woon ik in Londen en er gaan maanden voorbij dat ik ons huis op het platteland niet zie. Ik denk dat het te maken heeft met het feit dat ik niet zo vaak op van die vervelende 'ons kent ons'-feestjes te zien ben, de Britse tabloids nooit iets interessants over mij hebben kunnen schrijven en men daarom dat stempel – saai en *country-life* – op mij heeft geplakt. Het is wat makkelijk, maar wel zo duidelijk: Bryan Ferry is een *country-gentleman*, dus daarover hoeven we verder niet na te denken. Op zich zou ik er blij mee moeten zijn, want het bespaart me een boel ellende en onzin. En ik was er ook een tijdlang blij mee. Maar op een gegeven moment gaat het ècht irriteren. Kortzichtig en ook nog onjuist. Ga een willekeurige vrijdagavond of zaterdagavond uit in Londen en je hebt als journalist al een volledig ander beeld.»

Het is opmerkelijk hoe goed geconserveerd Ferry er voor zijn 50 jaar uitziet. Hij maakt een *crispy* indruk en de jaren lijken weinig sporen te hebben getrokken, een paar kraaiepootjes en rimpeltjes daargelaten. Ferry houdt het imago waarover hij zich zo beklaagt dan ook zelf min of meer in stand. Want stappen en andere ondeugden mogen momenteel dan wel weer deel van zijn leven zijn, hij heeft kennelijk wel zijn grenzen bereikt.
«Ik vind het erg belangrijk om een vinger aan de pols te houden van wat er ondergronds gebeurt. Ik wil niet indutten en dezelfde fout begaan als veel andere muzikanten: muziek maken die niets meer te maken heeft met de tijd waarin we leven. Dat is het bekende generatiekloof-verhaal: mensen worden ouder, komen aan de verkeerde kant van de generatiekloof terecht en vinden de muziek van nu niets meer. Ik heb dat niet. Ik probeer alles zo goed mogelijk te volgen en ik moet je eerlijk zeggen dat ik de muziek van nu energieker, spannender en inventiever vind dan ooit. PJ Harvey vind ik fantastisch, de hele *Bristol-scene* vind ik geweldig, Björk, Gavin Friday, Pulp en Tim Simenon vind ik zeer oké, de Future Sound Of London vind ik het summum en ook in de dansbeweging kan ik me goed vinden. Ik hou van *groovy* muziek, maar ik zal nooit proberen diezelfde muziek na te maken, ik laat me er hooguit door beïnvloeden. Momenteel ben ik zelfs bezig met het andere uiterste: een orkestrale plaat. Maar ik vind het heerlijk om naar danceclubs te gaan en te voelen wat er gebeurt. Het is alleen vervelend dat het nachtleven zo laat begint. Waarom gaan clubs niet al om acht uur open en is het om negen uur niet gewoon leuk en vol? Wat is het toch voor onzin dat het pas na twee uur 's nachts echt knallen wordt? Weet je, ik heb mijn slaap gewoon nodig om er de volgende dag niet als een zombie uit te zien.»

Toch een beetje uitgeblust dus? «Nee, dat heeft er niets mee te maken. Maar ik merk gewoon dat ik niet goed functioneer zonder acht uur slaap. Bovendien is het zo dat mijn uiterlijk me toch ook wel wat waard is. Niet dat ik superijdel ben, maar ik voel me lekkerder als ik tevreden ben met mijn uiterlijk. En het nachtleven heeft daar nu eenmaal geen goede invloed op. Mede daarom ben ik een jaar of zes geleden gestopt met roken. Pats, in één keer gestopt, terwijl ik ruim twee pakjes per dag rookte. Op foto's van vroeger hangt bijna overal een rookgordijn om mij heen, of heb ik een sigaret in mijn hand. Ik taal er nu niet meer naar en ik voel me beter dan ooit. Wat het geheim van mijn uiterlijk is? Ik weet niet, het is me zo gegeven. Ik slaap veel, ik ben veel buiten en ik sport een beetje. Matig met drank? Nee, dat ben ik niet. Uit eten gaan is een van mijn favoriete bezigheden en ik vind het heerlijk om dat weg te spoelen met een mooie Grand Cru. En nog één...»

The secret life of Bryan – *Mr. Style* – Ferry is vijftig en *grunge*.

Erger is, dat zijn verschijning symptomatisch lijkt voor zijn recente werk: optredens die onopgemerkt voorbijgaan en maar liefst twee verzamel-CD's met Roxy Music-klassiekers. Mr. Ferry, verklaar u nader.

211

top **Vol. 9 Winter 1996**
EDITOR David de Leeuw
ART DIRECTOR Sandor Lubbe
ILLUSTRATOR Vaiyaz Jafri

bottom **Vol. 6 Spring 1996**
EDITOR Willem Baars
ART DIRECTOR Sandor Lubbe
PHOTOGRAPHER Willem Baars

Fur you

by Cometti & Matthias Vriens

Vol. 8 Autumn 1996

ART DIRECTOR
Sandor Lubbe
PHOTOGRAPHER
Cometti
STYLIST
Matthias Vriens

I LIKE TO WATCH

PHOTOGRAPHY ANDREW MCKIM | ART DIRECTION MATTHIAS VRIENS

Vol. 9 Winter 1996

ART DIRECTOR Matthias Vriens
PHOTOGRAPHER Andrew McKim

Winter 1996

DESIGNER
Yeow Tan

DESIGN FIRM
Design Studio

CLUB 21
1   **Summer 1996**
2   **Winter 1996**

EDITOR   *Christina Ong*
CREATIVE DIRECTOR   *Giovanni Pinna*
FASHION DIRECTOR   *Christopher Cheong*
PHOTOGRAPHER   *Simon Harsent*
PUBLISHER   *Club 21 Pte. Ltd.*

Singapore

1

2

3

4

5

6

3 **Summer 1996**	4 **Winter 1996**	5 **Summer 1996**	

3   **Summer 1996**

DESIGNER   *Yeow Tan*
PHOTOGRAPHER   *Daniel Zheng*
DESIGN FIRM   *Design Studio*

4   **Winter 1996**

FASHION DIRECTOR   *Christopher Cheong*
DESIGNER   *Yeow Tan*
PHOTOGRAPHER   *Tomek Sikora*
DESIGN FIRM   *Design Studio*

5   **Summer 1996**

DESIGNER   *John Finn*
PHOTOGRAPHER   *Wee Khim*
DESIGN FIRM   *Rice Bowl Pte Ltd.*

THE HARD SELL

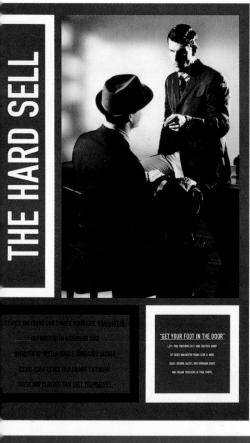

"SALES PITCH"

SHE WEARS: WOOL DRESS BY JILL STUART.
HE WEARS: PLAID SUIT BY BILL TORNADE, BOTH AT BLACKJACK.

"DRESS FOR SUCCESS"

TODAY'S TAILORING CAN CHANGE YOUR LIFE. GUARANTEED.

GET NOTICED IN A CHECKER SUIT.

SMARTEN UP WITH A SINGLE-BREASTED JACKET.

EXUDE CONFIDENCE IN A SKINNY CARDIGAN.

THESE ARE CLOTHES THAT SELL THEMSELVES.

"GET YOUR FOOT IN THE DOOR"

"A QUESTION OF TASTE"

"NEVER TAKE NO FOR AN ANSWER"

ALL CLOTHES AT GIORGIO ARMANI.

"NEW AND IMPROVED"

STRIPED COAT AND CHECKED TROUSERS BY COMME DES GARCONS
FROM CLUB 21 MEN. SHIRT AND TIE AT GIORGIO ARMANI.

---

opposite page 6	**Winter 1996**		**Winter 1996**
FASHION DIRECTOR	*Christopher Cheong*	*FASHION DIRECTOR*	*Christopher Cheong*
DESIGNER	*John Finn*	*DESIGNER*	*Yeow Tan*
PHOTOGRAPHER	*Simon Harsent*	*PHOTOGRAPHER*	*Juli Balla*
DESIGN FIRM	*Rice Bowl Pte Ltd.*	*DESIGN FIRM*	*Design Studio*

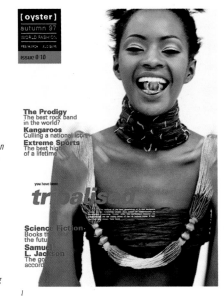

Oyster

1 **Autumn 1997**
2 **Spring 1996**

EDITOR IN CHIEF	*Monica Nakata*
EDITOR	*Madelienne Anderson*
ART DIRECTORS	*1 Sean Flanagan,*
	2 Nick Morgan
PHOTOGRAPHERS	*1 Ursula Steiger,*
	2 Carmen Kemmink
FASHION EDITOR	*Kelvin Harries*
HAIR & MAKEUP	*1 Daniel Sandler,*
	2 Dotti
STYLIST	*Fabienne Apert*
DESIGN FIRM	*New Moon*
PUBLISHER	*3D World Publishing*

Australia

1

2

**COMME DES GARÇONS' RECLUSIVE
GOLDEN CHILD, JUNYA WATANABE,
MEETS EXCLUSIVELY WITH OYSTER.**

1. feeding

3. lazer girl

4. fantasy *5

**IN 1984 WATANABE TOOK A JOB AS A PATTERN
MAKER WITH COMME DES GARÇONS PUTTING HIM
IN CONTACT WITH A WOMAN WHO HAS BECOME
HIS MENTOR SPONSOR AND SOLE EMPLOYER**

4. flavour 1- plastic

Summer 1996

ART DIRECTOR	*Sean Flanagan*
PHOTOGRAPHER	*Tim Robinson*
FEATURES EDITOR, WRITER	*Michelle Katz*
HAIR & MAKEUP	*Ken Arthur*

Summer 1996

ART DIRECTOR	*Nick Morgan*
PHOTOGRAPHER	*Pete Thiedeke*
STYLISTS	*Craig Borham,*
	Pele Thiedeke

1	**Spring 1996**		2	**Spring 1996**
ART DIRECTOR	*Nick Morgan*		ART DIRECTOR	*Nick Morgan*
PHOTOGRAPHER	*Tim Robinson*		PHOTOGRAPHER	*Jez Smith*
DESIGN CO-ORDINATOR	*Cheryl Anderson*		STYLIST	*Michael Bechara*
			HAIR & MAKEUP	*Dotti*

Soled to Techno

Walking the beat with high-tech sole.

Sneakers... who could live without them? They're as diverse as the feet that wear them and they will escort you anywhere. Current features include the angled edge sole from DCSHOECOUSA, forefoot flex grooves from Fila and the hexalite cell courtesy of Reebok, providing cushioning and control for explosive performance in all walks of life.

Marguerite Evans

REEBOK
Model: Bullet (womens)
RRP $139

ACUPUNCTURE
(available from D-POI)
RRP $189.90

FILA
Model: Barricade XT Low
RRP $129.95

PUMA
Model: Cell speed
RRP $140

DCSHOECOUSA
Model: Rudy Johnson
RRP $125
Trade Enquiries Kwala Skateboards
Available at all good skate shops.

Photography: Tim Robinson

oyster (p.23)

Autumn 1997

ART DIRECTOR *Sean Flanagan*

PHOTOGRAPHER *Tim Robinson*

PRODUCE *Marguerite Evans*

[oy8]
in profile

Spppsss℘
with Madellienne Anderson

cum quat may

Rebecca Paterson & Megan Salmon are fashion designers with a label like no other - Spppss℘

> "We'll do anything with our fabrics, Let's see what happens when we put the fabric on the floor and have a party."

Spppss℘ try to pronounce it and it either elicits a curious frown or an eruption of laughter, followed by the inevitable "but what does it mean?" Well think of these words: "See-throo, Texture Twist, Navel Ring Boot Leg, Big Girl Gun, wet stretch and CUM QUAT MAY."

Still confused? That's OK, it isn't meant to be understood in its entirety. These are just some of the words that embellish Spppss℘'s swing tag, in an expression of laughter. Spppss℘'s love of layering shape, fabric, texture and colour reflects the mood of the Deconstructionists and the Japanese designers in particular, Rei Kawkaibo of Comme des Garçons, who is their mentor.

It is with this clue that we can attempt to decipher the play on words on their swing tag. CUM QUAT MAY. Cum, comes from Comme des Garçons. Cum Quat originates from the fruit kumquat and is a reflection of the rich fruity palette of their designs and of course comme what may, an indication of their innovative approach to Australian fashion design.

Rebecca and Megan both trained as fine artists in Perth and only launched Spppss℘ at the beginning of this year. Despite their late start, they've developed a most unusual range of clothing. I say unusual because at first glance they appear a strange blend of science fiction, industrial and tutti frutti.

If this doesn't make any sense, try Rebeca's explanation: "They are physical clothes, to do with the senses. I love food and designing these clothes are almost like eating fruit; crispy, wet and juicy. There are lobes, a steak somewhere in there, and what about a chocolate flake designer cake?"

That pretty much explains the tutti frutti aspect.

The science fiction angle must come from Megan's love of Star Trek. True to her Trekky heart, she designs shapes that are simple and wearable. Spppss℘'s respect for Japanese textile engineers, particularly Junichi Arai, whose influence is reflected in their close attention to fabrics.

They spend an inordinate amount of time treating their fabrics, experimenting with everything from stripping chemical to car engine rust. Rebecca jokes: "We'll do anything with our fabrics. Let's see what happens when we put the fabric on the floor and have a party."

Spppss℘'s are flattering designs in spite of the unconventional mixing and matching. In their collections you'll find a see-through industrial inspired dress to wear over a bright yellow trapeze dress. A 3/4 length dress to wear over Capri pants. Wet, stretch Lyra skirts and tops, cut up and sewn back together with the seams on the outside. And some body hugging pieces cut flatteringly, thanks to Megan's swimwear design background.

There are fabrics that bounce back when you crush them. Others that you can take out of the washing machine and watch dry within five minutes. Producing these fabrics may be labour intensive but Rebecca and Megan insist that their pieces be affordably priced.

Soon you may see a retail outlet called Spppss℘. This will be Rebecca and Megan's concept store. A vehicle for explaining to their buyers that their outfits, although off-beat, are also easy to wear, being casual, elegant and directional all at the same time. For now, Spppss℘ is available through Museum and Akira Isogawa in Sydney and Elle in Perth.

See stockists for details.

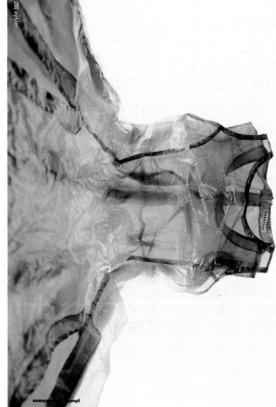

photo: Tim Robinson

[p.20] oyster

Spring 1996

ART DIRECTOR *Nick Morgan*

PHOTOGRAPHER *Tim Robinson*

waterproof©

BRAVE
AUTUMN WINTER 1997

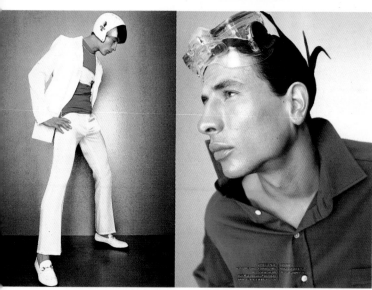

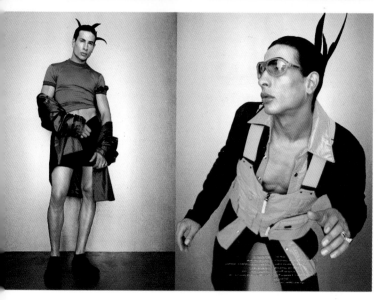

Spring 1996

ART DIRECTOR	Nick Morgan
PHOTOGRAPHER	James Houston
STYLIST	Kim Payne
HAIR & MAKEUP	Budi Juspandi

Autumn 1997

ART DIRECTOR	Nick Morgan
PHOTOGRAPHER	Nick Samartis
STYLIST	Alex Zabotto-Bently
HAIR	Campbell Macauley
MAKEUP	Chris King

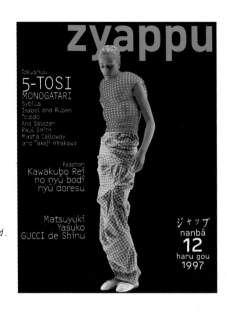

zyappu
Vol. 12 Spring 1997

EDITOR　　　　Kaoru Ijima
ART DIRECTOR　Shuzo Hayashi
DESIGNER　　　Shuzo Hayashi
PHOTOGRAPHER　Goro Arizona
DESIGN FIRM　　Neoplan
PUBLISHER　　　Korinsha Press & Co., Ltd.
　　　　　　　Japan

Vol. 10 Autumn 1996

DESIGNER
Masataka Murai
PHOTOGRAPHER
Goro Arizona

1

2

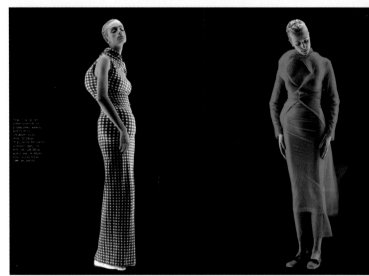

3

1　**Vol. 12 Spring 1997**
DESIGNER　　　*Masataka Murai*
PHOTOGRAPHERS　*Rika Noguchi (left),*
　　　　　　　Ryu Tamagawa (right)

2　**Vol. 12 Spring 1997**
DESIGNER　　　*Shuzo Hayashi*
PHOTOGRAPHER　*Noboru Kikuchi*

3　**Vol. 12 Spring 1997**
DESIGNER　　　*Takashi Sato*
PHOTOGRAPHER　*Goro Arizona*

Vol. 9 Summer 1996

DESIGNER *Shuzo Hayashi*
PHOTOGRAPHER *Noboru Kikuchi*

Vol. 10 Autumn 1996

DESIGNER *Takashi Sato*
ILLUSTRATORS *1,2,3 Yuka Asakura,*
1 Kaoruco,
Tsuyoshi Hirano &
Fred Jacquet,
Ed Tsuwaki,
Junichi Hakamaki,
Nobuko Terada,
Hiroshi Tanabe

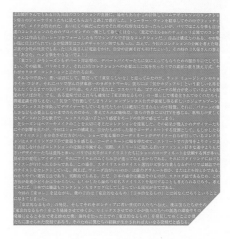

「東コレ」雑感　平川武治

今年も「東コレ」と呼ばれる不思議な「村祭り」の様なコレクションシーズンが終わった。東京ファッションデザイナー協議会（略CFD）がメイン主催団体であり、そのメンバーは現在43社で構成されている。この団体の大半とその周辺の新人デザイナーたち、あわせて73メンバー約が今回の「東コレ」の実態であった。実際にはこのCFDの設立発起人である三宅一生を筆二世代設計事を務めた山本耀司は去年来、この「東コレ」には参加していない。メンバーであり、多分、発言権を強く持っている彼らが「東コレ」への参加を中止し、いちじるくこの自体の存在に不協和音を感じて凝縮したコムデギャルソンが単独で、この東京でも上質なコムデギャルソン・スタンダードをいつも前衛的な発想の元に発表し続けている現状は、別の面からもこのデザイナー、川久保玲に大なる評価を与えた。このせ旧CFDが「自由な発想」を捨て切るとした職業もら名いのだが、その認識に取り集まってくる途中でヒエラルキーを構造化してしまっているのではないだろうか。平川が観たコレクション・ベスト#4

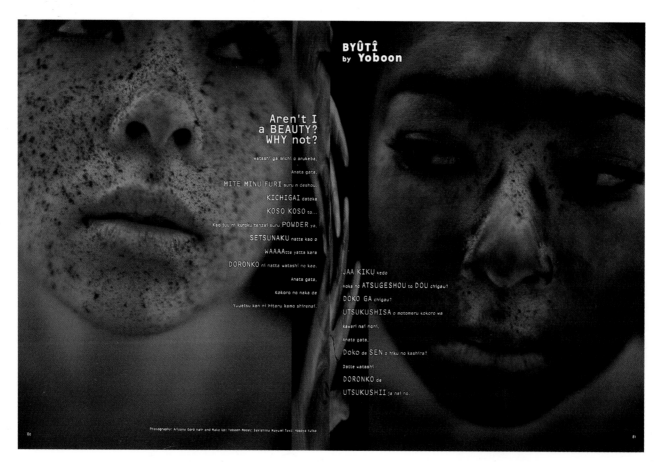

Aren't I a BEAUTY? WHY not?

watashi ga michi o arukeba,

Anata gata,

MITE MINU FURI suru n deshou.

KICHIGAI datoka

KOSO KOSO to...

Kao juu ni kuroku tenzai suru POWDER ya,

SETSUNAKU natte kao o

WAAAAtte yatta kara

DORONKO ni natta watashi no kao.

Anata gata,

Kokoro no naka de

Yuuutsu kan ni hitaru kamo shirenai.

BYÛTÎ by Yoboon

JAA KIKU kedo

hoka no ATSUGESHOU to DOU chigau?

DOKO GA chigau?

UTSUKUSHISA o motomeru kokoro wa

kawari nai noni.

Anata gata,

Doko de SEN o hiku no kashira?

Datte watashi

DORONKO de

UTSUKUSHII ja nai no.

Photography: Arizona Goro Hair and Make Up: Yoboon Model: Sakishima Mayumi Text: Hosoya Yuiko

top **Vol. 12 Spring 1997**
DESIGNER *Takashi Sato*

bottom **Vol. 12 Spring 1997**
DESIGNER *Makoto Tekawa*
PHOTOGRAPHER *Goro Arizona*

The Joint Live of ISABEL and RUBEN TOLEDO – Spring '97

Hair Color : Danilo Fake Hp : James Kaliardos for kieul loops Cosmetics : MAC Afro-Cuban Music : David Abir

Atamano saki kara ashi no saki made, torikakomu kuuki,
sokokara umareru kanjou mademo ga shin no messéji o motsu ISABEL TOLEDO.
Shinrai shiau nakama tachi to tomo ni
tsukuri age rareta kono korekushon. *It's bloody ALIVE!*

Draped
Suspender
Dresses in
TOLEDO
Rayon
Jersey
and
Silk
Georgette

Vol. 12 Spring 1997

DESIGNER   *Takashi Sato*
ILLUSTRATOR   *Ruben Toledo*

Evil Eye
Hair piece
in Copper-
Silver by:
Gabriella
Kiss
for
ISABEL
TOLEDO

Aquamarine
Drop Earing
by : Ted
Muehling
for
ISABEL
TOLEDO

TOLEDO
1997

Draped and
Suspended
Dresses in
Silk Jersey
and Silk
Georgette

Shoes in
Cotton
Brocade
Antique
Fabric
by: Manolo
Blahnik
for
ISABEL TOLEDO
Hand Dyed
Stockings
of Silk

3 Silk
Jersey
Dresses

Fashion
ファッション

Scene
1 **Oct./Nov. 1996**
2 **Mar./Apr. 1997**

EDITOR   Deborah Bee
ART DIRECTOR   Gerard Saint
DESIGNERS   Gerard Saint,
                Jane Bramwell
PHOTOGRAPHERS   1 Johnathan
                Mannion N.Y.,
                2 Huggy
                Regnarsson
STYLISTS   1 Gayle Rinkoff,
                2 Deborah Bee
DESIGN FIRM   Big-Active Ltd.
PUBLISHER   Get Seen
                Magazine Ltd.
                UK

1

2

opposite:
lipstick:
Ullas Röda

EXPOSED REVAMPED, REVIVED AND
RARING TO GO — RED MARKS ITS RETURN WITH A
VENGEANCE. FLASHBACKS OF NAFF EIGHTIES
FILMS AND HIDEOUS IMAGES OF AGEING BEAUTY
QUEENS DIED LONG AGO. RED HAS BEEN
JUSTIFIABLY RESUSCITATED BUT THIS TIME
REINCARNATED WITH A NEW VERSATILITY. GLOSSY
AND MATTE INTERTWINE TO CREATE A FRESH
APPROACH AND A WHOLE NEW CONCEPT IN COLOUR.
FORGET ALL THOSE INHIBITIONS. APPLY BY SIMPLY
SMEARING, SMUDGING AND LITERALLY SLAPPING
IT ON. THERE ARE NO RESTRICTIONS.
ACCESS ALL AREAS.

Photography by Eva Mueller • Beauty by Linda Burns

80   scene

BABYDOLL
Overstated underwear
-big knicks and boned bras upstage
this season's sheets.

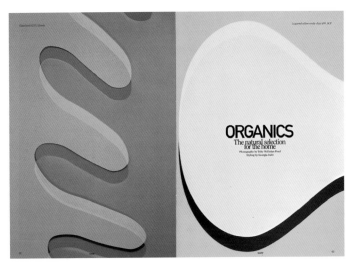

ORGANICS
The natural selection
for the home

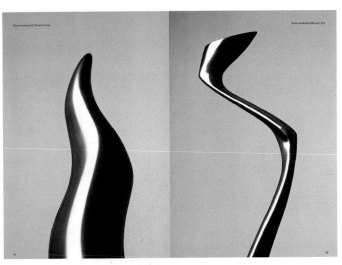

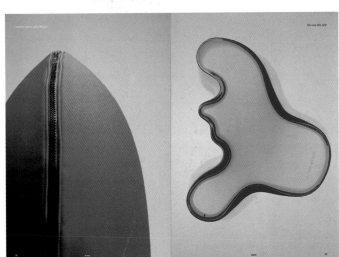

Mar./Apr. 1997

DESIGNERS   *Jethro @ Squid,*
              Gerard Saint
PHOTOGRAPHER *Steve Shaw*
STYLIST   *Deborah Bee*

Mar./Apr. 1997

PHOTOGRAPHER *Toby McFarlan-Pond*
STYLIST   *Georgia Juêtt*

opposite page   **Mar./Apr. 1997**

BEAUTY EDITOR   *Linda Burns*
PHOTOGRAPHER   *Eva Mueller*
SHOOT DIRECTOR   *Linda Burns*

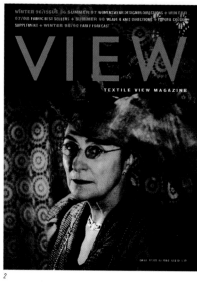

TEXTILE VIEW MAGAZINE

1 **Vol. 35 Autumn 1996**
2 **Vol. 36 Winter 1996**

EDITOR	*David R.Shah*
ART DIRECTORS	*Miriam van Loosdrecht,*
	Moniek Rump
PHOTOGRAPHER	*Grant Wilson*
PUBLISHER	*Metropolitan Publishing BV*
	Netherlands

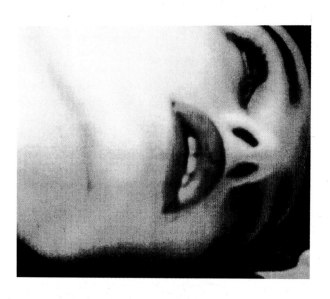

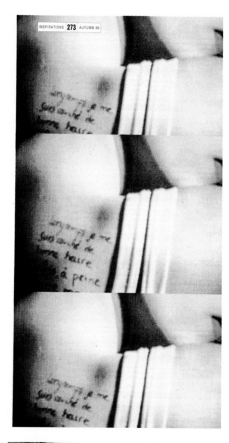

sensual

a fleur de sens

to follow your heart

to give yourself up to sensations and emotions
to give free reign to your senses

to wake up desire
to let eroticism bloom
to be overwhelmed by beauty

to revel in poetry and the mystery of the body
to rediscover the art of seduction

to abandon yourself to the
extremes of womanhood
to feed on pleasure
to drown yourself in fantasy

voluptuous

Vol. 35 Autumn 1996

DESIGNER	*Studio Edelkoort*
PHOTOGRAPHER	*Studio Edelkoort*

NOW THAT THE ONLY RULE IS TO MAKE YOUR OWN RULES, it is hardly surprising that a bit of everything was on offer. And in that offer, there was a lot of familiar looks such as tweed, Donegal, velvet, jersey, suede etc. But familiar and conforming though those stories seemed, there is nothing old fashioned about them. *Old categories such as 'natural', 'synthetic', 'pure', 'city', 'sportswear' have completely disappeared with totally new textile balances and families are being created where the look is one thing but the reality is another.* Tweeds come purple with a nervous soft crêpe touch: stretch wools and even silks are being used to create a new level of sportswear for chic city dressing. It's all very exciting and completely different to the minimal and techno we have got used to. The question is: "are browns and tweeds or purple and velvet what the consumer actually wants or what we stylists think they want. (See Womenswear and Menswear Introduction). And even when we think we know what the consumer wants the problem is only just beginning for *what counts now is mixing the stories together in a hugely novel often street inspired way. Remember there are no more rules, only the rules you make. That is why at the end of this feature we show pages of mixes bringing together elements from previous pages in a new way.*

COLOURS Universally sampled were *the browns*. These ranged from luxury camel through caramel and honey to chestnut red hues and dark peat. Then came a new feeling for ornamental in a haute-couture gamma of *reds and purples* with lipstick reds, Schiaperelli pinks, fuchsia and imperial purple. In complete contrast come the greens bringing a military feeling to fashion in winter olives, khakis, plus brighter verdant hues. The *greens* were often complemented by yellow, lemon and lime. Black is still around. Stylists talk about brown being the new black, but black is still black and remains popular for stretch, techno and sophisticated drape dressing. It is also a key mix with brights. TOUCH The key to the season is softness whether in luxury blends, chenilles and velours or the new tweeds. Even high-twist crêpes have a much gentler feel. Second in importance is weight and drape bringing a new feeling to stricter fashion dressing through diagonals, tricotine and stretch. Sanding and brushing remains an important aspect of sportswear. Some clean and satinised looks remain to sportswear. SEE PAGE 248 ▶

Vol. 36 Winter 1996

DESIGNERS
1,3 David R. Shah,
2 Studio Edelkoort,
4 Marie C. Viannay

PHOTOGRAPHERS
2 Studio Edelkoort,
4 David Burton

fabrics

1

FEMALE FUN REVENGE

TECHNO NATURE

TECHNO NOMADS

2

THE BLOSSOMING

BROWNED OFF WITH CARDEDS Is the menswear business making the same mistake today as it did three years ago when it failed miserably in trying to thrust ecru and non-dyed linen down the consumer's throat. For, just as the market was settling down nicely to another season of black 'modernistic' suits in a whole variety of new stripes and avant-garde Sixti and Seventies inspired checks, along come carded tweeds. *It is true that we have not seen carded Shetlands for a long time. But it is also true that the old fashion adage of 'four years of cardeds to one of worsteds' has been completely reversed.* Not only that, they are being presented in far from ea colour ranges starting with browns for the US and European fashion markets complemented by a range of yellows and blues for the German area and vibrant brights for younger market According to the fashion world, 'brown is the new black' and magazines are pushing it like crazy. But then you try telling that to consumers between 30 and 60 years old especially in Norther climes who will immediately counter with: "Brown, tried it before. It doesn't suit my complexion or my hair. It looks dowdy. It reminds me of Seventies furniture." Worse still, stro group buyers argue that history has shown them brown never sells well. Brights are anoth matter. Germany, Benelux and Switzerland are famous for the love of bold colouring. B again, it is one step too far not just to turn from black to bright yellow and even poster red i one leap but also to go from suits to jackets. Understandably, the fashion world finds itself in bit of a cleft stick. Sales are difficult. The decline in business might have halted, but it does n mean that business is picking up. Retailers are demanding something different. The indust as ever, is ready to oblige. They have come up with a package of tweeds that are completely ne in their touch and lightness or in their flatness and compactness. Also, when boldly mixe with strong coloured shirts and accessories in turquoise and lime, brown suddenly becom exciting. However, the step is still dramatic and fast. The consumer needs time to catch up wi the industry. Until he does, he will still go for what he knows best!

menswear

3

Vol. 35 Autumn 1996

DESIGNER
Lilian Vos

PHOTOGRAPHER
Lilian Vos

ILLUSTRATOR
Sandra Kiwiet

THE PLEASURE ZONE You are about to enter Textile View's Pleasure Zone With a flick of your finger, each of the following spreads will take you, the reader, through t w simple pleasures o' every day life. Those very same pleasures whose practices are too often neglected or truly forgotten. Let's try to re-enact some of them and travel at their ability to revitalise and rejuvenate our fatigued time-tight routines. PLEASURE IN NATURE nature's offerings. Abandon yourself to the freshness of greens in cool surface fabrics with ultra smooth finishes, foplins, ery, new twills, cottons mixed with roda coats and pyramisine, matt and flat or lightly iridescent and crépey jersey and Elite-like surfaces in polyamide or viscose. PLEASURE IN SHADOW TIME and finding the time to have time to relax and enjoy a chic, sophisticated and controlled rarity of materials and colours. Chic, fresh linen, impeccable cottons, starched knits, alpacas, fagotting, holes and crinkly textures that are barely there. PLEASURE IN LEWESS committing oneself to a romantic liaison between the sensual and the strict; intimate marriages that provoke passion between cool wools and lurex and between severe darks and seductive pastels. PLEASURE IN LANGUOR as it is revealed that laughter is the most effective stress reliever. Faded colours are cheered up and brightened up by precious stripes and luxurious glitz of an exotic provenance. Also important are metal inlays. PLEASURE IN CREATION re-colouring and recapturing the possibilities of mixing yarns to create new tweed textures and intimated patterning. Printed yarns and chequered effects, contour tweeds with mélange spots and bouwette effects, warp knitting for a knitwear nexus, three-dimensional flowers and irregular surfaces.

4

forecast

Vol. 34 Summer 1996

DESIGNER   *Denise Ford*
DESIGN FIRM   *DuPont(UK) Ltd.*

autumn winter 97.98
The Tactel Effect Colour and Fabric design direction for performance sportswear

activated brights accent a cool palette while
chalk white contrasts with metal greys in clever
surface treatments for new technical structures.

Vol. 34 Summer 1996

DESIGNER   *Rony Platenkamp*
ILLUSTRATOR   *Roland Arnassalon*
DESIGN FIRM   *M A Deymann*

CLICK ON: BEAUTY EVOLUTIONISED Gender confusion? Everyone, today, can have the experience of living as the other sex. On the Internet global network, romantic and sexual electronic conversations proliferate. Only, next time you log on, beware who you touch screens with. One of the most common phenomena in these electronic conversations is for people to adopt an identity different to their own. With the popularisation of plastic surgery, genetic engineering and electronic image retouching, gender identity poses so many new possibilities and sexual options. Even neologisms like 'transgender' are appearing as recognition of the fluidity of post-modern identity. One of the most important lessons to come out of this movement has been the collapse of stereotypes about gender identity resulting in a divorce between one's biology and psychology, or between one's body and one's sexual identity. Gender has a way of adapting to personality the same way that nature is sometimes tamed by culture. The world is ready for its next evolutionary step. As the biological body is merging with the electronic world, we are moving to an era beyond fixed gender, indeed, beyond human identity. The post-modern world will be post-gender perhaps even post-human. But don't get confused! VIEW offers you some fashion information for the junior market explaining new gender appearances in nowadays society. INFERNO the culture of fighting spirit. The burnt dry feeling of the desert. Protective army-like fabrics in warm browns, greys and burnt oranges with bright accents. VIRTUAL DELIGHT the culture of longing for unity in sexuality. A romantic, sweet story in a virtual world. Plastics and transparent fabrics in soft skin colours dark purples and browns. HYPERDERME the culture of uniformity and tenderness. An easy-listening story about the music of the '60s and '70s. Technical fabrics are mixed with cotton denims and twills. A mix of clear blues with a bright touch. CYBER REALISM the culture of connection and communication. A futuristic cyborg story in light fabrics and jerseys. Airbrushed colours in yellows and browns with bright accents. CROSS TOWN TRAFFIC real life in big cities all over the world. Fabrics feature pigment dyed denims combined with nylon. Clean checks and stripes in dark neutrals. KIDZ: WWW/SURFERS the culture of speed and movement, like surfing into the world wide web. High-tech weaves in bright colours with all kinds of greens and yellows combined with blue, pink and black.

CONCEPT: RONY PLATENKAMP GRAPHICS: M.A. DEYMANN ILLUSTRATIONS: ROLAND ARNASSALON

juniorwear

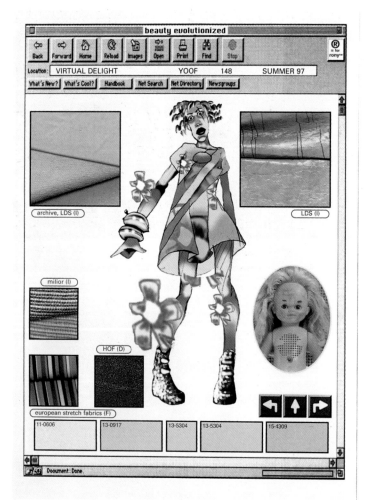

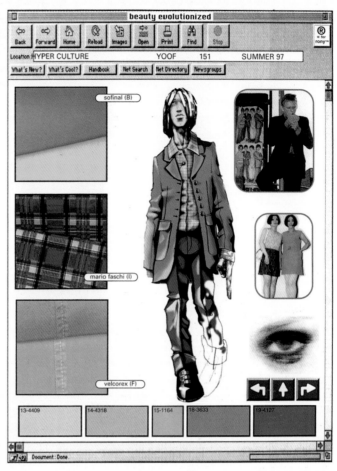

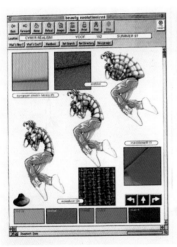

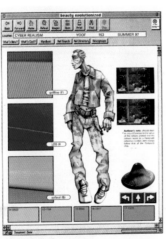

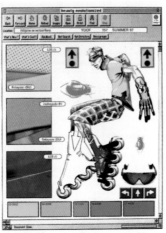

frieze

1 **Vol. 32 1997**
2 **Vol. 29 1996**
3 **Vol. 31 1996**

EDITORS   *Matthew Slotover,*
           Thomas Gidley,
           Amanda Sharp
DESIGNER   *Harry Crumb*
PUBLISHER *Durian Publications Ltd.*

UK

1

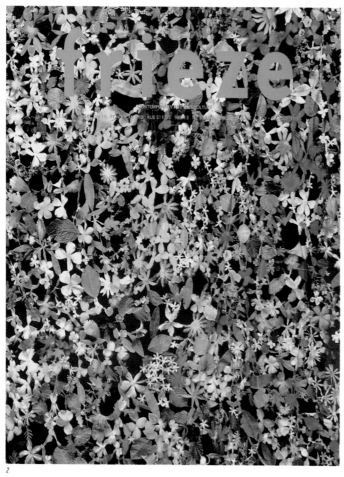

2

3

ible Air

brams talks to Gordon Thompson III, Vice-President
search, Design and Development at Nike Inc. about street
e, shoelaces and odd-sized feet

Shoe portraits by Matthew Andrews

Seasonal Change

Benjamin Weissman on Jennifer Pastor

e Chosen Few

Gidley confesses to an obsession with (certain) shoes

THE MANCUNIAN CANDIDATE

Michael Bracewell on Barry Adamson

Who's That Girl

Glenn O'Brien on Alex Bag

3

1	**Vol. 31 1996**
ART DIRECTOR	*Harry Crumb*
2	**Vol. 32 1997**
ART DIRECTOR	*Harry Crumb*
PHOTOGRAPHER	*Matthew R. Lewis*
3	**Vol. 29 1996**
DESIGNER	*Harry Crumb*

Vol. 32 1997

DESIGNER *Harry Crumb*
PHOTOGRAPHER *Matthew Andrews*

(not only)black+white

1 **Vol. 15 Oct. 1995**
2 **Vol. 23 Feb. 1997**

EDITOR *Karen-Jane Eyre*
CREATIVE DIRECTOR *Marcello Grand*
DESIGNERS *1 Christopher Holt,*
  2 Tim McIntyre
PHOTOGRAPHERS *1 Aldo Fallai,*
  2 Peter Lindbergh
DESIGN FIRM *Studio Magazines*
PUBLISHER *Studio Magazines Pty Ltd.*

Australia

1

2

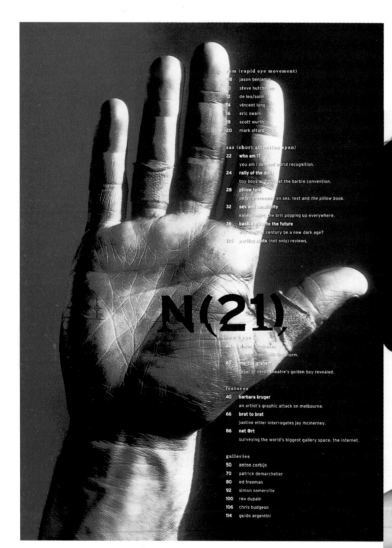

Vol. 21 Oct. 1996

DESIGNER *Tim McIntyre*
PHOTOGRAPHER *Jez Smith*

Vol. 23 Feb. 1997

DESIGNER *Tim McIntyre*
PHOTOGRAPHER *Jez Smith*

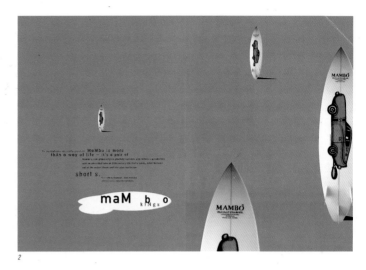

hep to be

.ny

john

depp

maM b o
kings

short s.

N C

Ni co la th Artes

CORPOREAL PUNISE

ME N1

(net) her
world

DOES THE INTERNET
HAIL A BRAVE NEW WORLD,
OR VIRTUAL IMPOTENCE?

INTER NET

GRUNGING IT UP AND PLAYING HOLLYWOOD DOWN,
ETHAN HAWKE IS SO COOL HE'S HOT

serious

CO O l

1	**Vol. 11 Feb. 1995**
DESIGNER	*Christopher Holt*
PHOTOGRAPHER	*Albert Watson*

3	**Vol. 23 Feb. 1997**
DESIGNER	*Tim McIntyre*
PHOTOGRAPHER	*James Houston*
HAIR & MAKEUP	*Lucy Caldock*

5	**Vol. 14 Aug. 1995**
DESIGNER	*Christopher Holt*
PHOTOGRAPHER	*Arunas*

2	**Vol. 11 Feb. 1995**
DESIGNER	*Christopher Holt*
PHOTOGRAPHER	*Jenny van Sommers*

4	**Vol. 13 Jun. 1995**
DESIGNER	*Christopher Holt*
PHOTOGRAPHER	*Sonia Post*

6	**Vol. 11 Feb. 1995**
DESIGNER	*Christopher Holt*
PHOTOGRAPHER	*David Rose*

kravitz

With his fourth album *Circus*,
Lenny Kravitz confirms his status as America's soul rock ringmaster.

Pippa Leary finds him hangin' in New Orleans.

Vol. 15 Oct. 1995
DESIGNER *Christopher Holt*

kristen mcmenamy in katharine hamnett, 1991, Juergen teller:

Although the London fashion pack now cite low-life documentarians Nan Goldin and Larry Clark as their primary influences, only Juergen Teller actually started his career as a documentary photographer. Since 1990, Teller has clinically exacted a raw sexuality and penetratingly crude humanity from his harshly-lit subjects. His eponymous first book is filled with starkly realistic portrayals of individuals and places he has seen in the course of his career – a career that catapulted Teller from a tiny German violin-making village to the high streets of the world's fashion capitals.

juergen teller is published by taschen

kristen mcmenamy in katharine hamnett, 1991, juergen teller:

pHotogrApher | 08

Vol. 23 Feb. 1997

DESIGNER   *Tim McIntyre*
PHOTOGRAPHER *Juergen Teller*

CREDITS
Vol. 2 1996

EDITOR — *Frank Bierens*
ART DIRECTOR — *Marjolijn Ruyg*
DESIGNER — *Marjolijn Ruyg*
PHOTOGRAPHER — *Marc de Groot*
PUBLISHER — *Uitgeverij Credits*
Netherlands

Vol. 2 1996

PHOTOGRAPHER — *Marc de Groot*

Lieve Credits, ik weet het, we laten je niet met rust. Misschien hebben we een beetje met je gesold de laatste tijd, maar neem van mij aan, met de beste bedoelingen. In ieder geval: je inhoud stáát, dus die hebben we dit keer niet rigoreus omgegooid. Maar je vorm, tja… We hebben je maar weer eens in een nieuw jasje gestoken. Hopelijk een outfit waar je niet snel uit zal groeien, maar dat verwachten we niet. Je zogenaamde superspreads vragen om een vorm waarmee dit unieke formaat ook ten volle wordt benut. 'Monumentaal', noemt vormgeefster Marjolijn Ruyg de grafische oplossingen. 'Vet', zou ik zeggen. In ieder geval ben je die 'slick' Italiaanse meubeltjes-achtige vormen kwijt en breng je de boodschap zo hard en direct mogelijk, zonder je zorgen te maken over de streling van het oog. Want dat is een erfenis uit de jaren tachtig die we nu maar eens van ons af moeten schudden. Het begin is vrij tekstueel, het tweede deel met de superspreads is daarentegen weer vrij visueel, met onder meer een portfolio van Marc de Groot die - heel bescheiden - zijn tijdsdocumenten geen eeuwigheidswaarde toekent. Zoals voortaan voor ieder nummer, mogen dit kwartaal twee toegepaste kunstenaars 'vrij werk' voor je maken. Nu zijn dat fotografe Cornelie Tollens en stylist Ruud van der Peijl, die voor de dag kwamen met het vierluik 'La vie sexuelle des plantes'. Dus Credits, het meest gerestylde blaadje van Nederland, je blijft *alive and kicking* en je zult je vast uiterst senang voelen in je nieuwe vorm. *Frank Bierens, hoofdredacteur*

Vol. 2 1996

PHOTOGRAPHER — *Marc de Groot*

Jessica Gijsel

TREND

iD.
INSTINCTIVE +
DEBONAIRE +
ECLECTIC +
NONCONFORMISTIC +
TEXTURAL +
IDEOSYNCRATIC +
TRANSMUTANT +
YOU =
IDENTITY

VORMEN

door Sybrand Zijlstra

BLAUWTJE

Pepsi-Cola — 1898
Pepsi-Cola — 1940
PEPSI — 1991
PEPSI — 1996

Altijd worden ze in ijltempo gemaakt, want de dj is altijd pas op het laatste moment bekend. In die creatieve *rush* doen vormgevers hun kleine experimenten en ontwikkelen ze hun ideeën. Flyers voor danceparty's zijn daardoor de motor van vernieuwing in vormgeving. Sinds het prille begin van de dance-feesten, houdt Discotheek RoXY die motor al draaiende.

PARTYCULTUUR BOOST NIEUWE VORMGEVING

Vol. 2 1996

MARC DE GROOT
MIJN TIJDSDOCUMENTEN ZIJN NIET VOOR DE EEUWIGHEID

Vol. 2 1996

PHOTOGRAPHER *Marc de Groot*

Vol. 2 1996

PHOTOGRAPHER *Cornelie Tollens*
STYLING *Ruud van der Peijl*

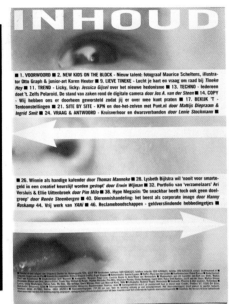

Vol. 3 1996

PHOTOGRAPHERS   Ari Versluis, Ellie Uyttenbroek

Vol. 3 1996

PHOTOGRAPHER   Fulco Smit Roeters, Ari Versluis, Ellie Uyttenbroek

PORTFOLIO 32

door Pim Milo

foto: Fulco Smit Roeters

EXACTITUDE ROTTERDAMSE VERZAMELWOEDE

EEN INTERVIEW MET ARI VERSLUIS EN ELLIE UYTTENBROEK

Hun verbondenheid spreekt al uit het gemeenschappelijk visitekaartje: Ari Versluis & Ellie Uyttenbroek Fotografie/Styling. 'Verzamelaars' had er ook nog achter kunnen staan, want beiden zijn werkelijk verzot op series. Individueel of samen maakten ze al series van vrouwengezelschappen en kaalgeschoren gabbers en ze zijn nu bezig met de reeks 'nichten in ruitjeshemden'. Als ook dat personage in beeld is gebracht, gaan ze op zoek naar slagers met stropdassen. 'Liefst nog met een bloedvlek op hun schort.'

EU: Ik heb in Rotterdam mode gestudeerd. Daarna heb ik een half jaar lang een collectie gemaakt. Al snel werd me duidelijk dat ontwerpen niet de kant was die ik op wilde. Het is zo'n vreselijk lang verhaal om iets te ontwerpen, te maken en vervolgens aan de man te brengen. Toen ben ik freelance voor een stylingbureau in Amsterdam gaan werken. Daar maakte ik voornamelijk trendprognoses. Op een gegeven moment wil je dan wel weer eens wat anders. Dus ik heb bij Oilily mijn map laten zien en ben daar onmiddellijk aangenomen. Freelance, wel te verstaan. Ondertussen wilde ik me met de styling voor fotografie bezig zijn. Ik heb voor Oilily een stand gemaakt waarop ik portretten van jongetjes wilde gebruiken. Zo ben ik met Ari in aanraking gekomen. Die fotografie voor die stand hebben we met zijn tweeën gemaakt, en daarna die PTT en wat je verder in onze portfolio kunt zien.

AV: Ik heb mijn fotografie-opleiding in Rotterdam gedaan. Toen ben ik naar Londen gegaan, waar ik stage liep bij Paolo Roversi. Eerst heb ik hem gebeld maar hij had geen plek. Toen ik toch in Londen moest zijn, heb ik zijn studio opgezocht en ben langsgegaan. Heb me voorgesteld, zijn map laten zien en ben komen. Kopjes koffie en twee inschrijven, je landt vel eens een cassette. Maar het is toch vooral: het bekijken van de dagelijkse praktijk. Hoe worden de modellen neergezet, wat is de belichting? Voel geleerd. Na verloop van tijd krijg je meer verantwoordelijkheden. Na een half jaar ben ik weer teruggegaan naar Nederland. Of ik erdoor beïnvloed ben? Het geniale aan hem vond ik, dat hij helemaal niet uit die hoek van de mode kvam. Op een gegeven moment is hij die mode gaan doen. En naar mijn gevoel zo ongelooflijk oké. Gewoon kool, dit is het. Wat Roversi doet met zijn polaroids, dat was uiteindelijk gewoon de regels aan zijn laars lappen. Door gewoon fouten te maken en meerdere belichtingen door elkaar heen te gebruiken en een bepaald effect te krijgen, dat zo'n vrouw helemaal geen ack meer had. Helemaal uitgebleekt. Prachtig. Dat vond ik allemaal erg inspirerend. Absoluut. Tegelijkertijd zie je: er was zoveel werk en d'r werd zoveel materiaal gebruikt. Op die ene plaat lagen soms veertig polaroids op de vloer die vervolgens allemaal de prullenbak ingingen en die eeo wes hat dan, te kijkt er naar en je trekt er je conclusies uit.

Ben je daar niet jaloers op?

AV: Nee, uiteindelijk niet. Ik vind het wel een prachtige rijkdom aan keuzemogelijkheden, maar in die eerste polaroids zag ik toch al dezelfde kracht zitten als in nummer veertig, die het uiteindelijk werd. Het is ook een heel mooi idee. Met die serie over gabbers of de home's in ruitjeshemden is het zo: zes opnames en dan staat het erop. Ja okee, je kan wel heel veel materiaal maken. Uiteindelijk belandt alles in de prullenbak. Dat is gewoon niet nodig. Het is zo'n...

rond modefotografie: veel schieten, veel maken. Jahan, weet je wel. Nee, je moet eerst bedenken wat je wilt. Vooraf bedenken en daarna schieten in plaats van andersom. Het werkt zo nu en dan wel, maar ik vind het gewoon zonde. Dus dat gaat altijd door mijn hoofd heen. Dat al beslist met mijn gereformeerde afkomst te maken hebben. Of het milieubewustzijn, de ecologie. Terug uit Londen ben ik gewoon aan het werk gegaan. In eerste instantie ze zelfstandig. Daarna heb ik een samenwerkingsproject gedaan met Gina Kranendonk en een boek gemaakt, Het Vrouwvengezelschap. Het was naar aanleiding van een schuttersstuk. Een tentoonstelling in het Frans Halsmuseum. Daar was Gina geweest en ze vond het belachelijk dat er nergens een vrouw op stond. Dat is toen uitgemond in driekwart jaar gakte en dat is een boek geworden. Eigenlijk een zelfde soort portretten als ik nu doe, maar op een andere manier. Meer een spiegel van de samenleving. Wat doen vrouwen? Het moesten allemaal vrouwen zijn, het moesten er meer dan drie zijn en er moest geen man aan te pas komen. Dan ga je eens kijken: wat is er te vinden? Dan kom je op de raarste plekken en in de meest idiote situaties. Dat boek leidde tot een tentoonstelling die op onvoorstelbaar veel plaatsen, onder andere in Amerika, te zien was. Dat heeft heel erg te maken met dat rare Nederlandse klooimokjes om in te tennissen terwijl... Het is ambivalent. Die gabbers zijn van groote markt, uiteindelijk. Toch wil Australian er niet mee geïdentificeerd worden. Dat merk wil zich niet aan die cultuurstroming ophangen: pillen slikken, XTC...

EU: Maar met dat soort opdrachten als voor Australian kun je wel weer vrij werk maken. Zodat we drie dagen in de week commercieel werk maken en twee dagen met onze eigen projecten bezig kunnen zijn.

AV: Ik ben de subsidiewegen, maar zal er niet snel een beroep op doen. Voor een subsidieaanvraag moet het plan namelijk vooraf beschreven worden en dan eenmaal beschreven is het al half dood. En ik vind echt dat het niet leeft. Ik vind het ook spannender om mijn eigen projecten te gaan voor je te vinmen, een beetje met ze aanwhoren en uitnodigen in de studio en daar een foto's maken. Op sommige foto's ben ik herretrets, andere zijn meer curieus dan het waanzinnige platen zijn. Maar dat heeft me niet toe, het is de rezameling waar het om gaat.

EU: Na die stand voor Oilily kregen we van de PTT een opdracht om jeugdculturen vast te leggen en dat was dan hiphop en skaten en weet ik niet wat allemaal. Toen zijn we die gabbers tegengekomen. We dachten echt: dit zie je nooit op een manier gecoverd die wij interessant vinden. Vier maanden zijn we elke scene ingedoken, naar de feesten toe en dan proberen die gasten voor je te vinmen, een beetje met ze aanwhoren en uitnodigen in de studio en daar een foto's maken. Op sommige foto's ben ik herretrets, andere zijn meer curieus dan het waanzinnige platen zijn. Maar dat heeft me niet toe, het is de rezameling waar het om gaat.

AV: Onze voorliefde gaat erg naar series uit, naar verzamelingen. Op een bepaald moment begin je daarmee, gaan we alletwee er ontzettend veel van verzamelen. Het is ook een heel mooi idee. Met die serie over gabbers of de home's in ruitjeshemden is het zo: zes opnames en dan staat het erop. Ja okee, je kan wel heel veel materiaal maken. Uiteindelijk belandt alles in de prullenbak. Dat is gewoon niet nodig. Het is zo'n...

in vinden omdat we het gewoon heel erg vervelend vinden om..., nou ja, we vinden mode heel erg interessant maar alles wat er omheen hangt, dat hele modellengebeuren veel minder. Dat is iets wat we eigenlijk niet te zien zitten. Het leukste is eigenlijk gewoon om wat op straat gebeurt naar de studio te brengen en er dermate in te duiken en het ook vast te leggen, dat het ook echt een tijdsdocument is. Dat het meer is dan alleen een nieuw jurkje verkopen. Kijk, met modellen werken is wel heel handig. Zo iemand neemt een standdje in en daar doe je het dan mee. Maar het is uiteindelijk veel interessanter om dat wat je oovalt in het straatbeeld, om dat te pakken en te krijgen en daar iets mee te gaan doen.

Dat kraagje dat die gabbers allemaal hebben, daar hangt het labeltje van Australian, wat van oorsprong een sjiek Italiaans sportmerk is dat die gabbers als kleding hebben gekozen.

EU: Het is peperduur spul. Kost f500, zo'n pak.

Hoe is dat met die gabbers begonnen, en toen is het uiteindelijk een reclameopdracht voor Australian geworden?

AV: We hadden die serie en toen begonnen we gewoon te raden. Het heet Australian, dus we dachten: 'Waar zit het dan?' Uiteindelijk bleek er een Nederlandse importeur te zijn en we kregen een commerciële opdracht voor hun schoenenlabel. Tja, die importeur houdt zich bezig met sjieke klooimokjes om in te tennissen terwijl... Het is ambivalent. Die gabbers zijn van groote markt, uiteindelijk. Toch wil Australian er niet mee geïdentificeerd worden. Dat merk wil zich niet aan die cultuurstroming ophangen: pillen slikken, XTC...

EU: Dat is ook heel moeilijk. Soms werk je een paar weken achter elkaar. We hebben aan een documentaire meegewerkt, twaalf minuten geportretteerd. We hebben er vier als het ware onder onze hoede genomen.

AV: Het is een soort van supergestileerde homevideo, elk kind een week lang gevolgd - wat ze doen, alles erop en eraan.

EU: De aan had alleen zijn kop vergabbord, de ander was echt gabber, een jaar of vijftien en zwaar aan de pillen en de speed. Een jongetje, helemaal aan de video en de 'film, een freak. Maar dat nam erg veel tijd in beslag. Daarnaast gingen we ook door met commerciële klussen,

onder andere voor Scapino-schoenen, word je helemaal opgeslorpt. Je bent al leiden aan het aanrennen. Je kunt je in helemaal niet meer kwijt. Dan vraag je: waar zijn we nou mee bezig, gaat het knikkers of gaat het om de creativiteit?

En na de gabbers?

AV: We zijn bezig met project 'Exactitude' voeren, en we zijn halverwege, het gaat al ever codes, kledingcodes, en we zijn nu met nichten in ruitjesoverhonden. Die je've gewoon uit bars en het nachtleven houdt een beetje het midden tussen een van semi-klassieke nicht en die kinky worts ze zijn hot of ze zijn het niet.

EU: Je ziet het ook echt, gewoon.

AV: En die portretteren we allemaal op de manier. Waarbij het er in dit geval ook om hoe ze staan, want die jeans zijn voor hun heel belangrijk. Ik let er dus op dat ze op de manier gaan staan. Want een vierkant hoort identiek te zijn, dat kijkt het prettigst leukste van zo'n serie, of dat nou slagers of ruitjesoverhemden of gabbers, uiteindelijk één foto. Het is dé gabber, dé slager.

EU: Het etiquette in kleding blijft mij, in dit geval erg bezighouden. Slagers met stropdar bijvoorbeeld.

AV: Dat moeten er ook weer veertig worden is meer in het zuiden van het land. Zo'n serie liefst nog een bloedvlek erop en dan dat beord en die stropdas. Dan die computer kids. Die hebben vierkante ogen van de le voor het scherm zitten. Dan ook nog ze oudenwetse obers. En wat te denken van aess-cultuur?

EU: Kledingetiquette is bij mannen veel te gor. Vrouwen zijn veel meer bezig met mee make-up dan mannen. Mannen zijn statische huh keuze. Ze gaan ergens voor en dat blij ook een tijd hetzelfde. Vrouwen laten het van hun gemoedsgesteldheid en de dag al ges. Er zitten zo'n tien van zijn kledinger ruïen in ons hoofd en die moeten er gaan komen, dat staat zo vast als een huis. Is al voel werk. Je moet ze in vinden, in aanspre contact leggen, het vertrouwen, winnen, naartoe halen.

EU: Ze vragen dan waar het voor is, maar u dclijk vindas ze het allemaal heel leuk at hier zijn.

AV: En als er dan zo'n type met van die rui komt, die neemt dan gelijk twaalf ruitjes mee EU: Wij vinden het ook leuk om op zo iemand te stappen en de vraag te stellen: 'Ben jij nicht die altijd ruitjesoverhemden eraagt? leggen we ze uit wat de bedoeling is. Menst reageren dan heel verschillend. Er zijn erbij het irritant vinden, die hebben genoeg aan kop, maar ze krijgen ze bijna allemaal ever drempel.

New kids: Inez van Lamsweerde, Diederick Koopal, Cor den Boer, Peggy Stein, Else

Sodderland, Jerome Esch, Maurice & Rob van Gijzelen, Herbert van Hoogdalem, Kees Klomp,

Benjamin Landshoff en Christien van Citters zijn enige van de mensen die wij in het verleden

in Credits portretteerden als Jonge Honden. Met het experimenteren met de formule verdween

deze rubriek. Dit nummer portretteren wij Liesbeth Bijlstra die vier jaar geleden ook in de

Jonge Honden-rubriek stond. Bij het herlezen van dat stukje vroegen wij ons af waarom wij

ooit met die rubriek zijn gestopt. Het was eigenlijk erg leuk, die nog nauwelijks bekende men-

sen die één, hooguit twee jaar bezig zijn en al onmiskenbaar hun sporen nalaten. Daarom

vanaf dit nummer: Jonge Honden Revisited. Hoewel... de naam doet inmiddels wel heel erg

denken aan busreizen naar Cannes. Dus die naam veranderen we; de eerste New Kids on the

Block zijn fotograaf Maurice Scheltens, artdirector Karin Heuter en illustrator Otto. Verder zijn

er dit nummer eigenlijk nauwelijks structurele veranderingen! *Frank Bierens, hoofdredacteur*

INHOUD

CREDITS

NUMMER 3 1996 _| FL. 10,- _| RECLAME _| FOTOGRAFIE _| MEDIA _| DESIGN

Vol. 3 1996

PHOTOGRAPHERS   *Ari Versluis,*
Ellie Uyttenbroek

Vol. 3 1996

PHOTOGRAPHERS   *Ari Versluis,*
Ellie Uyttenbroek

V.l.n.r. Voorstel voor Freecard TV-serie 'Einde Kind; TV Dits BV, Rotterdam Gabber, BLVD.

mÂp
1 **Vol. 7 1996**
2 **Vol. 8 1996**
EDITOR Robert Bergman-Ungar
ART DIRECTOR Robert Bergman-Ungar
DESIGNER Robert Bergman-Ungar
PHOTOGRAPHERS 1,2 Andrew MacPherson,
2 Nasa,
2 Eamonn J. McCabe,
2 Mark Laita
DESIGN FIRM Bergman-Ungar Associates
PUBLISHER MÂP Publications Inc.
USA/Switzerland

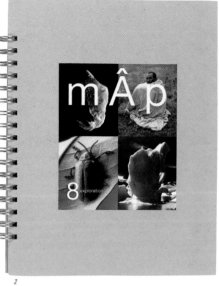

1

2

3 **Vol. 7 1996**
PHOTOGRAPHER Panasonic Corp
(National, Matsushita)

4 **Vol. 8 1996**
PHOTOGRAPHER Robert Bergman-Ungar

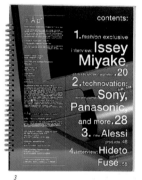

3

4

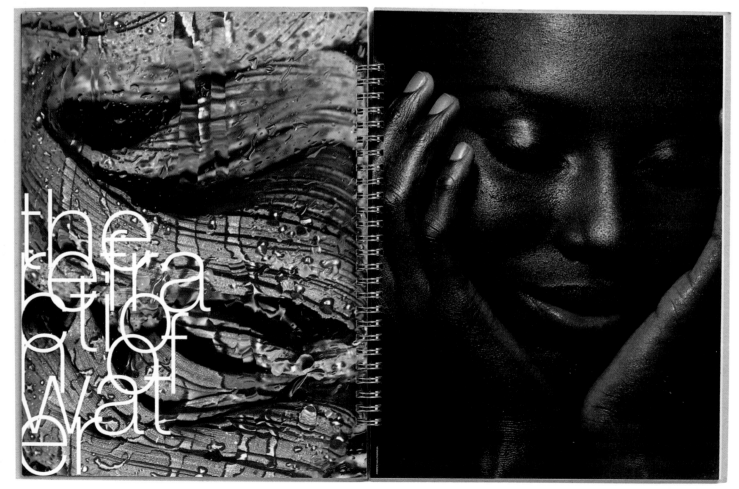

Vol. 7 1996
DESIGNER Robert Bergman-Ungar
PHOTOGRAPHER Andrew MacPherson

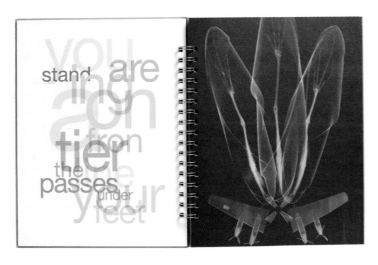

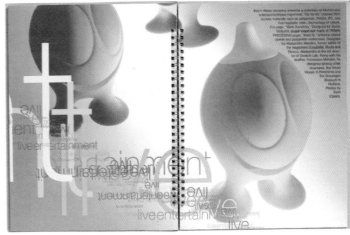

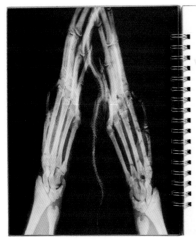

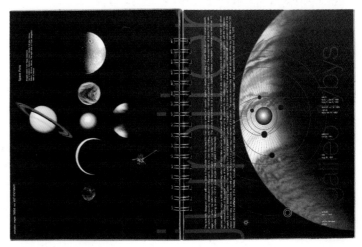

Vol. 8 1996

DESIGNER   *Robert Bergman-Ungar*
PHOTOGRAPHER   *Seiju Toda*

Vol. 7 1996

DESIGNER   *Robert Bergman-Ungar*
PHOTOGRAPHER   *Santi Caleca*

Vol. 7 1996

DESIGNER   *Robert Bergman-Ungar*
PHOTOGRAPHER   *Sony*

Vol. 8 1996

ASSOCIATE ART DIRECTOR   *Giles Dunn*
PHOTOGRAPHER   *Nasa*

HYPE MEGAZIN
Vol. 11 Winter 1994-95

EDITOR | *Henk Fischer Heyne*
ART DIRECTOR | *Henk Fischer Heyne*
DESIGNER | *Henk Fischer Heyne*
PHOTOGRAPHER | *Henk Fischer Heyne*
DESIGN FIRM | *Hype*
PUBLISHER | *Henk Fischer Heyne*

Netherlands

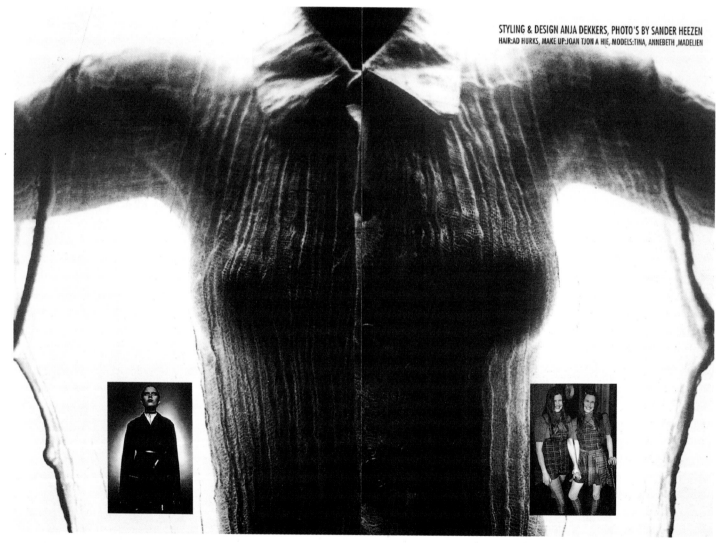

STYLING & DESIGN ANJA DEKKERS, PHOTO'S BY SANDER HEEZEN
HAIR:AD HURKS, MAKE UP:JOAN TJON A HIE, MODELS:TINA, ANNEBETH ,MADELIEN

Vol. 11 Winter 1994-95

DESIGNER | *Anja Dekkers*
PHOTOGRAPHER | *Sander Heezen*

NIGHTSWIMMING

A FEELING OF BEING TRANSPARANT

POWER
SEXUALITY
FREEDOM
MOVEMENT

LOOSELY

GET OUT OF THE
GROUP LIVING

BODY ✦

FIND WAYS TO ACT OUT FREEDOM   MIND

Vol. 11 Winter 1994-95

DESIGNER
Marieke Slinkert
PHOTOGRAPHER
Anna Tiedink

Vol. 11 Winter 1994-95

DESIGNER
Pauline v/d Heyden
PHOTOGRAPHERS
Calja de Bruyn,
Simone Golob

Vol. 11 Winter 1994-95

PHOTOGRAPHER
Martyn van der Griendt

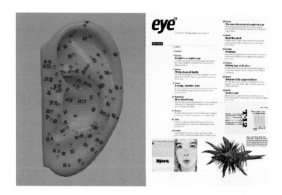

Vol. 23 Winter 1996

PHOTOGRAPHER Toby McFarlan-Pond

eye

Vol. 23 Winter 1996

EDITOR	Rick Poynor
ART DIRECTOR	Stephen Coates
COVER IMAGE	Edward Fella
PUBLISHER	Emap Business Communications

UK

Cornel Windlin is a fluent graphic stylist and a playful manipulator of communication codes.

This signifier is loaded

Signifiers don't come much more heavily loaded than Cornel Windlin's posters for the Rote Fabrik, a performance space located a couple of kilometres south of Zurich's city centre. Windlin's first public communiqué, based on a firing-range target, rounded up concert-goers with a pistol-brandishing silhouette. If this suggested the arrival of a designer who, conceptually at least, should be regarded as armed and dangerous, it paled beside a later creation, in which Zurich's good townsfolk were treated to a scarily alluring Uzi, presented against a brilliant yellow background.

It is easy to see how such hair-raising visual tactics might have come as a jolt to the peace-loving collective

2-4. Windlin conjures his concert posters for Rote Fabrik, a Zurich performance space, to "acts in a theatre". The aim was to give the centre as much street presence, and credibility, as possible, with dramatic and unpredictable shifts of mood and message, from tongue-in-cheek postcard naïvety for an open-air concert by the lake, to the mixed aggression of Windlin's use of gun imagery to announce American hip-hop bands – regular visitors to Zurich in the 1990s.

His Zurich audiences tend to like it, but his clients don't always get the point. *By Rick Poynor*

rote fabrik april '94

5-7. Windlin was his own client for Reefer Madness, the dance music club he co-founded in Zurich with two friends as a reaction to the city's night-life. The club had its own Rote watch-inspired logo (7) and the southerlised monthly events were announced by a stream of flyers in a variety of graphic vernaculars – such as fabric roll identification numbers (5) and the famous Mary Long cigarette packet (6) – mailed to interested parties.

that operates the lakeside centre, set up fifteen years ago to mollify Zurich's young people in the wake of city riots. Windlin is sure the automatic weapon poster lost him the job (though enquiries suggest this was not the case). But the willingness – or need – to believe the worst says something in itself. Client relationships are distinctly uneasy for Windlin. "It's always a problem," he says, "If I'm lucky I can get away with things – if it's a good client. If it's a bad one, then I'm the one who's going to walk away with the money, but I've lost the fight somehow. I don't seem to fit in. I don't seem to find people who are willing to do what I want to do." When he won a prestigious Swiss prize for the applied arts in

The portable art space

1. Spread from *Mining the Museum: An Installation* by Fred Wilson, designed by Charles Nix for the Maryland Historical Society, 1994.
2. Spread from *A Family Affair: Gay and Lesbian Issues of Domestic Life*, designed by Andrew Blauvelt for Atlanta College of Art Gallery, 1995.
3. Spread from *MONOLITH, between echo & HOPE*, designed by Willem Oorebeek and Felix Janssens for Witte de With Center for Contemporary Art, Rotterdam, 1994.
4. Spread from *Wherever You are on this Planet*, designed by Stéphanie De Vilder for Gerald van der Kaap's exhibition at the Stedelijk Museum, Amsterdam, 1996.

Designers who collaborate on artists' catalogues must negotiate a complicated web of personal and institutional interests. Even so some projects still succeed in questioning and subverting our expectations of what a catalogue is and should be. *By Anne Burdick*

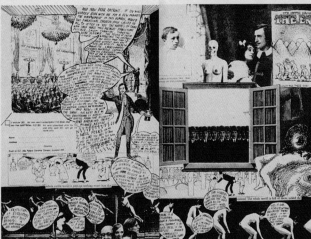

Archive

1969
OZ 16: THE MAGIC THEATRE ISSUE

Martin Sharp

In his memoir of the 1960s underground, *Hippie Hippie Shake*, writer and *OZ* magazine editor Richard Neville recalls the night that his friend and fellow Australian Martin Sharp, high on hash, proposed to take charge of the next issue of *OZ*. It would, Sharp said, be entirely visual, and working away on the project, night after night, assisted by film-maker Philippe Mora, the designer was true to his word. Sharp's "Magic Theatre" issue was recognised at the time as outstanding and holds up in retrospect as one of the most extraordinary visual artefacts of the psychedelic era. Sharp cast aside the conventional journalistic apparatus of discrete articles, headlines, supporting pictures and captions for a writhing 48-page collage-fusion of images and text. "Price of admittance your mind," his cover announces. "All men are madmen." And for much of its length Sharp's theatre feels more absurdist than magical, closer to an asylum than an auditorium, a tragi-

comic inferno of babbling media and human craziness that alternates between acidhead deathwish and occasional flashes of a more optimistic vision. Flouting copyright as a matter of principle, the "Magic Theatre" works by associative juxtaposition: a skull with copy from a Coty Dew Fresh lipstick ad; a crucifixion scene opposite DC's Justice League of America comic; a jailbreak headline above lines about the expulsion from Paradise. Panels from *Little Nemo in Slumberland* and the comix of Robert Crumb collide with images of John and Yoko, Hitler and the Queen, famine victims, human freaks, and the paintings of René Magritte. Running along the foot of each page to form a ribbon from beginning to end are Muybridge's locomotion studies, their silent naked figures brought to life by speech bubbles. As art critic Robert Hughes enthused: "Sharp has assembled one of the richest banks of images that has ever appeared in a magazine."

top **Vol. 22 Autumn 1996**

PHOTOGRAPHER *Anthony Oliver*

bottom **Vol. 24 Spring 1997**

A series of 30 prints that manifest an unusually close visual synthesis between type and image are the result of a four-year collaboration between Peter Anderson, a typographer and print-maker; Platon, a fashion photographer; and Claire Todd, a fashion stylist. The three, who all trained in London as graphic designers, had no client or brief, just a strong motivation to see where the collaborative process would lead.

When Platon first began working with Peter Anderson, any potential uses for what they might create were far from their thoughts. "It struck me that what Pete was trying to do with type, I was trying to do with images," says Platon. "Both our work is intricate but with an economy of gesture; there may be many elements on the page, but all are necessary. I gave Pete some of my images just to see what he'd come up with, and he disappeared with them for four months. I thought the whole thing had fizzled out. Then I got a call from him, and when I saw what he had done, we all realised that it was something new. We decided to collaborate and develop a visual language which explains fashion information in a new way, and blends typography and photography."

TYPE FASHION FUSION

A stylist, a photographer and a typographer celebrate the look and feel of exceptional clothes.

By Julia Thrift

Each image is inspired by a garment, chosen by Todd. Many of them, she explains, would not be featured in editorial fashion shoots – they are iconic, one-off pieces, and not integral to commercial collections. "This is paying homage to an individual garment, without having to worry about how it fits into a six-page fashion story."

During the four years in which they have been working together, fashion has moved from grunge to glamour, and the three have become increasingly secure as a team. As a result, later images differ from the early ones in both content and form. "When we started, we used to try and impress each other by doing something as finished as possible," says Platon. "Now, Claire will bring along things that are almost unresolved, I will photograph things in a way that is almost unfinished, and Pete will do type that has room to be taken a stage further. It allows a little gap for someone else to come in, and that enhances what we are doing."

Some of the images have been through numerous stages, with effects achieved in camera, during photographic processing, using etching, Letraset, computer typesetting and, finally, colouring.

Most have been output on an Iris printer, giving continuous tone direct from digital data. Printed on to thick art paper, the images have a soft, almost luminous beauty, a result of Anderson working closely with a repro company, Quicksilver, to push the technology as far as possible.

Despite his evident sense of achievement with the Iris prints, Anderson emphasises that it was the image which determined the process – whether in terms of originating the type or printing the image – and not the other way around. "I don't use a process for a process's sake," he says. "Whatever I'm trying to communicate sets what I use. It's dictated by the subject matter. I'm anti-technique."

With Anderson's typography ranging from strident to sinuous, it comes as some surprise to discover that the words used are no more than the credits found on the fashion pages of any magazine. Far from seeing this as a cop-out, the three insist that it is essential to the project; that documenting everything from the name of the garment's designer to the price of the model's tights is all part of the narrative. "It's really important," says Platon. "This isn't about literature or poetry, it's information design. It's about telling a story about the dress." But if it really is intended as information design, then the project has a fundamental flaw. The images represent less a commentary on the fashion shown than a sensual response to it, and the information could only be accessed by the most determined viewer. Given the banality of what the words actually say, it seems unlikely that anyone will be that anxious to read them. If, on the other hand, the images are taken purely as visual poetry – as art – the emptiness of the words seems to reflect a lack of anything to say, as though the demand for expressive typography has outstripped the supply of ideas.

Nonetheless, as a self-financed portfolio piece, the project has done its job. Platon, Todd and Anderson have been commissioned by the Italian fashion house Moschino to create the advertising campaign for its couture collection this autumn. Maybe their work, once it has to function in the commercial world, will gain in conceptual depth, although whether it might also lose some of the refinement of these exquisitely crafted and subtly expressive images in the process remains to be seen. ●

"Gravitaz" is at Hamiltons, 13 Carlos Place, London W1, until 28 September.

Vol. 22 Autumn 1996

ART DIRECTOR *Stephen Coates*
TYPOGRAPHER *Peter Anderson*
PHOTOGRAPHER *Platon*
FASHION STYLIST *Claire Todd*

GIANT FAKE FUR COAT VIVIENNE WESTWOOD
AUTUMN/WINTER 1995 MADE TO ORDER SHOOT NO2

1. This image, called "Moped", was inspired by Moschino's autumn 1996 couture collection, although it will not be used as part of the new advertising campaign.
2. One of the first images from the collaboration: Platon's flower-like photograph of an unfinished garment borrowed from the Royal College of Art's fashion department inspired Andersen to add typographic "roots".
3. John Lennon's comment in the 1960s that he was a "rocker" – a mixture of a mod and a rocker – led Andersen to create type in the shape of a mod scooter for this image of a girl in Moschino biker wear.
4. As a reaction to Platon's shots of clothes by young British designers Owen Gaster and Hussein Chalayan, Andersen used type to turn the images into bubbles. The bubbles, he says, are a metaphor for the designers, rising from obscurity and ready to burst upon the world.

5. The model's comment that wearing this underskirt by Red or Dead made her feel like a cloud inspired this airy back-lit shot. The typographic "rain" was too delicate and complex to output digitally, so the image was litho-printed.
6. A chrysalis-like dress by Issey Miyake encouraged Andersen and Platon to study close-up film footage of insects to ensure that the typographic "legs" of the emerging butterfly looked realistic.
7. Swamped in an enormous fake fur coat, the model has been turned into a scuttling insect with type that combines photography, etching and computer manipulation.
8. The fabric of this Issey Miyake suit seems to be melting, so Platon and Andersen collaborated to create "melting" type. The process began with a font which was re-drawn on-screen, and then subjected to various photographic manipulations such as reverse solarisation.

rana

| 1 | **Vol. 1 1994** |
| 2 | **Vol. 2 1996** |

EDITOR	Frogteam/Frogdesign
ART DIRECTOR	Frogteam/Frogdesign
DESIGNER	Frogteam/Frogdesign
PHOTOGRAPHER	1 Hashi
ILLUSTRATORS	2 Max Sims, Technolution
DESIGN FIRM	Frogteam/Frogdesign
PUBLISHER	Rana Publishing

USA

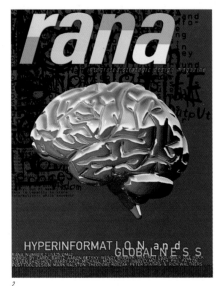

1

2

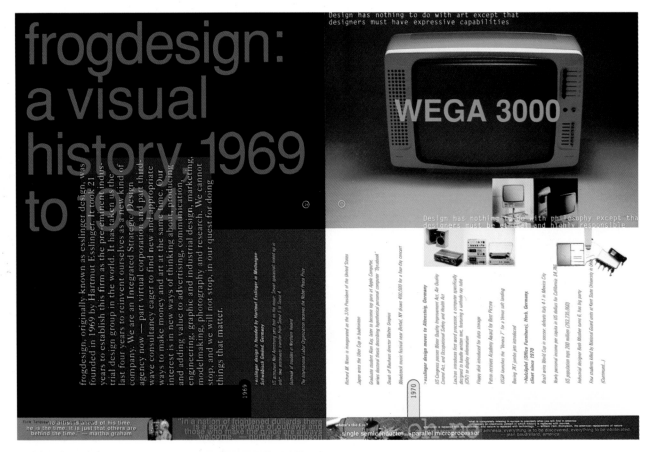

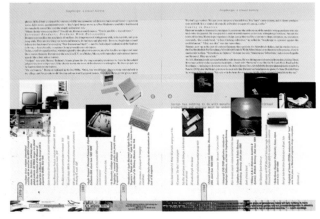

oh *ah*

—"In any case, when a man must be afraid to drink freely from his country's rivers and streams, that country is no longer fit to live in... time then to move on, to find another country or — in the name of jefferson — to *make* another country." — edward abbey, *desert solitaire*

---

cyberfrogs

language that emphasized interactive scenarios, the possibility of implied travel, and the potential mind-bending opportunity of experiencing time and space in a new way.

By contrast, as we looked at designing for HMD environments, we focused on the immersive nature of VR. By seeing HMD-based VR in this way, we created another design language that emphasized new information interfaces, three-dimensional layering of on-screen information, techno-organic form-making, and software-based instrumentation options.

Where It's Going

It has become clear that a new level of ergonomics is needed — one that merges psychological and physical data. People must be comfortable sitting, standing or moving within the new VR technology, but there must be mental comfort as well. I envision placing multi-cultural ergonomic data of all types into VR-driven CAD domains as a way of more richly conceptualizing space, form, material and texture. Such an approach would provide a sensory data domain that would allow us as designers to get around, on top of, and inside of our designs in a way we can only wonder about presently.

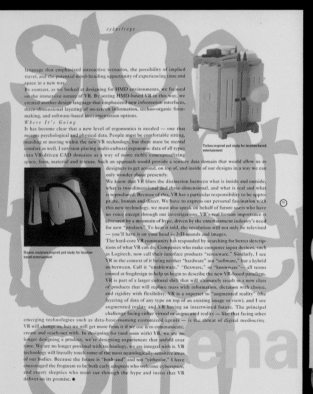

Techno-inspired pod study for location-based entertainment

Organic sculpture-inspired pod study for location-based entertainment

We know that VR blurs the distinction between what is inside and outside, what is two-dimensional and three-dimensional, and what is real and what is reproduced. Because of this, VR has a particular responsibility to be appropriate, human and direct. We have to express our personal fascination with this new technology, we must also speak on behalf of future users who have no voice except through our investigations. VR's real human importance is obscured by a mountain of hype, driven by the entertainment industry's need for new "product." To hear it told, the revolution will not only be televised — you'll have it on your head in 3-D sounds and images.

The hard-core VR community has responded by searching for better descriptions of what VR can do. Companies who make computer input devices, such as Logitech, now call their interface products "senseware." Similarly, I see VR in the context of it being neither "hardware" nor "software," but a hybrid in-between. Call it "enableware," "flexware," or "knowware" — all terms coined at frogdesign to help us begin to describe the new VR-based paradigm. VR is part of a larger cultural shift that will ultimately result in a new class of products that will replace mass with information, dictation with choice, and rigidity with flexibility. VR is a superset to "augmented reality" (the layering of data of any type on top of an existing image or view), and I see augmented reality and VR having an intertwined future. The principal challenge facing either virtual or augmented reality — like that facing other emerging technologies such as data-base-roaming customized agents — is the threat of digital mediocrity. VR will change us, but we will get more from it if we use it to communicate, create and reach-out with. In designing for (and soon with) VR, we are no longer designing a product, we're designing experiences that unfold over time. We are no longer proximal with technology, we are integral with it. VR technology will literally touch some of the most neurologically-sensitive areas of our bodies. Because the future is "both-and" and not "either/or," I have encouraged the frogteam to be both early adopters who welcome cyberspace, and crusty skeptics who must cut through the hype and insist that VR deliver on its promise. ●

BOTH
AND not EITHER/OR

WARNING: Always carry protection. Develop point-of-view. Stay wrinkle-free. Hide in plain sight. Drink only from simultaneous data streams. Attack success, conspire against identity, believe only cross-pollinated hybrids. At all times, seek oxymoronic lifestyles.

Imagine the virtual reality experience of a whole new generation of video games — you bond with the machine as your body intuitively and deeply moves with the action. *Imagine* that trigger-based joysticks give way to squeezable, friendly, finger-size controls — allowing tight control of visual and auditory information flow through easy hand gestures.

Imagine the virtual reality experience of education anywhere, anytime you want it — you can focus without distraction because you are "inside" your digital textbook.

Imagine what each component might be — a joystick that feels like a favorite stone, a console detailed like a well-made car, a head-mounted display that kids wear like a baseball cap because it's so cool.

Imagine selective texture combinations — intense finger interactions might offer soft, movable pads; headsets might have flip-up visors for easy exits, and articulated details so you know where and what to grab.

Imagine the techo-emotive potential of the head-mounted display environment — where the player has seemingly edgeless game fields to play within, and where 3-D seeing and hearing is believing.

what pattern connects the crab to the lobster and the orchid to... — gregory bateson, *mind and*...

be obscure clearly — e.b. white

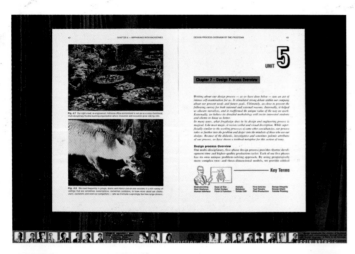

left   **Vol. 1 1994**
right   **Vol. 2 1996**

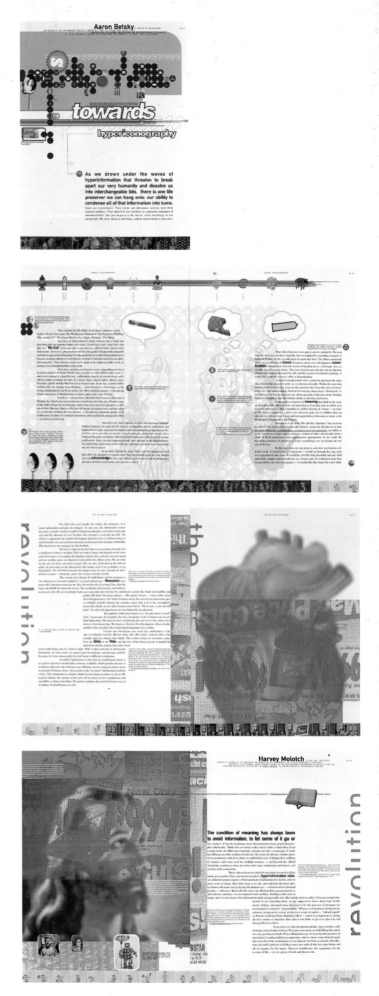

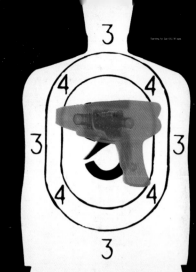

ANYWHERE

1

Afterwor

"The painting of portraits, used to transmit through the ages extremely co nesses of persons, has entirely gone out. Bronze shields are now set up ments with a design in silver, with a dim outline of men's figures; heads are exchanged for others, about which before now actually sarcastic epigr been current: so universally is a display of material preferred to a recogniz ness of one's own self. And in the midst of all this, people tapestry the wal picture-galleries with old pictures, and they prize likenesses of strangers for themselves they imagine that the honour only consists in the price, for to break up the statue and haul it out of the house with a noose. Cons nobody's likeness lives and they leave behind them portraits that repre money, not themselves." — Pliny the Elder, *Natural History*, trans. by H.
In our anywhere, anytime hyperinformation economy, it seems like the more thing more that they change. But that's not always the case. Sometimes the more things more we latch onto a standard to anchor us. Jaron Lanier has challenged all of us inv ducing microprocessor-based products to consider what civilizations we disallo choose one technology over another. Windows® is an obvious example to consider. prodigies does it negate? Isn't every soaring monument to what we have done als tombstone for what we have not? Even if such provocative questions have no immed Lanier's voice rings as true as Pliny the Elder's did, and it provides food for thought preparations for our next issue, *nine* Number 3 will focus on retro-futuristic design a tomization in business and culture. All like-minded students, ethical leaders and c are invited to participate in the (r)evolution.

Vol. 2 1996

ILLUSTRATORS
3 Frogteam,
4 Matthew Clark

3

PURE ART

Our business takes place in the "Anywhere, Anytime Hyperinformation Economy," a system predicated on fundamental reformulations of time (to market), speed (to sale), and distance (to customer). But the key to this new economy still lies in old wisdom: the integration of observations, concepts and results through teamwork. Only through such integration does vision meld with practicality. Because there's more information than any of us wants, intuition and market awareness are now key components of business intelligence. In spite of the hardware and software advances of the last few years, fundamentally appropriate technologies such as the written word are thriving, even exploding — as Paul Saffo has noted — like kudzu vines at the edges of the digital revolution. Our metaphor isn't the info highway where consumers hurtle along, but the info pond where like-minded visitors come to dive in, swim and be immersed. In short, hyperinformation is a medium (like air or water) that we live in and move through, and *rena* is a step toward the realization of Alan Kay's "n-dimensional information spaces." We aspire to nothing less than an open architecture of ideas, a flexible navigation of mediaways, and an Integrated Strategic Design approach that is geared to optimizing feature, function, brand and identity convergence. ISD has become a critical management system for product conception and delivery for companies operating on what Tom Peters calls the edge of change, control and chaos. For these companies, our goal is to expand the definition of what "design" can do to create understandable, desirable, and ultimately meaning-rich solutions that offer the scarcest resource of all in our anytime, anywhere hyperinformation economy — passionate point of view.

Introductio r

Vol. 2 1996

ILLUSTRATOR
1 Matthew Clark

2

4

IDEA 261

アイデ.ア

特集：トランス・デザイン
Special Feature: **Trance Design**

INTERNATIONAL GRAPHIC ART 1997-3

世界のデザインの誌 誠文堂新光社

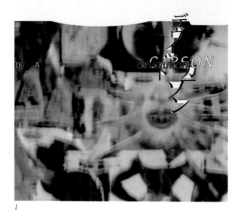

IDEA Magazine

1 **Vol. 261 Mar. 1997**
2 **Vol. 258 Sep. 1996**

EDITORS   *Hidemichi Yoshida,*
Manabu Koseki,
Tomoko Miyazaki

DESIGNERS   *1 David Carson,*
1 Aki Oe

ARTIST   *2 Shinro Otake*

PUBLISHER   *Seibundo Shinkosha*
Publishing Co., Ltd.

Japan

1

2

meanwhile, working in the underworld

Tomato / Underworld project "Skyscraper," personal work by John Warwicker and Karl Hyde, 1994.

UNDERWORLD. BORN SLIPPY, record sleeves for new single by Underworld. Design by Jason Kedgley, 1995.

P.12-13 Personal work by Graham Wood, 1995.

14

Words From Underworld

hey the dancers were very good
tomato:harmonious
     yeah
tomato:25 to 7
     very round
tomato:a drift into cheese
     very modern
tomato:(attack/gently)
     i don't think we missed anything
tomato:or
     by being in the middle
tomato:degenerated
     do you?
tomato:better
     no
tomato:a thing of beauty
     and that old woman
tomato:a valve
     yeah
tomato:you got a valve?
     she was really struck on him
tomato:is what you is
     yeah
tomato:is what you done it
     where is it who is it?
tomato:growing
     its karen
tomato:the music
     do you remember the jacket i was wearing
tomato:nutter
     and the bottoms?
tomato:fuck abaart
     it was like silver orange green
tomato:twist knob
     it was quite good
tomato:yes pull it
     what that james was wearing
tomato:aaaaahh
     yeah
tomato:what change oh
     they showed that on the television
tomato:2 chocolate kiss
     yeah the one with the green
tomato:tiny doll
     and the chaps dancing
tomato:tiny outstretched miniature
     i cant remember that
tomato:glitter doll
     ill have to get the video out
tomato:each new happiness
     and then i thought about it
tomato:shrine
     no hes not very popular
tomato:thankyou thankyou
     but has a very good accountant
tomato:healing dirt
     but the thing is
tomato:beer dog floodlit
     you know this woman in southend
tomato:am the cure
     i feel better
tomato:Mmmm
     dyou
tomato:long fingers
     think
tomato:inner thigh
     she can do these
tomato:yellow stain so
     alterations
tomato:pull down your
     for me
tomato:we only do it in half pint
     their school uniform
tomato: £2.50
     the straight skirt
tomato:is big
     oooh thats good
tomato:is long
     you can order the recordings
tomato:on your jeans
tuna?
     post free
brown?
     £2.50
granary?
     but its
or
     ever such a good idea you know
white?

ワーズ フロム アンダー・ワールド

ダンサーたちはヴェリーグッド
トマト：ハーモニアス
     yeah
トマト：25対7
     とても丸い
トマト：流れ流れてチーズになる
     とってもモデム
トマト：(攻撃しろ、おだやかに)
     取り逃がしたものはないはずだ
トマト：変質した
     そうかい？
トマト：前よりいい
     no
トマト：美しいもの
     それにあのばあさん
トマト：バルブ
     yeah
トマト：バルブを持ってるかい？
     彼女は彼に夢中だった
トマト：それは君自身
     yeah
トマト：それは君がやったこと
     どこにある？だれだ？
トマト：伸びざかり
     それはカレンだ
トマト：音楽
     僕が着てたジャケット覚えてる？
トマト：変人
     それに、ズボンは？
トマト：fuck abaart
     シルバー・オレンジ・グリーンみたいだった
トマト：ツイスト・ノブ
     非常によかった
トマト：そう、それを引っ張る
     あのジェイムスは何着てた？
トマト：aaaaahh
     そう
トマト：どんな変化だ
     テレビでやってた
トマト：2チョコレート・キス
     そう、グリーンのやつ
トマト：ちっちゃい人形
     ヤブも踊ってる
トマト：広がったちっちゃいミニチュア
     思い出せない
トマト：ピカピカ光る人形
     ビデオを取り出さないと
トマト：それぞれの新しい幸せ
     僕はそれを考えた
トマト：聖堂
     あまり人気がない
トマト：ありがとう、ありがとう
     優秀な会計士がいる
トマト：熱い泥
     だが大事なのは
トマト：ライトアップされたbear dog
     おどしてもムダだ
トマト：私は君んだ
     君はサウスエンドのこの女を知っている
トマト：Mmmm、気分がよくなった
     そうかい
トマト：長い指
     考えろ
トマト：内股
     彼女はできる
トマト：黄色いシミ
     変更
トマト：君のを引き下ろせ
     僕のために
トマト：われわれは半パイントでできるだけさ
     だよな
トマト：2.50 ポンド
     彼女たちの学校の制服
トマト：大きい
     フレアのないスカート
トマト：長い
     おお、それは結構
トマト：君のジーンズについてる
     そのレコードは注文できる
ツナ？
     送料無料
ブラウン？
     2.50 ポンド
穀食？
     しかし、それは―
それとも
     君の素晴らしいアイディアだね
ホワイト？

Tomato / Underworld project "Skyscraper," personal work by John Warwicker and Karl Hyde, 1994.

tomato 15

Vol. 252 Sep. 1995

TITLE   *Hyper Design Unit: Tomato*

EDITORS   *Hidemichi Yoshida,*
Manabu Koseki

DESIGNER   *Manabu Koseki*

VISUAL MATERIAL   *Tomato*

TEXT   *Underworld*

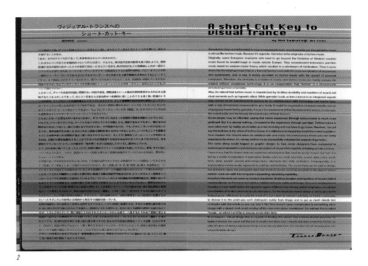

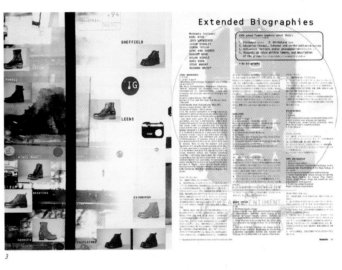

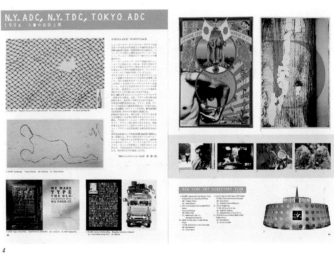

1   **Vol. 258 Sep. 1996**

TITLE   *Elements-Re·Elements*
EDITORS   *Hidemichi Yoshida, Manabu Koseki, Tomoko Miyazaki*
ART DIRECTOR   *Gento Matsumoto*
PHOTOGRAPHER   *Yoichi Inoue*
ILLUSTRATORS   *Keiji Ito,Sarubrunei*
VISUAL MATERIAL   *Keiji Ito*
DESIGN FIRM   *Sarubrunei*

2   **Vol. 261 Mar. 1997**

TITLE   *Trance Design*
EDITORS   *Hidemichi Yoshida, Manabu Koseki, Tomoko Miyazaki*
DESIGNER   *Manabu Koseki*
TEXT   *Noi Sawaragi*

3   **Vol. 252 Sep. 1995**

TITLE   *Hyper Design Unit: Tomato*
EDITORS   *Hidemichi Yoshida, Manabu Koseki*
DESIGNER   *Manabu Koseki*
VISUAL MATERIAL   *Tomato*
TEXT   *Tomato*

4   **Vol. 258 Sep. 1996**

EDITORS   *Hidemichi Yoshida, Manabu Koseki, Tomoko Miyazaki*
DESIGNER   *Kaori Mori*
VISUAL MATERIAL   *The Art Directors Club (New York)*

1

2

3

4

	Vol. 252 Sep. 1995
1,2	
TITLE	Ichiros
EDITORS	Hidemichi Yoshida, Manabu Koseki
ART DIRECTORS, DESIGNERS, ILLUSTRATORS	Ichiros (Ichiro Higashiizumi, Ichiro Tanida)
TECHNICIAN	1 Aki Oe

3	**Vol. 252 Sep. 1995**
TITLE	Noriyuki Tanaka 1995 1/2
EDITORS	Hidemichi Yoshida, Manabu Koseki
ART DIRECTOR	Noriyuki Tanaka
DESIGNER	Hideo Kawamura
DESIGN FIRM	Noriyuki Tanaka Activity
VISUAL MATERIAL	Noriyuki Tanaka

4	**Vol. 261 Mar. 1997**
TITLE	David Carson-Shift of Power / Devolution
EDITORS	Hidemichi Yoshida, Manabu Koseki, Tomoko Miyazaki
DESIGNER	Manabu Koseki
VISUAL MATERIAL	David Carson

"Bargain of the year"

In the course of creating art work, there are many elements which affect an
人のアーティストが、作品を生み出すプロセスには、作品に登場しているものはもと
artist. They are things which might appear in the work, but also things
より、それら以外にも影響を受けた数多くの物事が存在する。作家が自らの身体を通し
related to the artist's feelings, interests and daily life, etc. It can be
て、心に焼き付けた多くのエレメントの一つひとつ一例えば、感情、興味、日常生活な
said that all these elements combined together make up one's individuality as
どに痕跡を残しているモノやコトなどーは、まさに作品を生み出すための「個」の総体
an artist. In this experimental project, Keiji Itoh explained to the other
と言えよう。このプロジェクトは、それらのエレメンツを通して他のクリエイターが伊
participating artists, which elements figure prominantly in his work, and the
藤桂司というアーティストの「個」に深く入り込み、それを分析・解体、さらに再構成
artists in turn reused those same elements in their own ways to produce their
して作品化する、といういままでにない実験である。伊藤桂司の「個」が他の身体へと
own new works. In this way, aspects of Itoh's individuality are transplanted
移植され生まれ変わる、それをリ・エレメンツと呼ぶことにしよう。これから数回にわ
and reborn in the other artists' works.
たるシリーズでこの実験的プロジェクトをご紹介していきたい。（このプロジェクトに
The title "re-elements" is a Japanese construction using abbreviated English
関する解説は48ページ）
words to mean "reused elements." IDEA will present these "re-element" works
in the next few issues. (for commentary see p.48)

ICHIRO HIGASHIIZUMI IN THIS PAGE, EMPLOYING KEIJI ITO'S METHOD. ("METHOD" MEANING KEIJI ITO MI HAS DRAWN ILLUSTRATIONS WAS INTERPRETTED SELFISHLY BY HIGASHIIZUMI.)

LEFT PAGES ARE MR. ITO'S "ELEMENT"
RIGHT PAGES ARE "RE-ELEMENTS" BY ICHIRO HIGASHIIZUMI

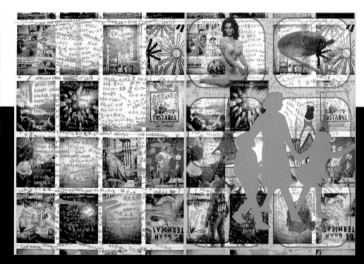

Vol. 252 Sep. 1995

TITLE	*Elements-Re·Elements Vol.1*
EDITORS	*Hidemichi Yoshida,* *Manabu Koseki*
CREATIVE DIRECTIOR	*Keiji Ito*
ART DIRECTORS, DESIGNERS, ILLUSTRATORS	*Keiji Ito,* *Ichiro Higashiizumi*
VISUAL MATERIAL	*Keiji Ito*

I. D.
Vol. 43 Nov. 1996

EDITOR *Chee Pearlman*
ART DIRECTOR *Tony Arefin*
DESIGNER *Andrea Fella*
PHOTOGRAPHER *James Wojcik*
PUBLISHER *I.D.Magazine*

USA

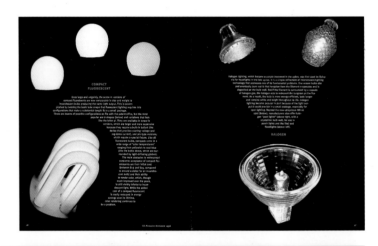

The International Design Magazine

I.D.

NOVEMBER 1996

**Wolf in Sheep's Clothing:
Selling to Gen-X**

**Roger Black:
The Real and the Virtual**

**European Cars:
Born in the USA**

**Apples Are Not the
Only Fruit:
Learning to Love the PC**

Lights

Switching on to the
Latest in Bulb Design

Vol. 43 Nov. 1996

PHOTOGRAPHER *James Wojcik*
WRITER *Mark Branch*

Let There Be Light Bulbs

By Mark Aiden Branch   Photography by James Wojcik

**COMPACT
FLUORESCENT**

HALOGEN

**HIGH-INTENSITY
DISCHARGE**

High-intensity dis-
charge (HID) is the
umbrella name for a
family of lighting
types that produce
light by passing an
electrical current
through a gas or
vapor under pressure.
They range from the
eerie amber glow of
low-pressure sodium,
which has virtually
no ability to render
color and is mostly
used for lighting
warehouses, tunnels
and roadways, to the
intense white light of
metal halide. The
oldest use of this tech-
nology dates back to
1901, when the first
mercury-vapor lamp was
invented. Long used for
street lights, mercury
vapor has largely been
replaced by more efficient
high-pressure sodium (left).
The newest in the HID
family is metal halide, whose
white light and relatively
good color rendering is popular for such uses as stadium
lighting (far left). Further
improvements in color rendering and a dramatic minia-
turization of metal halide
bulbs have made them
increasingly popular for
indoor uses, typically in
high-ceilinged spaces.

The oldest
and most famil-
iar light sources,
incandescent bulbs
are available in thou-
sands of shapes,
sizes and configurations
for the narrowest of
specialized uses. Chrome-
top bulbs (right) are used
in open fixtures to prevent
glare (in pendant lights in
restaurants, for example).
Sylvania makes a shatter-resis-
tant and moisture-resistant bulb
for outdoor use (center right) and a
two-watt "flicker bulb" with a two-
dimensional cartoonlike flame inside that
glows and flickers when turned on (bottom). On the more utilitarian
end of the spectrum, a small company called Bulbrite makes
a nine-watt exit-lamp bulb (left) composed of ten
smaller bulbs linked together.

INCANDESCENT

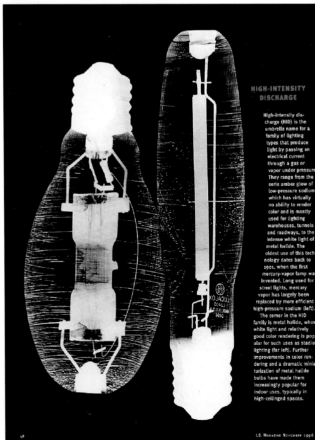

The Red
and the Black

As Will Hearst's @Home network lifts off, the world's best known publication designer is applying his trademark style to its front pages. I.D. Magazine asks: How did the irrepressible Roger Black become a new media mogul? By Peter Hall

Vol. 43 Nov. 1996

WRITER
Peter Hall

TROJAN HORSES

As megacorporations continue to masquerade as upstarts, package designers create an aesthetic of smallness.

By Leslie Savan & Dan Bischoff

You're an **independent individual, bold, discriminating, and, hey, you gotta admit. hip. Sure, you're willing to spend $4 on a cup of java or a** pack of smokes, **but not for some mass-market, over-the-counter slop. You'll buy only if the product (whatever it is) has been** honey-roasted in Dijon-flavored **kilns according to an ancient recipe. And you can't find that stuff just anywhere. You know what you really want?**

Vol. 43 Nov. 1996

WRITER
Leslie Savan

Learning From LaLa Land

How do European automakers make sense of the American market? By setting up shop in California. By Phil Patton

"When you come here, there is a tremendous culture shock. L.A. is a bubbling pot of intense changes and fads. You look out and see a woman traveling at 70 miles an hour putting on makeup."

Vol. 43 Nov. 1996

WRITER
Phil Patton

VIEW ON COLOUR
Vol. 9 1996

EDITOR	*Lisa White*
ART DIRECTORS	*Anthon Beeke,*
	Lidewij Edelkoort
DESIGNERS	*Anthon Beeke,*
	Borinka Beeke
PHOTOGRAPHER	*Maurice Scheltens*
STYLING DIRECTOR	*Graham Hollick*
DESIGN FIRM	*United Publishers S.A.*
PUBLISHER	*United Publishers S.A.*

France

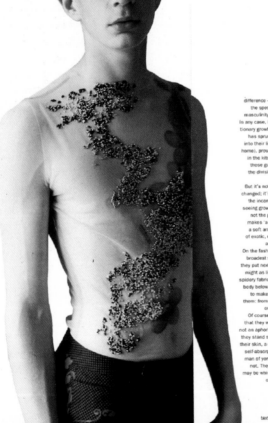

les fleurs du mâle

There's a new kind of masculinity about, sprouting defiantly from the compost of pop culture's image of manhood. The likely 'new lads' who've held sway for so long with their beer-swilling, babe-chasing, ball-gaming ways have turned out to be just the hollow men. Just the same old macho men dressed up - albeit quite nicely - in the emperor's ephemeral clothing. But as their credibility crumbles, signs of a new species are popping up all over. Abandoning the traditional testosterone tenets of power, success and physical prowess, this new breed doesn't so much want to bend gender, but break it's hold altogether. It's not about new definitions but the inverse: a softening up, a blurring of distinctions and lines.

Of course, this is not the first time that set notions of masculinity have been brought into question. Far back in the French 1650's, female courtesans, tired of the coarseness of Henri IV's men, demanded new property and sexual liberties for themselves, and a new gentleness from their menfolk. As a result, delicacy and decorous respect became the ideals of manhood for a small but influential group. *Les Précieux* donned long white wigs, popped beauty spots on their cheeks and swished seductively along in luxuriously embroidered frock coats. And they were a hit with the ladies of court. While not necessarily a style statement for today, *Les Précieux* made clear that, as Rousseau would later put it, "The male is only male at certain times." Or, more precisely, 'masculinity' is not fixed, but in a state of constant flux.

That idea was axiomatic to the so-called Men's Liberation movement of the 1970's. A result of, and reaction to, the advances made by feminism, the men's movement tried to deconstruct what it saw as an all-powerful 'hegemonic masculinity', that rigid set of subconscious rules governing how 'a man' should think, act and appear. Unfortunately, these early ideological days also gave rise to a mythopoetic, hormonally potent men's movement which ended up celebrating the essential

difference - and de facto superiority - of the male of the species. Even now, the words 'bond' or 'deep masculinity' send shivers down skinny boys' spines. In any case, it's from this soil - and its noxious reactionary growth, ladism - that a new, fluid masculinity has sprung. Men are now getting a little softness into their lives. They cry uninhibitedly on TV (and at home), proudly take care of the kids, happily get out in the kitchen and rattle these pots and pans. For those guys, in these economic and social times, the division of labour is a laboured division which is better filed under 'd' for defunct.

But it's not just the way men fill their roles that has changed; it's also the way they fill their bodies. Once the incarnation of masculine strength, we are now seeing grown men with the bodies of boys (or rather, not the gym-constructed corps we've been taught makes 'a man'). Like the early adolescent, there's a soft ambivalence, an openness to a whole world of exotic, erotic possibilities ahead. And erotic they are, these unpumped-up objects of desire. On the fashion front, there's a new sensuality, in the broadest sense. Men are thinking more about what they put next to their skin - though what they slip into might as likely be latex as lace. Gauzy, shimmering, spidery fabrics that cling just enough to show the easy body below. Intricate print shirts: just like mum used to make you wear for Sunday best. Florals, lots of them: from big succulent rosebuds to exotic orchids, or rambling brambles entwining the wearer.

Of course, it's not just what they wear, but the way that they wear it. Chins-up-stomachs-in-chests-out is not an aphorism close to this new breed's heart. Sure, they stand straight, and tall, but there's a softness to their skin, a curvaceousness to their bodies, a dreamy self-absorption in their eyes. Unlike the defiant rock-man of yore, they don't really care if we're looking or not. They don't need our gaze as affirmation. They may be whimsical, but they're far from effete. Echoes of *Les Précieux*, perhaps, but not precious.

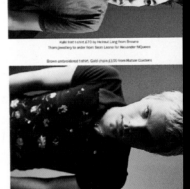

Beaded flesh top (mail order) from Alexander McQueen tel: 44-171-729 0537 customised with silk flowers.
Printed trouser to order from Hannah Mac Gibbon tel: 44-181-960 7316

text **Stephen Todd** photography **Josh van Gelder** styling **Alistair Mackie** hair **Lisa Eastwood for Aveda**
makeup **Sharon Dowsett for Aveda** models **Elvis at Take 2, Daniel at Boss, Ben, Simon**

Vol. 9 1996			
PHOTOGRAPHER	*Josh van Gelder*		
STYLIST	*Alistair Mackie*		

opposite page left **Vol. 9 1996** *opposite page right* **Vol. 9 1996**
PHOTOGRAPHER *Cora* PHOTOGRAPHER *Koto Bolofo*
STYLIST *Charlotte Stockdale*

FARMER FRESH

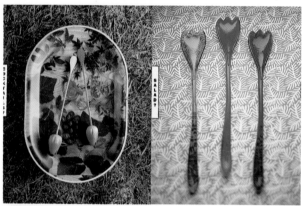

Vol. 9 1996

PHOTOGRAPHER Saram Morris

Vol. 9 1996

PHOTOGRAPHER Lon van Keulen

opposite page top **Vol. 9 1996**

PHOTOGRAPHER Lon van Keulen

opposite page bottom **Vol. 9 1996**

PHOTOGRAPHER Goran Dejkoski

SEEDS
OF
DESIRE

Bennett underscores that wild carrot seeds should only be used by women who are prepared to get to know their bodies and establish a working relationship with them. 'There's a little trick here – it's making us pay more attention to our cycles,' Bennett says. And the more attention we pay, the more likely we are to conceive when we want to and not conceive when we don't want to. This is a terrible method for somebody who doesn't want to pay attention.' Women for whom convenience is a top priority, who would rather not be vigilant about when they ovulate and menstruate, should stick with scientifically proven contraceptives. Another important, if obvious, point to remember: wild carrot seeds offer no protection whatsoever against sexually transmitted diseases.

But for those who understand the risk of the unknown, the seeds offer a natural alternative to more widely publicised methods of birth control. 'We're the pioneering generation,' Bennett says. 'We will in confidence be able to pass this to our daughters and their daughters, and so on. That's my hope.'

Queen Anne's Lace (wild carrot or Daucus Carota L.) is sold by the ounce at most herb suppliers. In London, contact Neal's Yard Remedies, (44) 171-379-7222; in New York, contact Green Terrestrial in Milton, (1) 914-795-5238 (they ship anywhere in the world and accept Visa and MasterCard) or Angelica's in Manhattan (1) 212-529-4335 (they do not mail order). To ensure that the seeds do not lose their potency during storage, it is best to keep them in a glass jar with an airtight seal. Do not keep them in paper. For information on a one-year 'grass roots study' of wild carrot seeds for contraception, write to Robin Rose Bennett, Wise Woman Healing Ways, South Mountain Pass, Garrison NY 10524 USA.

gesterone inhibitor. 'It has the same type of effect that RU486 does,' Riddle says. The theory is that the turpenoids in the seeds block crucial progesterone synthesis. In effect, what it does is cause implantation not to take place, or if it has shortly occurred, to dislodge it.'

How to take them? Once a day during your cycle, measure a small amount, approximately a teaspoon, of the seeds, chew slowly so that the volatile oils in the seeds are released, and swallow. (They resemble little bug-like scarabs, and they taste hard, dry, crunchy, and quite bitter, like tough old carrots.) Variations on this theme include taking the seeds post-coitally or taking them a few days before ovulation, during ovulation, and a few days after. Wild carrot seeds are definitely not for everyone. There are contraindications: women going through periods of 'intense hormonal activity' (coming off the pill or other anti-fertility medication; after a pregnancy, miscarriage, or abortion; or during menopause) must not rely on them at first for contraception. These individuals should wait anywhere from three to six months until their normal cycle is re-established, during which time they should rely on a barrier method of contraception.

So far, the only reported side effect of ingesting the seeds is mild gastric distress in some cases – similar to what happens when one eats, say, beans. Still, it's important to remember that the long-term effects of using wild carrot seeds daily are not fully known. Adriane Fugh-Berman, MD, a physician with the Office of Alternative Medicine at the National Institutes of Health in Bethesda, Maryland, sounds a note of caution. 'I would be concerned about long-term use of anti-progestins,' she says. 'Plants have pharmacologically active substances which can be beneficial or negative, and people shouldn't assume that something is harmless because it's in a plant rather than in a pill.'

...– perhaps even millennia – women all over ... have successfully avoided pregnancy by eating the seeds of Queen Anne's Lace (a.k.a. wild carrot), a flowering herb that grows profusely in many areas of the world. In fact, in rural India the taking of wild carrot seeds for contraception is a current practice that dates back two thousand years; anecdotal evidence suggests that Chinese and Navajo women also use this method of birth control. So why don't more people know about this? The answer is simpler: western doctors set no store by folk medicine that hasn't got scientific research to back it up. And no western research has been conducted on Queen Anne's Lace because there is no incentive for such study, given the existence of hormone medications (the birth control pill and Depo-Provera), the medical community's fear of liability, and the lack of potential profit margins for drug companies. (Wild carrot occurs commonly in nature; hormone medication requires a prescription. Think about it.)

Robin Rose Bennett is a New York-based herbalist in the 'Wise Woman' tradition and a respected teacher, author, and lecturer. She explains that wild carrot (Daucus Carota L.) is a 'stimulating aromatic' used in herbal medicine as a tonic for the urinary system; it is also used to dissolve kidney and bladder stones, and as a digestive aid. Here's how wild carrot seeds appear to work as a contraceptive: by making the eggs slide out of the uterus. 'What it seems to do is make the lining slippery in a way that the egg can't implant,' Bennett says. 'Yet when you're not taking wild carrot seeds, the egg implants just fine.' According to historian John Riddle, author of Contraception and Abortion from the Ancient World to the Renaissance (Harvard University Press, 1992), pharmacology studies conducted in China and India indicate that wild carrot sees act as a pro-

text **Julia Szabo**   photography **Lon van Keulen**

COSMETICS

**A blooming face
is one with roses
in the cheeks –
or perhaps daffodils,
tulips, anemone
or columbine.
Since antiquity,
blush has been used
to infuse healthy colour
in the visage but,
whether it was fucus
or ochre, berries
or roots,
the chosen hue
has always been
a flush of red or pink.
The cosmetic concentration
has recently been
on eyes, lips and nails,
and it is time
to bring some
of the diversity
of colour and pattern
seen in these areas
to the tempting surface
of a blank cheek.
A feeling for flowers
inspires us
to translate the complex
layers of patterns,
textures and colours
found in petals
directly on the cheekbones
in a manner
that is highly evocative
of dusky blossoms.
Through this unusual blend
of colour and shape,
the entire face
will be transformed
into an enticing blossom,
eliciting looks that might
just make one blush...**

**title borrowed from
George de Feure,
artist and designer,
whose drawings of women
becoming the flowers
they symbolised
were significant
of the early
Art Nouveau years**

Orchidée feminiflores

Pansy

images **Goran Pejkoski**

baseline

1	**Vol. 20 Jan. 1996**
2	**Vol. 21 Jul. 1996**
3	**Vol. 22 Dec. 1996**
EDITORS	*Hans Dieter Reichert,*
	Mike Daines
ART DIRECTOR	*Hans Dieter Reichert*
DESIGNERS	*Hans Dieter Reichert,*
	Dean Pavitt,
	1,2 Simon Dwelly,
	2 Kai Herse,
	3 Peter Black,
	3 Loïc Lévêque,
	3 David Scadding
ILLUSTRATOR	*3 Susanna Edwards*
PHOTOGRAPHERS	*1 John Chippindale,*
	1 HDR Design,
	2 David Arnold
	2, 3 Studio 2
DESIGN FIRM	*HDR Design*
EDITORIAL BOARD	*Martin Ashley,*
	Misha Anikst,
	Colin Brignall,
	David Ellis,
	Alan Fletcher
PUBLISHER	*Bradbourne Publishing Ltd.*
	UK

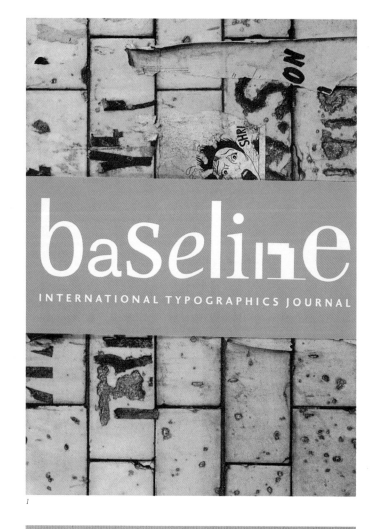

1

2

3

FORM+ZWECK

1	**1995**
2	**1993**
3	**1994**

EDITOR	*Form+Zweck*
CREATIVE DIRECTORS,	
ART DIRECTORS,	
DESIGNERS,	
ART DIRECTORS &	
ILLUSTRATORS	*Daniela Haufe,*
	Detlef Fiedler,
	Sophie Alex
PHOTOGRAPHERS	*1 Cyan,*
	3 Edward
	Muybridge
PUBLISHER	*Form+Zweck*
	Germany

1   2   3

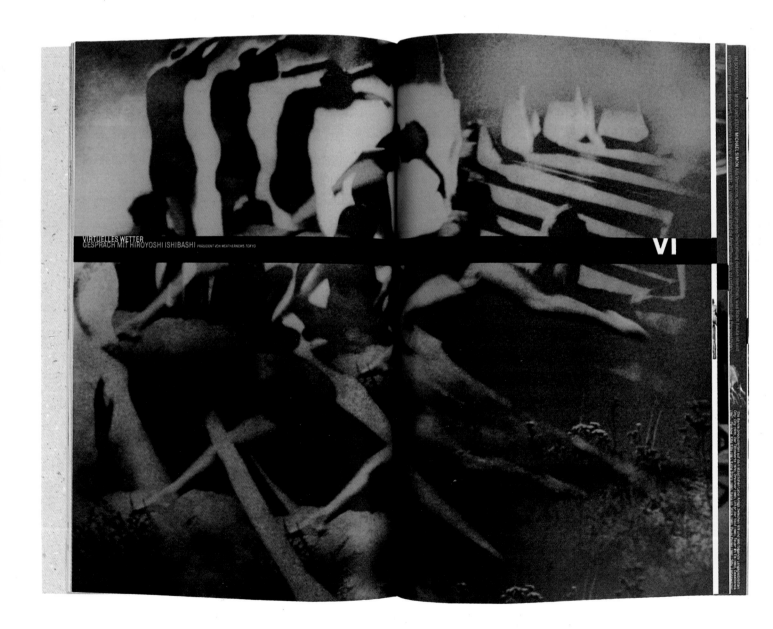

1993

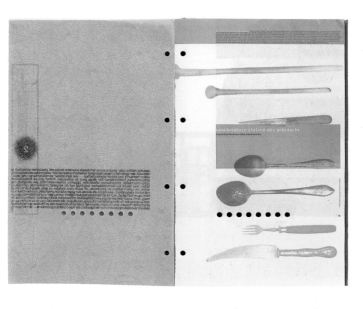

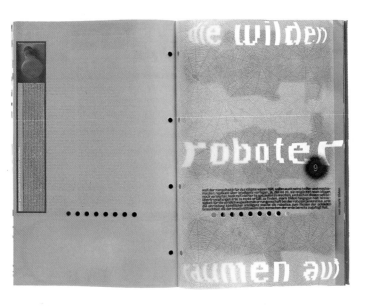

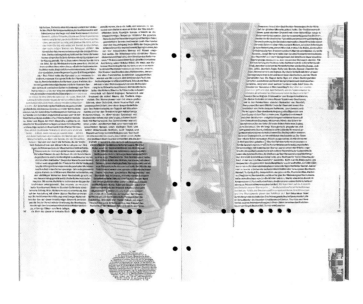

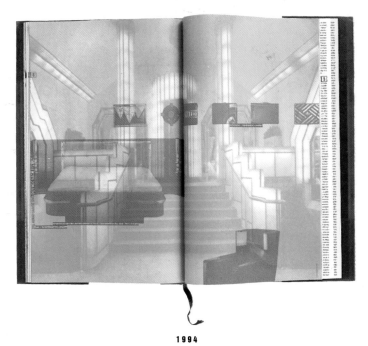

1995

1994

CONTRAST
Jan. 1997

EDITORS	*Liz Chase,*
	E.B.Eddy Paper
CREATIVE DIRECTORS	*Terrance Zacharko,*
	Theresa Zacharko
ART DIRECTOR	*Zacharko Design Partnership*
DESIGNER	*Terrance Zacharko*
PHOTOGRAPHER	*Terrance Zacharko*
DESIGN FIRM	*Zacharko Design Partnership*
PUBLISHER	*Island Paper Mills*
	Canada

hey noah,
HOW WE MEASURE WEALTH DEPENDS UPON DIFFERENCES –
economic, social, or cultural.
I THINK WEALTH CAN MEAN DIFFERENT THINGS TO DIFFERENT PEOPLE.

IT MAKES ME WONDER
TO WHAT EXTENT ARE WE INFLUENCED BY WHAT WE SEE AND
TO WHAT EXTENT ARE WE INFLUENCED BY WHAT WE DO?

SO IN A WAY, SOCIETY FUNCTIONS ON
the measurement of wealth.

IT FORCES US TO CONSTANTLY TAKE 'MEASUREMENTS,'
OPENING US TO A WEALTH OF EMOTIONS: GREED AND INADEQUACY.
OVERWHELMED BY THESE KINDS OF EMOTIONS,
WE ARE TEMPTED TO LOSE SIGHT OF WHAT IS IMPORTANT –

I THINK WHEN WE DIG DEEPER,
WE CAN BE OPEN
TO MANY SIMILARITIES.

THE CHALLENGE IS TO FIGHT
AGAINST THESE TOOLS THAT POKE FUN
AND MOCK REAL LIFE SITUATIONS, BELITTLING THE
**human mind
and spirit.**

yeah,
WE HAVE DIFFERENT BACKGROUNDS, **morals, lifestyles,** AND EXPERIENCES.
SOME OF US HAVE SO MUCH AND SOME HAVE SO LITTLE.

KATE,
I THINK WE SHOULD BE MORE INFLUENCED
BY WHAT WE DO...BUT UNFORTUNATELY,
WE ARE MORE EASILY INFLUENCED BY
WHAT WE SEE.

OR IN A LOT OF WAYS,
IT DOESN'T FUNCTION.

...AND ENVY,

OUR UNDERSTANDING OF EACH OTHER. WE ALL MUST EAT,
DRINK, AND SLEEP. WE COME FROM
THE SAME THING AND WE SHARE THE SAME PLANET,

IF WE UNDERSTAND WHAT FACTORS HAVE SHAPED ONE ANOTHER,
PERHAPS THIS NEED TO MEASURE CAN SOON BECOME IRRELEVANT.
THE YOUTH OF TODAY ARE VERY DIVERSE. IN A CULTURE OF FAST FOOD
AND TALK SHOWS, WE ARE FACED WITH A **tremendous challenge...**

YOUTH IS THE FUTURE. THE WAY WE MEASURE WEALTH TODAY
WILL DETERMINE THE WAY WEALTH IS VIEWED TOMORROW.

Jan. 1997

DESIGNERS	*Kate Elazegui,*
	Noah D.Gaynin
PHOTOGRAPHER	*Jonathan Londres*
DESIGN FIRM	*The School of the Art*
	Institute of Chicago
MENTOR	*Ann Tyler*

Jan. 1997

DESIGNERS   *David Sterling,*
Mark Randall

DESIGN FIRM   *World Studio*

inside

PHOTOGRAPHERS   *Bill Bernstein,*
Geoffrey Croft,
Angela Fisher,
David Austin,
Erich Lessing

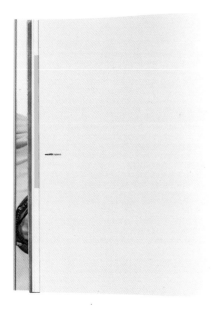

Jan. 1997

DESIGNER   *Ute Zscharnt*

PHOTOGRAPHER   *Ute Zscharnt*

DESIGN FIRM   *Grappa Design*

inside

TYPOGRAPHER   *Ute Zscharnt*

Jan. 1997

DESIGNERS   *Rod Roodenburg,*
David Coates,
Dawn Newton,
Matt Heximer,
Judy Bau

PHOTOGRAPHER   *Perry Danforth*

DESIGN FIRM   *Ion Design*

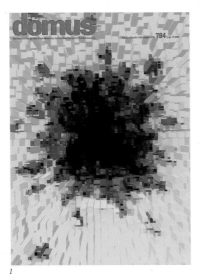

1

2

3

domus

1 **Vol. 784 Jul./Aug. 1996**
2 **Vol. 789 Jan. 1997**
3 **Vol. 791 Mar. 1997**

MANAGING EDITOR *François Burkhardt*
ART DIRECTOR *Giuseppe Basile*
DESIGNERS *1 Uwe Loesch,*
2 Gert Dumbar,
3 Shinro Otake
PUBLISHER *Editoriale Domus S.P.A*

Italy

Vol. 784 Jul./Aug. 1996

PHOTOGRAPHER *Michel Denance*

16 Progetti Projects

Domus 784 Luglio/Agosto July/August '96

Renzo Piano

Testo di Charles-Arthur Boyer
Fotografie di Michel Denance e Studio Gui

Text by Charles-Arthur Boyer
Photographs by Michel Denance and Studio Gui

Cité Internationale, Lione

Cité Internationale, Lyon

Progetto: Renzo Piano – Building Workshop: Renzo Piano,
Paul Vincent (associato)
Collaboratori: C. Calafell, A. Chauya, A. Gallissian,
M. Howard, A. El Jerari, M. Henry, C. Jackman, J.B. Mothes,
E. Novel, M. Pimmel, J.A. Polette, M. Salerno,
A.H. Téménidès, B. Tonfoni, W. Vassal
Associati al progetto complessivo: Michel Corajoud,
T. Boursier-Mougenot, Cartelin-Ricard-Bergeret, H. Cocagne,
G. Mormina, T. Rolland, C. Valentinuzzi, Alain Vincent,
Syllabus con Stéphanie Bernard

Project: Renzo Piano – Building Workshop: Renzo Piano, Paul
Vincent (associate)
Collaborators: C. Calafell, A. Chauya, A. Gallissian,
M. Howard, A. El Jerari, M. Henry, C. Jackman, J.B. Mothes,
E. Novel, M. Pimmel, J.A. Polette, M. Salerno, A.H. Téménidès,
B. Tonfoni, W. Vassal
Overall project associates: Michel Corajoud, T. Boursier-
Mougenot, Cartelin-Ricard-Bergeret, H. Cocagne,
G. Mormina, T. Rolland, C. Valentinuzzi, Alain Vincent,
Syllabus with Stéphanie Bernard

A metà degli anni Ottanta "l'urbanistica è stata derubata dall'architettura". Le antiche regole e i sistemi della progettazione urbana sono stati soppiantati da nuovi e imponenti "grandi progetti" dell'architettura. Anche Lione ha seguito questa via del rinnovamento, e allora – undici anni fa – il Renzo Piano Building Workshop vinse il concorso per la Cité Internationale. Un pezzo di città, con vari nuovi utilizzi. Strutturato intelligentemente in maniera mista, ampliabile e futuristica. Adesso è un frammento eroico, che attende uno sviluppo. La sua forza architettonica è grande, ma sarà sufficiente per attirare nuovi "vicini"?

In the mid-eighties "urban planning was stolen by architecture". The old planning rules and systems had to give way to architecture's new, imposing "major projects". Lyon also followed this path of urban renewal and at the time – 11 years ago now – Renzo Piano Building Workshop won the competition for the Cité Internationale. A little piece of city with many new functions. An intelligently mixed development. It can be extended and adapted to future needs. At the moment it is a heroic fragment waiting to be developed. Its architectural power is great but will it be sufficient to attract new neighbours?

La prima parte della Cité Internationale di Lione, assegnata per concorso al Renzo Piano Building Workshop nel 1985, sorge dopo soli diciotto mesi dall'apertura del cantiere lungo l'ansa del Rodano. Comprende per ora un centro per congressi, dei palazzi per uffici e i nuovi edifici del Museo d'arte contemporanea, e rappresenta una sfida politica, economica, sociale e culturale per una delle più importanti metropoli regionali francesi, alla ricerca di una nuova ispirazione vitale.
Distesa tra una delle anse del Rodano e il parco più famoso della città, quello della Tête d'Or, la Cité Internationale è emblematica dei nuovi monumenti urbani che, dall'inizio degli anni '80, vanno sorgendo nelle grandi città francesi. Nîmes in questo campo ha fatto da battistrada. Poi Lille (con il progetto Euralille di Rem Koolhaas), Montpellier, Marsiglia, Strasburgo, Nantes, Bordeaux... si sono imbarcate in questa direzione, con maggior o minor fortuna e abilità, moltiplicando gli edifici amministrativi, culturali o di servizio. Per acquisire una dimensione europea e la posizione di guida che aveva perso a vantaggio delle vicine Nîmes, Montpellier, Grenoble, la città di Lione ha dunque affrontato, a una decina d'anni, una ridefinizione completa della propria immagine economica e culturale attraverso una serie di "grandi progetti" architettonici e urbani: il Musée des Beaux-Arts di Jean-Michel Wilmotte, l'Opéra di Jean Nouvel, la place des Terreaux di Daniel Buren e Christian Drevet, la stazione di interconnessione TGV/aeroporto di Santiago Calatrava, gli ingressi e la stazione della metropolitana di Jourda & Perraudin... La Cité Internationale, ubicata a nord-est della città su un terreno occupato in precedenza dagli edifici della fiera internazionale di Lione costruiti a partire dal 1918 e da un Palazzo dei congressi realizzato negli anni '60, è parte di questa politica. Il programma molto complesso (224.000 mq di infrastrutture, servizi, uffici e costruzioni residenziali) dieci anni fa fu oggetto di un concorso. Renzo Piano lo vinse con una proposta più misurata che audace. La sua Cité Internationale si presenta come un frammento di città composto da una doppia schiera di padiglioni autonomi ordinati e collocati lungo un percorso pubblico centrale lungo 1,3 chilometri, parzialmente coperto. Questa frammentazione permette accortamente molti passaggi pubblici trasversali

che danno fluidità e permeabilità all'insieme del sito e si inscrivono come riferimento obbligato alle 'traboules' lionesi, rete complessa e parallela di vicoletti e passaggi che si insinuano tra gli edifici e dentro di essi in certi vecchi quartieri cittadini come quello della Croix-Rousse.
L'accesso principale a ogni edificio avviene, dal lato del Rodano, da un viale urbano accoppiato a un percorso alberato, che ci si è già occupati di sistemare (ideazione di Renzo Piano, con il paesaggista Michel Corajoud e gli organismi del dipartimento del Rodano). Una passeggiata ordinata d'alberi, dal lato del parco, garantisce un percorso secondario. I primi edifici del primo lotto di lavori sono oggi fuori terra: cioè il Palazzo dei congressi e due palazzi per uffici; poi, un po' discosto, il Museo d'arte contemporanea, solitario perché manca il complesso cinematografico destinato a fronteggiarlo, oltre a un albergo di prestigio e altri uffici che lo collegheranno alle realizzazioni precedenti. Come vuole ancora la tradizione lionese, il rigore di scrittura di cui Renzo Piano ha dato prova nelle altre opere francesi, come l'IRCAM e il complesso residenziale parigino di rue de Meaux, qui è più moderato, sfumato, anche se adotta lo stesso vocabolario di mattone, vetro e metallo. In realtà le 'assicelle' di terra cotta (elementi di facciata analoghi al mattone forato, ideati e studiati appositamente da Renzo Piano) si allungano e si addolciscono, le facciate si fanno più spesse, i volumi interni si condensano e si frammentano, le coperture metalliche e di vetro si incurvano. Ma anche se uno stupefacente spirito di sintesi ha presieduto al progetto di Renzo Piano per un quartiere internazionale che cerca di coniugare cultura e commercio, svago per famiglie e servizi d'alto livello, bisogna tenere che la situazione politica lionese, così come la situazione economica francese o addirittura mondiale, non consoterano al progetto di compiersi interamente. E che restino unicamente, eroi solitari e inoperosi, gli edifici ora terminati. Sarebbe un peccato per motivi sociali, perché questo nuovo quartiere cittadino non può costituirsi che nella globalità e nella molteplicità del programma e dei servizi. Ma anche per motivi architettonici, perché ogni elemento ha bisogno di un complementare e della continuità dell'insieme per essere perfettamente coerente, adempiere al proprio ruolo e giustificare la propria scrittura.

1 Il modello del progetto complessivo (modello: J.P. Allain, Olivier Doizy. Foto: Michel Denance).
2 Dettaglio di una facciata, che evidenzia la doppia 'pelle' della struttura: al paramento in mattoni è accostata una pannellatura di vetro (foto Michel Denance).

*1 The overall project model (model: J.P. Allain, Olivier Doizy. Photo: Michel Denance).
2 Detail of a facade, showing the structure's double 'skin'. The brick screen is flanked by glass panelling (photo Michel Denance).*

Leapfrog – Progettare la Sostenibilità

Leapfrog – Designing Sustainability

The planet is going through a particularly delicate period. Domus wishes to reflect on this disturbing but stimulating subject of sustainability, which concerns every one of us. We open the debate in a theoretical key, and report on the various forms of responsible action being taken within the framework of design in its broadest sense.

Ezio Manzini
Progettare per la sostenibilità
Leapfrog: anticipazioni di un futuro possibile

Fulvio Ferrari
Materiali eco-performativi
Tra ricerca, tradizione e cultura
Eco-performing materials
Research, tradition and culture

Vol. 789 Jan. 1997

PHOTOGRAPHER   1 Simona Pesarini
ILLUSTRATOR   Giuseppe Basile
DESIGN FIRM   3 Haasa

Vol. 789 Jan. 1997

PHOTOGRAPHER   4 Authentics (left)
ILLUSTRATOR   5 Sonia Pellegrini
DESIGN FIRM   4 Authentics (left)

Claude Fussler **Come migliorare l'efficienza ecologica del prodotto**
How to improve the product eco-efficiency

Mika Pantzar **Consumi e sostenibilità nel mondo occidentale**
Consumption and sustainability in the western world

Fumikazu Masuda **Il trionfo dello spirito sulla materia**
Spirit over matter and the evil of incompleteness

PHOTOGRAPHERS 　1 *Cesare Colombo,*
　　　　　　　　 2,3,4 *Gionata Xerra,*
　　　　　　　　 5 *Ramak Fazel*
ILLUSTRATOR 　　*Enzo Mari*
DESIGN FIRMS 　 2 *Enzo Mari Per Alessi,*
　　　　　　　　 3,4 *Driade,*
　　　　　　　　 5 *Cleverline (NL)*

DESIGNERS 　　　*Radi Group (left),*
　　　　　　　　 Jacob de Baan (right)
PHOTOGRAPHERS 　*Radi Group (left),*
　　　　　　　　 Toine van den Nieuwendijk (right)
DESIGN FIRMS 　 *Jacob de Baan per Quasar (right)*

"Il design o è plusvalore culturale o non è design" Dialogo con Enzo Mari

"Either design is a cultural plus-value or it isn't design" Dialogue with Enzo Mari

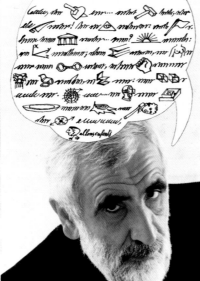

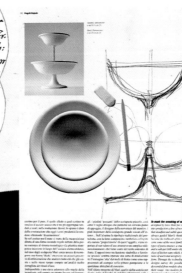

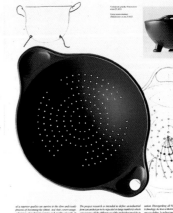

Portacavi, copricavi, interruttori e spine. Un problema periferico

Wireducts, wire covers, switchs and plugs. A peripheral problem

Lampada mobile non elettrica

Non-electric mobile l...

Jacob de Baan

Dalla Corea una nuova fioritura dell'arte tessile

Chung Kyung-Yeun, "l'artista con i guanti", sta conquistando un posto di primo piano nel panorama dell'arte tessile internazionale grazie alla sua ricchezza immaginativa, al suo talento per i materiali e al suo personalissimo tocco.

From Korea, textile art renewed

Chung Kyung-Yeun, "the artist with the gloves", has risen to the highest ranks of international textile art, thanks to the imaginative wealth of her talent, to her intelligent feeling for material and to her idiosyncratic touch.

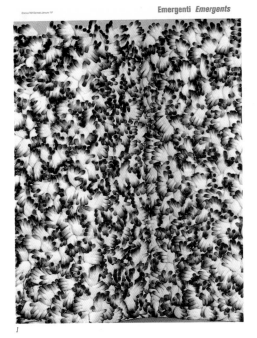

Prova di memoria *Rehearsal of Memory*, CD-Rom

del britannico Harwood, sovvertendo i canoni tradizionali di interfaccia che vogliono un'informazione facile e immediata richiede al fruitore un impegno emotivo e partecipativo, che ben si sposa ai particolari contenuti di questo lavoro.

Rehearsal of Memory

The CD-Rom by Britain's Harwood, subverts the traditional interface canons calling for easy, immediate information. This work demands more of the beholder emotionally and participation-wise, and the harmonises well with its unusual contents.

"Esposizioni. Letteratura e architettura nel XIX secolo".
Philippe Hamon.
CLUEB, Bologna, 1996
(pp. 278, L. 32.000).

di Gianni Turchetta

"Package Design 3. Corporate Identity. L'identità di prodotto per l'immagine aziendale e di marca".
Giovanni Brunazzi.
Testo italiano e inglese.
Antonio Ghiorzo Editore, Milano,
1995 (pp. 190).

di Giuseppe Raimondi

"Interiormente figure".
Paolo Thea.
Testo, Torino, 1995 (pp. 284, L. 40.000).

di Damiano Minishi

… oltre l'etichetta

Vol. 789 Jan. 1997

DESIGNERS   1,2 *Chung Kyung-Yeun* (left),
2 *Graham Harwood* (right)

Vol. 791 Mar. 1997

ILLUSTRATOR   *Antonio Talarico*

145

METROPOLIS
1 **Sep. 1996**
2 **Oct. 1996**
3 **Nov. 1996**

EDITOR   *Marisa Bartolucci*
ART DIRECTORS *Carl Lehmann-Haupt,*
              William van Roden
PHOTOGRAPHER   *3 Kristine Larsen*
PUBLISHER   *Bellerophon*
              Publications Inc.
              USA

1

2

3

SPIRIT SCHOOL TOWN ACTION MEMORY BUILDING PLACE HOME

what is community? ?? ???????

Images of community from Bay Ridge, Brooklyn, right.

photography by kristine larsen

PRIVATE PROPERTY

TRUTH

RESPONSIBILITY

It's time we talked about our communal life.

by Marisa Bartolucci During the Republican convention in August, the African proverb "It takes a village to raise a child," which also happens to be the title of Hillary Rodham Clinton's best-selling book, became the target of political attack. In his acceptance speech for the presidential nomination, Bob Dole insisted that "it takes a family, not a village, to raise a child." At first, it seemed rather extraordinary that an African proverb could emerge as a topic for national debate, a symbol perhaps of America's waxing multiculturalism. But, in fact, this rather contrived assault demonstrated something quite troubling in our nation: the confusion (or is it obliviousness?) of politicians in both parties about community's changing meaning and its role in our lives, and what the consequences may be for our future. Whether or not one agrees with Hillary Rodham Clinton that a village's involvement is essential to good child-rearing is moot, because we don't live in tightly knit, interdependent communities anymore. Even in Africa, they are fast disappearing.

As Stephen Doheny-Farina, a professor of technical communications at Clarkson University in Potsdam, New York, observes in his excellent book *The Wired Neighborhood* (Yale University Press, 1996), what this proverb "winds up meaning is that it takes an active and well-rounded mix of interacting co-located interest groups to raise a child." By which he means a school, a PTA, youth associations, sports groups, a church, and so on.

The notion of community, as writer and farmer Wendell Berry refers to it, as "a placed people" is as endangered today as the Amazon rain forest—and it's arguable that their concurrent demise is no coincidence. We have become "a knowledge society," writes Doheny-Farina, "a society of mobility." Of course, Americans have been on the move since frontier days, yet we still formed stable communities. The difference now is that we have become financially, intellectually, and emotionally mobile as well.

Consider a family that has lived for several generations in the same house in a small town in a still largely rural part of Maine. You might imagine that there is a real continuity to its members' lives, and in some respects you'd be right; but there have also been tremendous dislocations. The fresh produce the family buys from their longtime neighborhood grocer no longer comes from the local farmer (he now grows only fancy varieties of potatoes, and sells much of his crop out of state) but from throughout the world, with tomatoes from the Netherlands, melons from Israel, and bananas from Ecuador. The father teaches at the local school as did his father and his father's father before him, but the mother works for the branch office of a Japanese multinational. For entertainment, the family likes to watch television, especially *Baywatch*, and reruns of *Dallas* and *The Brady Bunch*, shows that put them in imaginative contact with utterly different places, people, and situations but that often seem more vivid, more compelling, more real than those in their own lives. Though this family may well have strong ties to its community, its members have nevertheless become what Doheny-Farina calls "globalized individuals." They depend far more "on large-scale markets and technologies" for their lives and livelihoods than on their neighbors. And so it is with each and every one of us.

Many see this development as progress. As Doheny-Farina mentions, not long ago several high-tech luminaries, including Alvin Toffler and Esther Dyson, authored an electronic document known as "The Magna Carta for the Knowledge Age," which proclaims: "The central event of the twentieth century is the over-

throw of matter....The powers of mind are everywhere ascendant over the brute force of things." With a giddy zealousness that recalls Marinetti and the Italian Futurists, they declare the supremacy of physical wealth to be at an end and the convergence of time and place all but superfluous. Cyberspace, they continue, "will play an important role in knitting together the diverse communities of tomorrow, facilitating the creation of 'electronic neighborhoods' bound together not by geography but by shared interests."

Shared interests are at the crux of the matter. They imply not just affinities, but rights and privileges. What these boosters of the virtual envision are not so much communities as cliques and clubs. While mutual interests help constitute communities, at their most fundamental communities are about shared responsibilities. "In physical communities," writes Doheny-Farina, "we are forced to live with people who may differ from us in many ways. But virtual communities offer us the opportunity to construct utopian collectives...of interest, education, tastes, beliefs, and skills." Independent of time and place, cyberspace is less a communal than a public realm; it is a domain where unencumbered selves pursue their own concerns. ▶ 71

Nov. 1996

EDITOR   *Marisa Bartolucci*
PHOTOGRAPHER   *Kristine Larsen*

In ancient times, the hospital began as a hall for dreamers,
where the sick received divine cures in their sleep. In the Middle Ages,
it was a haven for the indigent and the ill. By the Enlightenment, it was called
a "curing machine." The changing values of society have always been reflected
in the hospital's evolving mission and design. Now, as prayer is increasingly
thought to be as important to healing as the latest medical technology,
what form will tomorrow's hospital take?

Oct. 1996

EDITOR

Marisa Bartolucci

the evolution of the hospital

by Eric Darton   Long before Le Corbusier called the home a "machine for living," the eighteenth-century scientist Jean-Baptiste Le Roy proposed building a hospital that would be "a curing machine." It seemed logical, the human body was already being regarded as a machine, so why not the place that ministered to its ailments? Inherent in this rationalist conception were many of the blood-and-guts paradoxes at the core of the modern hospital. Can an institution designed for efficiency truly provide compassionate healing? Can it be a refuge, and still admit selectivity? These tensions between utopian expectation and harsh reality have shaped the hospital's mission and design from its inception.

Today, of course, they are most evident in the drive to ration care and drastically cut costs. This development has forced 664 of the nation's hospitals, or some 10 percent, to merge in the past year, while others for their specialization, and those that fail to compete successfully close. In Philadelphia alone, six hospitals and a medical school have shut down in the past two years. In the short term, this is sure to mean less access to health care for a wide spectrum of people, especially the poor and the elderly. The long-term prognosis, however, is less clear.

While there are many social and medical pressures forcing change upon the hospital, the most crucial may be the growing revolt against the mechanistic conception of the body and of medicine itself. An increasing number of physicians, health-care professionals, and patients are contending that medicine is essentially an art that must concern itself not just with the physical complaint but with the whole person, body and psyche. Thus, the very existence of the modern hospital as a curing machine, designed to treat medical conditions, not individuals, is being called into question.

Western medicine emerged out of a belief in the healing connection between mind and body. In ancient Greece, and later across the Hellenized world, the roles of priest and physician were integrated. In the temples of Asclepius, the god of healing, were "halls for dreamers." Sheltered by porticoes opened south toward the sun, and lulled by the gurgling mineral springs in which they had bathed, sleeping patients received Asclepius's proscribed cures in their dreams, and when they awoke, his injunctions were administered by the physician-priests. In addition to halls for dreaming and treatment, the Asclepian complex at Pergamum in the second century B.C. offered mud baths, a theater—presumably for drama's cathartic powers—

icff

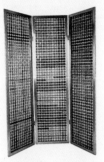

IAAE utilized outdated reels of 35mm processed film to weave this screen, appropriately titled Terra and One-Half Nineces.

T.E.M.T. designer Rodney Allen Trice took to the streets of Brooklyn to find the old tires and inner tubes he used to make El Kactor de Charles Muertos.

The Fair & Saucer Sconce by Christopher Parkhouse reemploys the melamine cups, saucers, and bowls of the 1950s.

refurnishings

Be it through economy of materials or multiplicity of functions, many works at the 1996 International Contemporary Furniture Fair embodied sound and sensitive design practices.

by Diana Friedman   Consideration, not ostentation. This was the message at the eighth annual International Contemporary Furniture Fair (ICFF), held in May at the Jacob K. Javits Convention Center in New York City. Of the more than 400 companies exhibiting at the show, which is produced by George Little Management Inc. and sponsored by Metropolis, a preponderance demonstrated a heightened awareness of how they are designing. From the large manufacturers to the one-person design studios, from the student displays to the special exhibitions. Earth-friendly materials, eco-conscious fabrication, and an emphasis on usability were very much in evidence. Such mindful design strategies can translate into lower production costs, and judging from the excitement expressed by the 10,000 attendees, value is precisely what architects, designers, manufacturers, retailers, and the public are looking for.

Without a doubt, most furnishings are still made out of wood. But with the growing awareness of the extent and consequences of deforestation, the demand for once coveted hardwoods like mahogany and rosewood is decreasing. In response, furniture makers are looking to plywood, particleboard, and veneer as less expensive alternatives. Not long ago, these materials were deemed pedestrian and cheap—inferior to solid hardwoods. But in the wake of this new-sprung experimentation, fresh sensibilities are emerging. There was, for instance, a spare, buoyant quality to many of the wood furnishings at the Fair—table and chair legs were

more attenuated than chunky; profiles, on the whole, were less imposing. The proliferation of molded plywood designs, such as the wildly contoured lounge chair from Detroit-based Grei Interiors and the willowy stacking chair by Danish designer Peter Karpf for Standnavian Design Inc., also reflects this new, economical way of looking at wood.

Other designers seem to favor recycling existing timber. Brooklyn designer Patrick Moore, for instance, restores much of the pine he uses for his furniture from demolished buildings, accentuating the salvaged look by adding handcrafted aluminum latches and hinges of his own design. Meanwhile, to make his graceful pedestals and stools, Chris Lehrecke searches out fallen trees in upstate New York. After strip-

The birch plywood Puzzle Chair designed by David Kawecki for 3D Interiors requires no hardware or tools to assemble.

Zenoldscype's Cactus umbrella stand is filled with grass and Nevada grass cacti that rely on rainwater for sustenance.

Sep. 1996

EDITOR

Diana Friedman

work of a new crop of Dutch design talent   can now be sampled at MOMA's newly   remodeled café

The spare and quirky

DUTCH TREAT
[h]

Apr. 1996

EDITOR

Marisa Bartolucci

BY LAURIE ATTIAS To complement the Museum of Modern Art's exhaustive Piet Mondrian retrospective last fall, Paola Antonelli, the associate design curator, thought about giving the museum's brasserie-style café a daring Dutch look, something downright Rietveldian. But, as Antonelli admits, "It was a little scary picturing black and white and primary colors everywhere"—especially for museumgoers already dizzy from studying Mondrian's Broadway Boogie-Woogie and desperate for a caffeine fix.

Called in to consult on the project, Rayn van der Lugt, then New York's Dutch consul for Cultural Affairs this month has assumed the post of director at the Groninger Museum), suggested instead something less severe, but no less stunning: a sleek, modern canteen that would at once showcase recent developments in Dutch design and blast away the old stereotypes of it being all flat, uncompromising rationalism.

As it happens, the star elements of the new

decor—the lighting fixtures—verge on the surreal. Lean back as you sip your espresso, and you may spy Tejo Remy's whimsical Milkbottlelamp, 12 sandblasted, standard glass bottles suspended from the ceiling. In another corner of the room, there are industrial designer Rody Graumans' chandeliers, bundles of 85 bare bulbs suspended from knotted black wires and connectors. And in the glass-enclosed area that overlooks MOMA's famous sculpture garden hang Henk Stallinga's Blisterlamps, composed of transparent lampshades, each encasing a small, round, red bulb.

The young designers responsible for these skillful couplings of the austere and innovative are part of an Amsterdam-based group known as Droog Design (Dry Design). The name seems oddly fitting for inhabitants of a country whose existence depends on a complex system of canals and dikes, regulated by an intricate network of drains and pumps. It also reflects the dryness of their wit, which at times borders on the absurd, especially in its curious combinations of humble materials: Stallinga's lamp shades, ►77

Opposite page, industrial chandeliers by Rody Graumans of Droog Design illumine one section of the new café at New York's Museum of Modern Art. The tables are by the design firm Spurs and the chairs are by a frequent collaborator, Piet Hein Eek. At far left, reminiscent of Droog Design's "quarter mentality," is a chest of drawers by Tejo Remy. This page, top, elsewhere in the café, the Blisterlamps of Droog Design's Henk Stallinga are as alluring at night, another section is defined by Remy's hanging Milkbottlelamps (seen in close-up at left), and by Eek's stools and tables.

147

KENCHIKU BUNKA
1 Vol. 52 Jan. 1997
2 Vol. 51 Dec. 1996

EDITOR   *Takaaki Tomishige*
DESIGNER   *Tetsuji Bang!*
PROVISION OF PHOTOGRAPH   1 *Nobuo Hozumi*
PHOTOGRAPHERS   2 *Arnaud Baumann,*
                2 *Sipa Press,*
                2 *Gaston Bergeret*
PUBLISHER   *Shokokusha*
                Publishing Co., Ltd.
                Japan

1

Vol. 51 Dec. 1996

2

Vol. 52 Jan. 1997

モダン・ストラクチュアの冒険
構造デザインをキーワードに近代建築　を読み直す

Le Corbusier

The Unbuilt Jean Nouvel 100 Projects

Text: Olivier Baissière

Vol.3

ジャン・ヌーヴェル 100プロジェクト Vol.3
テキスト：オリヴィエ・ブウシエール

No.10 TÊTE DÉFENSE
PARIS FRANCE / SKETCH   1980

Le Corbusier
Article-16
板倉真研一

ル・コルビュジエと日本の近代様式
影響作品の形態論的考察

No.18 PARC DE LA VILLETTE
PARIS FRANCE / INTERNATIONAL COMPETITION (WITH PIERRE SORIA, GILBERT LEZENES)   1982

Vol. 51 Dec. 1996

PHOTOGRAPHER   1,2 Philippe Ruault

Vol. 51 Dec. 1996

PHOTOGRAPHER   4 Gitty Darugar
PROVISION OF PHOTOGRAPH   5,6 Architectures Jean Nouvel

ELLE DECORATION
Mar. 1997

EDITOR — Ilse Crawford
CREATIVE DIRECTOR — Sue Skeen
ART DIRECTOR — Debi Angel
PHOTOGRAPHER — James Merrell
PUBLISHER — Hachette / Emap
Magazine Ltd.

UK

Mar. 1997

PHOTOGRAPHERS
1 *James Merrell,*
1 *Steve Dalton,*
1,2 *Christoph Kicherer,*
2 *Josh van Gelder,*
2 *Tim Evan-Cook,*
2 *Verity Welstead*

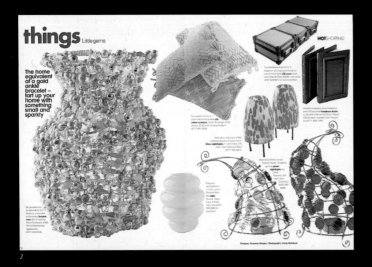

3 **Mar. 1997**

PRODUCER — Suzanne Stankus
PHOTOGRAPHER — Verity Welstead

4 **Mar. 1997**

PRODUCER — Deborah Morant
PHOTOGRAPHERS — Nigel Shafran,
Mario Pignata-Alonti

Mar. 1997

EDITOR — Deborah Morant
PRODUCER — Deborah Morant
TEXT — Gilda Williams (left)

RICHARD BRYANT /ARCAID

From the outside it looks like just another Victorian house. But once inside you're in unfamiliar territory. Whatever happened to the entrance hall for a start? Or corridors leading off rooms? Where has the kitchen gone? Why aren't the bedrooms in the usual place?

The Victorians, who had a place for everything, as well as putting everyone in their place, would never manage to find their way around a modern conversion. Nineties lifestyle demands futons in the front room, kitchens under the eaves where the maids would once have lived, no pantries, larders or dining room — in fact, hardly any rooms at all. Everyone's lives have changed and these modern interiors now reflect the changing demographics or what the Sunday supplements would refer to as 'lifestyle'.

First sign of the changing times was the gargantuan kitchen which gobbled up the dining room. Now the modern kitchen looks set to become the living room as well. Whatever its role, family and friends all converge and converse around the stove, which is the modern-day equivalent of the hearth. Kitted out with the latest labour-saving appliances in clunky, assertive, steely good looks, it now has the most important role in the house. And the most space, which is why it's often weirdly sited.

Dining under the stars without a boarding pass is a one-off that architectural duo Matthias Sauerbruch and Louisa Hutton (partners in life as well as business) designed for their own house. They moved the kitchen/living/dining room from the basement to the entire top floor of their London home. 'The house is completely upside down,' says Hutton. First they raised the roof, then they glazed it.

Now they live among the stars under a roller coaster of glass in what Louisa lyrically calls 'our sky garden'. For sure, they didn't put their kitchen up three flights of stairs for the ease and convenience of supermarket shopping. 'It was a slight reaction against the Victorian house we live in, with relentless divisions on every floor, the same two rooms and staircase winding through,' Hutton admits. 'Creatively, we wanted to make something of what we'd been given,' but like all lifestyle decisions these days, it was also a practical one. Along with many other metropolitan couples, instead of slogging it out in the city, they work from home. In ascending levels of privacy, the house develops from their street-level architectural practice with its drawing boards, scale models and clients.

Conversely, going out to work all day means there are no child-free zones at home anymore. Now you won't find the playroom, nursery or TV room in the working mother's household, as children today are not only seen, but herded into grown-up spaces as part of communal living. 'There's often too much fuss made over children's space,' says architect Sophie Hicks, who is scornful of kid-glove treatment of kids and who doesn't even have stair gates to block out her own three children. 'If you don't want to look at the load of plastic

'rubbish' which children like, then contain it, as we do. In our kitchen-diner we blow up an inflatable dinghy for the baby, Olympus, and all her stuff and just chuck things back into it.'

Art lovers, of course, always like open spaces. But as the children grow up, there is a noticeable trend for older couples — referred to by estate agents as 'empty nesters' — to move out of their overstuffed dinky little town houses and sell the Louis-something chairs and gilded clocks to collect art. Then they employ architects to throw the partitions into a skip so they can admire their collection. What people find sexy now is communal living, big time. Walls and doors have gone the way of Laura Ashley wallpaper and guest towels that match the bathmat.

Minimalist architect Claudio Silvestrin, who has been commissioned to design the two Calvin Klein Collection shops which are due to open in London and Paris this spring/summer, finds it remarkable that he has been commissioned by a property developer to re-model a Mayfair mews house and reduce it from being a three-bedroomed house to two. 'Now light and space and ▷

This page: Architect Richard Roger's Georgian town house encapsulates, for many, the ideal of modern living. By eliminating the second floor in this traditional space, he created a modern sense of volume and light

Reconfiguring
space

In the late 90s, light and space are valued more than the room-count. Now the walls are coming down

41

1

ELLEDECO MARCH

Hot
stuff

to beat the gloom

hot Forge your own mix of *modern* classics

hot The fusion of rich fabric and concrete — opposites *attract*

hot *Enrich* the mix with accidental finds

hot *Kitchens* — what we want and how to get it

hot Drop everything now and go somewhere *warm*...our list of affordable getaways

2

	1	**Mar. 1997**
PHOTOGRAPHERS		Richard Bryant, Arcaid
TEXT		Nonie Niesewand

	2	**Mar. 1997**
PHOTOGRAPHER		James Merrell
TEXT		Anoop Parikh

MAISON Française
Vol. 485 1996

EDITOR	Nadine Jarousseau
CREATIVE DIRECTOR	Jean-Pierre Marche
ART DIRECTOR	Olivier Lepage
DESIGNER	Gilles Dalliere
PHOTOGRAPHER	Christine Soler
PUBLISHER	Publications du Moniteur

France

fêtes

Champagne dans le pigeonnier du château éclairé par une multitude de lampions et par une lanterne-lyre en carton découpé (Jean-Louis Mennesson). Seau à champagne en métal argenté (Siècle) et fleurs (Baptiste pour Liliane François).

Jeu de miroirs et de lumière avec cette applique en fer laqué noir (Dick Dumas, David Hicks). Fleurs (Baptiste pour Liliane François).

LE SIÈCLE DES LUMIÈRES

*En s'inspirant du lieu et en pensant aux fêtes,
Jean-Louis Mennesson a imaginé des éclairages pour
les soupers du Régent. Ou pour nos dîners à nous.*

Vol. 485 1996

PHOTOGRAPHER   Nicolas Millet

Torsten Neeland fait partie
de la jeune garde des designers
allemands. Tendance
minimaliste. C'est pour
un médecin de Hambourg
qu'il a imaginé cet
appartement d'esthète ascète
en plein centre ville.
Du véritable "sur mesure".

Place à l'espace

R

UNE LUMIÈRE COLORÉE

Vol. 484 1996

PHOTOGRAPHER Christoph Kicherer

LE XVIIIᵉ, UN STYLE QUI A LA GRÂCE

C

Vol. 485 1996

PHOTOGRAPHER Nicolas Millet

INTERNI
Jan./Feb. 1997

EDITOR	Gilda Bojardi
ART DIRECTOR	Christoph Radl
DESIGNERS	Daniela Lambri, Daniela Nava
PHOTOGRAPHER	Miro Zagnoli
SCIENTIFIC LIBRARY PRODUCER	Molteni & C.
SCIENTIFIC LIBRARY DESIGNERS	Luca Meda, Chiara, Sofia Meda, Simone Cecchi
PUBLISHER	Elemond S.P.A.
	Italy

LE RIVISTA DELL'ARREDAMENTO

INTERNI

Abitare tra arte e design
Living with art and design
Incontro/Encounter
con/with Nino Cerruti
Morbide sedute/Soft landing

Sommario

Jan./Feb. 1997

A Carimate (Como), una casa essenziale ma ricca di sapore, con un *layout* architettonico flessibile e un progetto arredativo coerente.

In Carimate (Como), a home that is essential but full of impressions, with a flexible layout and coherent interior design.

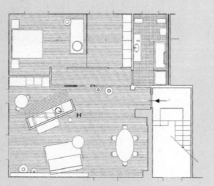

Dinamismi abitativi

progetto di/design by
Carlo Colombo
foto di/photos by
studio B.B.Emme

In questa pagina: la pianta della casa.
Nella pagina accanto: la camera da letto arredata con il sistema *Kyoto* di Carlo Colombo e il tappeto Carpet-rugs di Jasper Morrison, tutto di Cappellini.
On this page, the plan of the house.
On the facing page, the bedroom furnished with the Kyoto system by Carlo Colombo and the Carpet-rugs by Jasper Morrison, all by Cappellini.

120 Architetture d'interni

L'esperienza spaziale che la casa propone, superata la porta d'ingresso, crea un effetto di sorpresa: l'uniformità dei pavimenti in teck viene interrotta da una superficie in ceramica bianca che delimita lo sviluppo di un muro sghembo di colore blu notte. Nulla rivela la funzione di questa 'isola', posizionata in modo plastico nello spazio accogliere e minietizzare il blocco-cucina. Tutt'intorno, infatti, il paesaggio domestico è quello di un ampio soggiorno popolato di presenze diverse: mobili di produzione intimamente legati alla storia del design, oggetti d'affezione e piccoli ricordi di viaggio. Ma nella casa di Carlo Colombo il colpo d'occhio è d'obbligo: meglio dei molti prodotti da lui disegnati per diverse aziende dell'arredo, può infatti questo interno per esprimere la cifra del suo design sobrio, con un'anima vivace. "Ho ridotto l'arredo -spiega- a quanto mi occorre oggi, perché preferisco considerare la casa come un'entità che si costruisce vivendola, giorno dopo giorno". Il *layout* architettonico è stato comunque disegnato operando precise scelte, volte a consentire proprio l'espressione di un progetto arredativo in divenire. "Non volevo restasse traccia di quella tipologia

edilizia anni Settanta che aveva rigidamente determinato le funzioni abitative, all'interno di un appartamento di circa 95 mq", spiega Carlo Colombo. Così la ristrutturazione ha prodotto un'articolazione spaziale aperta, che si anima grazie a un gioco continuo di scorci visivi e di rimandi tra gli ambienti e il giardino esterno. Una dimensione fluida caratterizza la zona- notte, dove una parete mobile in legno consente di variare la superficie di due camere, secondo le necessità. Nella zona giorno questa percezione è ancora più evidente. Lì, infatti, l'effetto-corridoio prima esistente è stato annullato, demolendo due lunghi muri paralleli e sostituendoli da una parte con uno schema strutturale in metallo, lasciato a vista, dall'altro con una vetrata, scorrevole e fissa, ancorata nel pavimento, che permette una comunicazione diretta con la zona-notte. La leggerezza, la purezza e l'eleganza dell'insieme viene enfatizzata dal gioco dei contrasti compositivi: tra la fisicità eterea della partizione vetrata e l'immagine piena del muro sghembo, tra il bianco e il blu notte, positivo e negativo cromatico degli ambienti, tra il legno, l'acciaio e i tessuti, accostati in texture materiche dure e morbide. *(A.B.)*

La poltrona di casa: morbida, avvolgente, protettiva, meglio se colorata, è un vero e proprio 'miraggio' di fine giornata, che, una volta raggiunto, si trasforma in un'oasi di relax. Dalla più aggiornata vetrina della produzione emergono nuove forme sinuose, spesso accessoriate con schienali e braccioli tecnologici ed ergonomici. Il rivestimento -sempre sfoderabile- segue, nei colori e nelle finiture, i *trend* delle più attuali collezioni-moda

In poltrona, in poltrona!

foto di/*photos by*
Massimo Montagnoli
a cura di/*directed by*
Laura Ravaioli

An armchair at home. Soft, enveloping, protective, perhaps in a good colour. This is the mirage beckoning at the day's end. A mirage which becomes an oasis of comfort. From the most up-to-date showcase of production, new sinuous forms, often accessorized with technological, ergonomic backs and armrests. The covering -always removable- follows, in colors and finishes, the trends of the latest fashion collections.

Disegnata da Paolo Nava per Xom, la poltrona Saint Germain è rivestita con Trend, tessuto sfoderabile, disponibile nelle tinte unite, nei disegni e nei colori di collezione. La collezione comprende un divano due posti, un due posti grande e un tre posti, con pouf.
Designed by Paola Nava for Xom, the Saint Germain armchair uses Trend removable covers ,which can be in plain colours or in the collection's designs colours. The collection includes a two-seater sofa, a large two-seater and a three-seater, with pouf.

Jan./Feb. 1997

PHOTOGRAPHER Massimo Montagnoli

INTERIOR VIEW
Vol. 9 Jan. 1997

EDITOR	Lisa White
ART DIRECTOR	Lidewij Edelkoort
DESIGN DIRECTOR	Graham Hollick
DESIGNERS	René Knip, Patrick F van Dieren / Studio Anthon Beeke
DESIGN FIRM	United Publishers S.A.
PUBLISHER	United Publishers S.A.

France

Vol. 9 Jan. 1997

PHOTOGRAPHER   Stepman Abry

Vol. 9 Jan. 1997

PHOTOGRAPHER   Lon van Keulen
STYLIST   Graham Hollick

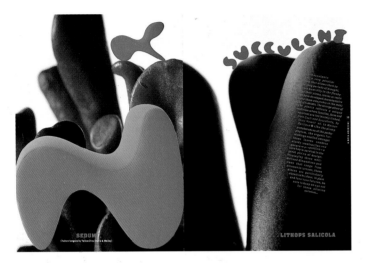

When you enter the fragrant Lush boutique your first impression is of a well-stocked delicatessen. But wait –the rounds of luscious cheeses are actually giant chunks of soaps, the iced-down salad bar is a mouth-watering selection of face masks and body scrubs, and the stacks of refrigerated chocolates are made to melt in the hands of a masseur. In fruit-and-vegetable bins are nestled a tempting range of bath ballistics that the body responds to immediately, especially the hands as they pop the colourful balls of pleasure into sweet sacks. Like food items, all of the Lush products are marked with a complete list of ingredients—minus the calorie count. Those products that correspond to the principles of a vegetarian lifestyle are clearly marked with a red V. ■ And to make matters better, packaging is kept to a minimum. The solid shampoos look as good as cookies but function like soap- no bottles necessary. The soaps themselves are cut to measure, weighed, wrapped in wax paper and closed with a price sticker. ■ "Our goal is to make good products that are effective, fresh, and have a sense of humour" explains Rowena Hofbauer, retail director of Lush. From the heavenly smell and soothing properties of the fruits, vegetables and essential oils, down to the colour of the product, everything is designed for maximum efficiency. ■ Though with the company has been making cosmetics and beauty products for over 20 years, the first Lush boutique opened in Covent Garden, London only two years ago. And its popularity has spread by word of mouth, making the four English, two Canadian and one Croatian boutiques buzz with the excitement of children in a sweet shop. Lush is still a cottage industry, however, with only 70 employees total, from the retailers to those who cook up all the products in an industrial kitchen in Dorset. But with its own quarterly newspaper, the *Lush Times*, and a mail-order service, bigger things are surely ahead. When can we expect the first Lush supermarket?

1 Massage Bars
With ingredients like cocoa butter, white and dark chocolate perfumed with a selection of peppermint oil, lavender and neroli oils, clove bud and cardamom oils, and rosemary and tarragon oils, these bars are made to melt with skin-to-skin contact. As practical as they are sensual, they have stimulated many a relationship...

2 Solid Shampoos
They look like home-made cakes and are indeed packed with fruits and vegetables, yet their solid ingredients being vitamins to your hair. They last for a very long time, don't waste space and packaging, and there is one for just about every hair type: The Poole Bar for swimmers; Dr. Peppermint for fine, falling hair; Gentle Lentil for dry hair and for children Fresh Berries for greying hair, Jumping Juniper for oily hair; and the Ultimate Shine with silver sparkles for partying. To name a few.

3 Bath Ballistics
These bath bombs dissolve with a spectacular fizz in the tub to bring you all the benefits of essential oils—plus more magical elements such as the rose petals of Tisty Tosty and the fortune numbers of Ching Ling Soo. From the wake-me-up lime oil and sea salt of the Slammer to the aphrodisiac vanilla, jasmine and vetivert essences of All that Jasmine, there is truly a ballistic for every mood...

Staff of Life Facial Exfoliator and Mask 4
Ingredients seaweed gel, kaolin, Fuller's earth, ground rice, talc, chlorophyll, lavender oil, lavender flowers, perfume.
Though recently a group of guys accidentally consumed a pot of More than Mortal Body Scrub (full of pineapple, rice and apricot kernel oil) as an after-party snack on toast (without suffering any side effects), the natural body products are truly meant for external use only. Which is easy to forget when confronted with a luscious lump of freshness.

Pineapple Grunt 5
Ingredients vegetable soap, propylene glycol, fresh pineapple, perfume, vetivert, crocin

and Honey Waffle Soaps
Ingredients vegetable soap, propylene glycol, honeycomb, ylang ylang, geranium oil, benzoin, perfume, crocin.
A monument to good washing, Cut from the most enormous, appetising rounds, the soaps are weighed and sold in wax paper like fresh cheeses. Both pineapple and honey soaps or the chunky Oatey Cakey have rough bits of fruit, wax or oatmeal that massage your body as you wash for hours–and bears. Red Rooster spice soap is so juicy red and redolent of orange and cinnamon that it takes a great deal of will-power not to pop it in your mouth for a taste.

photos by Diana Miller assisted by Lionel Acker. All glassware from the Conran Shop.

INTERIOR VIEW 9   127

CANVAS nobilis
CLUB taco
CANDY deschemaker
TICKING nina campbell
PYJAMA nina campbell
HESSIAN bisson brunest
CATALAN les toiles du soleil
TENNIS nya nordiska
KAFTAN nina campbell
TEA TOWEL les toiles du soleil
AWNING funcar
DECKCHAIR funcar

▶ key point fabrics 1997 STRIPES

top **Vol. 9 Jan. 1997**
PHOTOGRAPHER *Diana Miller*

bottom **Vol. 9 Jan. 1997**
PHOTOGRAPHER *Didier Griffoulière*

Vol. 9 Jan. 1997

PHOTOGRAPHER   *Lon van Keulen*

SUBLIME VOLUMES

Vol. 9 Jan. 1997

PHOTOGRAPHER   *Tyen*

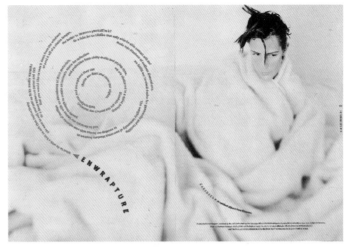

plénitude

Vol. 9 Jan. 1997

PHOTOGRAPHER   *Richard Vagnon*

Vol. 9 Jan. 1997

PHOTOGRAPHER   *Noelle Hoeppe*
STYLIST   *Nelson Sepulveda*

music
ミュージック

whaT

5   **Vol. 26 Oct. 1996**
6   **Vol. 28 Dec. 1996**

PHOTOGRAPHERS   *5 James and Matthew,*
                 6 Matthew Welch

huH
1   **Vol. 19 Mar. 1996**
2   **Vol. 20 Apr. 1996**
3   **Vol. 26 Oct. 1996**
4   **Vol. 28 Dec. 1996**

EDITOR   *Mark Blackwell*
CREATIVE DIRECTOR   *1,2 Vaughan Oliver / V23*
ART DIRECTOR   *Jerôme Curchod*
DESIGNER   *Scott Denton-Cardew*
PHOTOGRAPHERS   *1 William Hanes,*
                 2 Alison Dyer,
                 3,4 Matthew Welch
LOGO   *1 Timothy O'Donnell / V23*
DESIGN FIRM   *Ray Gun Publishing*
PUBLISHER   *Ray Gun Publishing, Inc.*
USA

1

Law Makers and Law Breakers

59

61

63

Vol. 19 Mar. 1996
CREATIVE DIRECTOR   *Vaughan Oliver / V23*
PHOTOGRAPHER   *Davies & Davies*

huH
marilyn manson

huH
this is a magazine about music. yeah. sight, whatever.

van halen

the presidents
of the united states
of america
interview by
soundgarden's
kim thayil plus a review by
first brother roger clinton

2   3   4

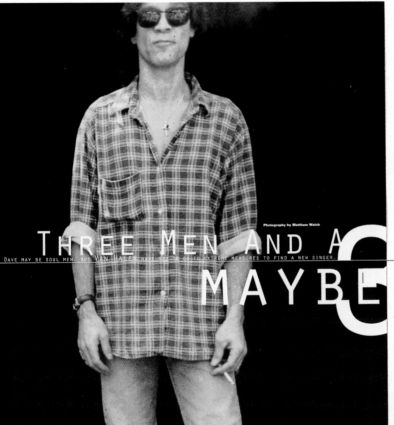

Photography by Matthew Welch

THREE MEN AND A
MAYBE

O DAVE MAY BE SOUL MEN, BUT VAN HALEN HAVE HAD A GO TO EXTREME MEASURES TO FIND A NEW SINGER,

SANDY MASUO SMOKES 'EM IF SHE'S GOT 'EM.

High up in the Hollywood Hills, beyond the marine layer hovering to the west and the smog build-up to the east, the harsh sounds of construction work intrude on the relative calm that surrounds 5150, the 24-track recording studio Eddie Van Halen built in his back yard 14 years ago.

"Right now I'm in the process of knockin' a hole out in the drum room to make it bigger," Eddie explains, having planted himself on the sofa in the comfortably air-conditioned studio lounge, pack of Camels at the ready, non-alcoholic beer in hand. An Indy 500 arcade video game sits idly to his right and a big screen to his left is silently transmitting images of real life racing. "We were experimenting and we thought we'd knock a hole out and make the drum room bigger. As soon as we're done with that then we'll start settin' up."

Now that the renowned guitarist, 41, has abandoned the beard and cropped hair he sported for the past few years, he doesn't look drastically different from the vintage photos that Warner Bros. is sending out with press information on volume one of The Best of Van Halen. His hair isn't quite as big, and it's flecked with gray and when he smiles the laugh lines are crisper, but he's still the same guitar god that Bill and Ted invoked during their excellent adventures.

Yet in person, the younger of the two Van Halen brothers seems more like one of Bill and Ted's more introverted buddies than a pop culture icon. You start to realize, as he grapples with his end of the interview that words really aren't his medium – "Music is just my way of expressing myself, the way I feel, just through notes," he says at one point – and when verbiage fails him, brother Alex, two years his senior, steps in to lend a hand. There's a certain old world sensibility about Alex beyond the faint traces of an accent that remain from the brothers' childhood in Holland. He speaks respectfully of Rod Stewart as a gentleman, and recounts the events of recent weeks as if the glove had been thrown down heralding a formal duel.

"We have an obligation to, as Ed would say, a God-given talent to make music. We also have an obligation to our audience, who we look at as more as friends than anything else, and that's why we are now responding," Alex's voice gradually takes on a purposeful, menacing edge. "There's only so much crap you can take, and I'll go on record as saying that if I hear one more lie from either Dave or Sam, I'm gonna come over to your fuckin' house and I'll kick your fuckin ass, okay? You don't talk about my family. You don't talk about my friends because I will kick your fuckin' ass. You got it?"

"And I'll be there with you," adds Eddie, seconding the emotion.

There's a certain oblique sense of irony wafting over Van Halen's official Halen's new frontman. The announcement capped off months of dramatic tension: Hagar's departure at the end of June, the studio flirtation with Roth in August that yielded two new tracks featured on the Best Of collection and the attendant titillating conjecture about a reunion tour, Van Halen's appearance with Roth at the MTV Video Awards in September (presenting an award to Beck), and speculation about Cherone – whose last album with Extreme was titled Waiting For the Punchline.

In the days following the announcement, the only people talking are Eddie and Alex. Hagar is out of communications range in Mexico for his annual birthday celebration, Cherone is declining interviews, and Roth isn't adding any comments to the open letter he sent out October 2 regarding what he concluded was his unwitting role in an elaborate Van Halen publicity stunt. In the letter he alleged that his one-time band-mates had hired a new singer prior to the MTV Music Awards and kept it from him because he had made it clear to Eddie that he did not want to appear on MTV as a band if Van Halen were not in fact reuniting. "Since neither Edward, Alex nor Michael (Anthony) have corroborated or denied the gossip," the letter reads, "I would like to go on record with the following: Eddie did it."

"We weren't saying anything at first," Eddie says.

"So far, Ed and I and Mike had decided to be complete and total gentlemen – take the high road to speak," Alex says. "There was a point in time where things got so out of wack, you know the comments and the press releases that some of these people make are so full of bullshit that we were advised that maybe we should take a little bit more of an aggressive stance. Meaning, very simply –"

"Tell the truth."

"These people were pissed off – Dave in particular," Alex explains. "There was more money thrown at the so-called reunion tour than probably the gross national product of East and West Germany put together. All right? There's no reason for us to do it for the money because the magic was not there. If it was there, and the fans and the audience would have liked it we'd have done it," Alex asserts. "But I can guarantee you it was not happening."

This seems far from the case when you listen to the two tracks that Van Halen recorded with Roth in August, "Me

Wise Magic" and "Can't Get This Stuff No More." The two songs don't so much pick up where they left off in 1985 as show off what they've both become since then. Roth's solo career might have fallen short of his glory days with Van Halen but he nevertheless has a one-of-a-kind voice and time has worn it in like a good pair of jeans – the rasp has a warmer edge, the growl a little more grit – the perfect match for the earlier vibe the band has absorbed in its years with Hagar. Unfortunately, even after ten years apart, the music still meshes better than the personalities behind it.

"There's things you can do in the studio that you can't do live," Eddie concedes, "and it's better left a memory. 'Cause if he is so concerned about the fans, he would have been there to do a video last Thursday, which he refused to do. But he would go on tour for the money, but we won't. That's not what it's about."

"Ed and I and Mike are not expecting to have somebody walk into the situation and be a puppet," Alex explains. "That's not the point at all, but if it gets to the point where things are so out of wack, where one person all of a sudden becomes so – let's say disrespectful, such as what happened during the MTV awards – you know it's time to say sorry pal, this ain't working. It's that simple."

"What's with these guys, man? They contradict themselves," Eddie says, edgy impatience creeping into his voice. "First Sammy in his own press release says he quit and then a week later he says he was fired. Make up your fuckin' mind. What was it? I mean, I know he quit. Dave says he was told that he was in the band and that's the only reason he did the MTV awards. Well four days later he did Howard Stern and said he wasn't in the band. It's just ridiculous. It's like we had to respond 'cause people are saying 'How can they both be wrong?' Well, I'm saying yes they're both fuckin' full of shit. They just are. They're both lying 'cause they're both ouching a bit."

"We prefer to remember the best of times," Alex says, resuming a more diplomatic tone. "The only reason I said what I did is because we're being pushed into a corner. But leaving that behind, every record that we have put out, there's nothing that we ever were embarrassed about, ashamed about, or that we did not do 110 percent to the best of our capabilities. And that included everybody."

In the Van Halen camp there's a clear line between personal and professional concerns. When Roth got out of hand during the MTV Music Awards and began mugging shamelessly, it was an intrusion of his own ego on a moment that was meant for the band. Likewise, Hagar's reluctance to tour seemed an indication that personal issues were infringing on his responsibility to the band. Any attempt on the part of either to justify or

33

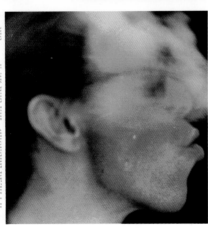

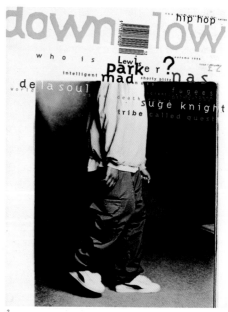

downlow
1 **Winter 1997**
2 **Autumn 1996**

EDITOR *Mat Carter*
ART DIRECTOR *Mark Diaper*
DESIGNER *Mark Diaper*
PHOTOGRAPHER *Jennie Baptiste*
DESIGN FIRM *Downlow Productions*
PUBLISHER *Downlow Productions*

U K

1

2

3

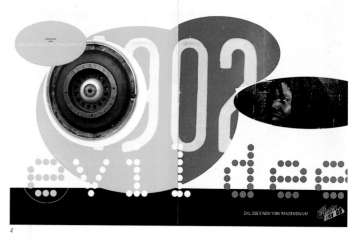

4

5

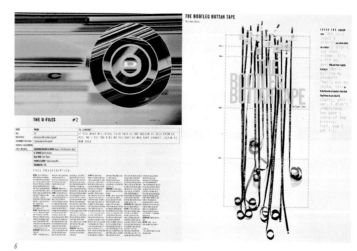

6

3 **Autumn 1996**

DESIGNER *Mark Diaper*
PHOTOGRAPHER *Alan Clarke*

5 **Winter 1997**

PHOTOGRAPHER *Jennie Baptiste*

4 **Winter 1997**

DESIGNER *Mike Davies*
PHOTOGRAPHER *Jennie Baptiste*
ILLUSTRATOR *Mike Davies*

6 **Winter 1997**

DESIGNER *Birgit Eggers*
PHOTOGRAPHER *Birgit Eggers*

1

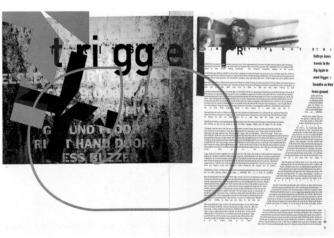

2   3

1   **Winter 1997**

DESIGNER   *Mark Diaper*
PHOTOGRAPHER   *Mark Diaper*

2   **Winter 1997**

DESIGNER   *Mark Diaper*

3   **Winter 1997**

DESIGNER   *Mark Diaper*
PHOTOGRAPHER   *Jennie Baptiste*
ILLUSTRATOR   *Mark Diaper*

BARFOUT!

BARFOUT!
1 **Vol. 19 Jan./Feb. 1997**
2 **Vol. 20 Mar. 1997**

EDITOR	*Jiro Yamazaki*
ART DIRECTOR	*Akihiro Soma*
DESIGNER	*Akihiro Soma*
PHOTOGRAPHER	*Koji Nomura*
PUBLISHER	*T.C.R.C. Co., Ltd.*
	Japan

1

2

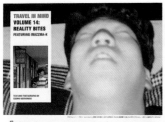

3

4

5

6

	3	**Vol. 19 Jan./Feb. 1997**
EDITOR		*Toshimitsu Aono*
ART DIRECTOR		*Akihiro Soma*
DESIGNER		*Akihiro Soma*
PHOTOGRAPHERS		*Toshimitsu Aono,*
		Akihiro Soma

	5	**Vol. 17 Oct./Nov. 1996**
EDITOR		*Koji Shimizu*
ART DIRECTOR		*Takashi Okada*
DESIGNER		*Takashi Okada*
PHOTOGRAPHER		*Noriko*
TITLE LOGO		*Masahiro Ogawa*

	4	**Vol. 19 Jan./Feb. 1997**
EDITOR		*Jiro Yamazaki*
ART DIRECTOR		*Mayumi Hirooka*
DESIGNER		*Mayumi Hirooka*
PHOTOGRAPHERS		*Karie Kahimi (left),*
		Akiyuki Terashima (right)
HAIR & MAKEUP		*Nobuaki Ehara*

	6	**Vol. 17 Oct./Nov. 1996**
EDITOR		*Jiro Yamazaki*
ART DIRECTOR		*Akihiro Soma*
DESIGNER		*Akihiro Soma*

Vol. 17 Oct./Nov. 1996

EDITOR	Toshimitsu Aono
ART DIRECTOR	Illdozer Graphuck
DESIGNER	Illdozer Graphuck
PHOTOGRAPHER	Tatsuya Kawai

Vol. 20 Mar. 1997

EDITOR	Koji Shimizu
ART DIRECTOR	Akihiro Soma
DESIGNER	Akihiro Soma
PHOTOGRAPHER	Koji Nomura
ILLUSTRATOR	Akihiro Soma

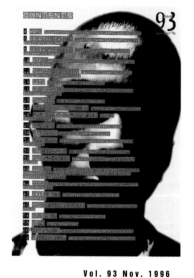

Hip-Hop Connection
Vol. 93 Nov. 1996

EDITOR	*Andy Cowan*
ART DIRECTOR	*David Houghton*
DESIGNER	*David Houghton*
PHOTOGRAPHER	*Deverill Weekes*
PUBLISHER	*Future Publishing Ltd.*

UK

Vol. 93 Nov. 1996

PHOTOGRAPHER   *Deverill Weekes*

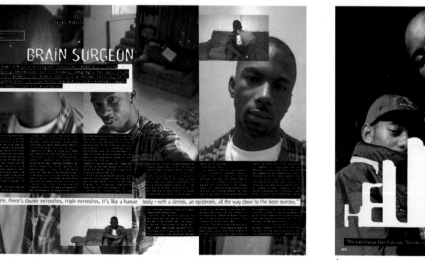

1   **Vol. 97 Mar. 1997**

PHOTOGRAPHER   *Paul Hampartsoumian*

3   **Vol. 93 Nov. 1996**

PHOTOGRAPHER   *Deverill Weekes*

2   **Vol. 92 Oct. 1996**

PHOTOGRAPHER   *Richard Reyes*

4   **Vol. 95 Jan. 1997**

PHOTOGRAPHER   *Stella Magloire*

straight no chaser
1 **Vol. 38 Autumn 1996**
2 **Vol. 39 Winter 1996**

EDITOR *Paul Bradshaw*
ART DIRECTOR *Swifty*
DESIGNER *Swifty*
PHOTOGRAPHER *Pav Modelski*
DESIGN FIRM *Swifty Typografix*
PUBLISHER *S.N.C.*

UK

3 **Vol. 35 Spring 1996**

EDITORS *Paul Bradshaw,*
Kathryn Willgress
DESIGNER *Fred Deakin*
PHOTOGRAPHER *Jonathan Oppong Wiafe*

5 **Vol. 36 Spring/Summer 1996**

EDITORS *Paul Bradshaw,*
Kathryn Willgress
DESIGNER *Swifty*
PHOTOGRAPHER *Pav Modelski*

4 **Vol. 38 Autumn 1996**

EDITORS *Paul Bradshaw,*
Kathryn Willgress
DESIGNER *Swifty*
PHOTOGRAPHER *Jonathan Oppong Wiafe*

6 **Vol. 37 Summer 1996**

EDITORS *Paul Bradshaw,*
Kathryn Willgress
DESIGNER *Swifty*
PHOTOGRAPHER *Jean Bernard Sohiez*

SPIN

| 1 | **Nov. 1996** |
| 2 | **Dec. 1996** |

EDITOR	*Craig Marks*
ART DIRECTOR	*Bruce Ramsay*
DESIGNER	*Bruce Ramsay*
PHOTOGRAPHERS	*1 Joshua Jordan,*
	2 Schoerner
PHOTO EDITOR	*Nancy Leopardi*
PUBLISHER	*Camouflage*
	Associates
	U S A

1

2

Nov. 1996

EDITOR	*Craig Marks*
PHOTOGRAPHER	*Joshua Jordan*

Painspotting The eels overcome their infinite sadness with some slippery pop. Photography by Tara.

Eel people, from left, Tommy Walter, Butch Norton, and Mark "E" Edwards.

Dec. 1996

EDITOR
Lee Smith

DESIGNER
John Giordani

PHOTOGRAPHER
Tara

brother from another planet

Dec. 1996

EDITOR   *Eric Weisbard*

PHOTOGRAPHER   *Ruven Afanador*

PHOTO EDITOR   *Bruce Ramsay*

With the masterpiece *Maxinquaye* and the new *Pre-Millennium Tension*, Tricky has become pop's most enigmatic genius, turning hip-hop into a hall of mirrors. Chris Norris goes off to see the Wizard.

Photographs by Ruven Afanador.

Tired of shabby skate and snowboard clothes for girls, a new wave of fed-up females have taken matters into their own hands. By Sia Michel.

Photographs by Einar Snorri and Eidur Snorri.

Dec. 1996

EDITOR
Craig Marks

PHOTOGRAPHERS
*Einar Snorri,
Eidur Snorri*

169

wax

1 **Vol. 7 Oct. 1996**
2 **Vol. 11 Feb. 1997**

EDITOR   *Anna Smith*
ART DIRECTOR   *Paul Gaines*
DESIGNERS   *1 Paul Gaines,*
                  2 Casa Hamid
PHOTOGRAPHERS   *1 Brian Sweeney,*
                  1 Dave Swindells,
                  2 Paddy Cook
PUBLISHER   *Mark Allen Publishing Ltd.*

UK

1

2

Feature

It's midnight at Athens airport. I'm with Darren from Matsuri Records - and we're two hours late, due to check out Japanese DJ/producer Tsuyoshi Suzuki at a club tonight. We're anxiously awaiting the promoter to take us there, but there's no sign of any trancers... shit, we don't even know where the club is. Then, after accosting several confused young men, we spot a six foot shaven-headed guy in a fluorescent yellow top. We don't even need to ask.

This is George, the promoter, who takes us to the hotel where we meet Tsuyoshi. Short and stylish, Tsuyoshi is easy to spot. What on anyone else would be a rather odd little goatee looks positively brilliant on his striking face, and he wears his flares and tight fitting t-shirt with a typically Japanese sense of style.

He and his friend DJ Keisuke - similarly groovily attired - greet me warmly. Tsuyoshi is immediately friendly and chatty - already setting himself apart from other "name" DJs by his habit of asking you questions with genuine interest, rather than just answering them.

We should be going to the club - but one of the world's most popular psychedelic DJs is hungry, so who are we to argue? Our party - including Sonia

complete with enormous mushrooms and lots of podiums. The crowd of Greek trancers are rather conservatively dressed compared to their British counterparts - more white shirts than tie-dye tops - but there's plenty of them. Even a few days after New Year, Tsuyoshi can pack 'em in.

At 3am, Manmademan take to the stage. As the couple bob behind their computer and mixing desk, their psychedelic sounds energise the watching crowd. We dance for an hour to their continuously mixed screaming trance. This is how a good trance PA should be - the music attracts more attention than the visual experience, everyone is dancing rather than staring blankly at the stage.

Then Tsuyoshi takes to the decks, beginning his four hour set with storming techno. Fans come intermittently to hang around the DJ booth, gazing in admiration. As time passes, the crowd starts to really warm up - things start off pretty late over here - and by 6am they're bouncing as Tsuyoshi carefully peppers his psychedelic techno with popular trance stormers.

A few more characters begin emerging in the crowd.

enormous meal. Tsuyoshi is cheerful and lively, though a little disappointed that they don't do rice.

He's falling asleep on the way back in the car, which I find a little disconcerting, given that we are due to do the interview on arrival back at the hotel. We've established that he's more comfortable having a chat than a strict interview format, so when he's woken up we join the others to chill in front of some Greek TV - which to our surprise has a station showing trance videos. We feel quite at home.

A natural topic of conversation is the growing popularity of the trance scene. While Tsuyoshi may be benefiting from it, he's anxious not to sell out. "What I can do is be careful that my music doesn't become cheesy," he says. "Even at Return to the Source me and Mark Allen play completely new stuff. It's not really hard stuff - but it's not commercial or anything. It keeps it fresh - no one's heard it before."

So what about DJs who play the poppier side of trance, like Paul Oakenfold and Danny Rampling? "They have to get commercial," he concedes. "This is their mission. But it's not my style. I can't release what I don't

> 'I can't relea[se]
> what I don't l[ike]
> for the mon[ey.]
> It's not my sty[le]'

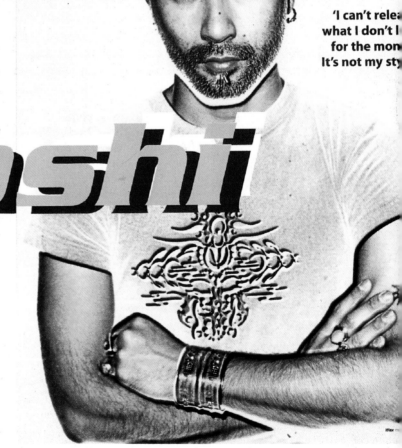

If there's one star in the trance scene, it's Tsuyoshi Suzuki. Anna Smith caught him on his psychedelic travels in Greece

Tsuyoshi

Photography **Paddy Cook, Danielle'a Buntman, Anna Smith, Vicki Couchman**

and Paul, aka Manmademan - head for a fast food joint. Tsuyoshi may be famous, but burgers are not beneath him. The only giveaway is when he asks the confused girl behind the counter to bring his food to the table.

Chips are downed and we set off for the club. Also, on the outskirts of a forest. The place is a fluoro haven,

including a groovy Hungarian Wax reader. There aren't too many dilated pupils about, possibly because a recent police crackdown in Athens has warned that promoters will be thrown in jail if any drugs are found on their premises. This really is a test for a DJ, and looking at the still busy dancefloor, I'd say Tsuyoshi had passed with flying colours.

I haven't spent much time with Tsuyoshi tonight, but not to worry, George has promised us a Greek meal the next night which, apparently, "we will never forget in all our lives." He's not one for understatement. As we set off, Tsuyoshi tentatively enquires if there are any Japanese restaurants in Athens, but sensitively acknowledges: "Another time." We're led into a cavernous traditional restaurant for an

like, I can't release for the money. That's the most important thing."

When I ask how he felt his set went down last night, he sighs. "I think it's the police problem and all that. Difficult. When I see this kind of club it makes me feel like I have to play a big hit track every track otherwise they don't dance." This man has clearly seen some good parties.

"I prefer to play outside to a club, under the sun," he admits. "It's just the vibe and everything. If you stay the whole of the winter time in Europe sometimes you can realize how much difference it makes. Everybody's smiling."

But there's not much danger of Tsuyoshi staying in one place for long. He's played Paris for New Year, and is going to Canada in a few days - followed by numerous other gigs away from his London home which he shares with wife Veronica, his partner John Perloff and Alison who also works for Matsuri.

"This year I'm trying not to book so much," he says wearily. "I used to play four times a week, like each in a different country. Thursday Amsterdam, after that France, after that Israel, maybe coming back to London to play, it's a bit too much. Maybe I've done a little bit

Vol. 11 Feb. 1997

ART DIRECTOR   *Paul Gaines*
DESIGNER   *Paul Gaines*
PHOTOGRAPHER   *Paddy Cook*

ART DIRECTOR Paul Gaines
DESIGNER Paul Gaines

ART DIRECTOR Paul Gaines
DESIGNER Casa Hamid

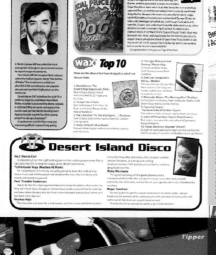

Vol. 11 Feb. 1997

ART DIRECTOR Paul Gaines
DESIGNER Casa Hamid

Vol. 7 Oct. 1996

ART DIRECTOR Dominic Rutterford
DESIGNER Dominic Rutterford

PREMIERE (FRENCH)

1	**Mar. 1997**
2	**Feb. 1997**

EDITOR	*Alain Kruger*
CREATIVE DIRECTOR	*Agnes Cruz*
ART DIRECTOR	*Marie Laure Cruz*
PHOTOGRAPHERS	*1 Stéphane Sednaoui,*
	2 Michel Figuet
PUBLISHER	*Hachette Filipacchi*
	Presse
	France

1   *2*

Mercredi 22 janvier 97. La nuit tombe sur Hollywood déjà gris sous l'orage. Le mythique Château-Marmont, tel le château du comte Dracula, surplombe toujours Sunset Boulevard. La pluie gouttant sur ses angles rappelle, au choix, l'antre de la famille Addams ou celle d'Edward aux mains d'argent. On comprend pourquoi Tim Burton et sa compagne et belle Martienne Lisa Marie y ont élu domicile. Nous débarquons avec quelques accessoires de *Mars Attacks!* «volés» dans l'après-midi à la Warner. Pendant le déchargement, Rosanna Arquette déboule avec son énorme 4 x 4 noir et manque de nous écrabouiller sans même s'en apercevoir. Dans la cuisine, Lisa Marie se laisse

Les Martiens attakkks!

Tim Burton nous réconcilie avec les envahisseurs.

maquiller, coiffer, pomponner pendant deux heures par ceux qui l'ont déjà transformée en Martienne pour *Mars Attacks!* Tim débarque enfin, avec leur chihuahua du Japon (lui aussi star dans le film). Les blagues fusent sur le quadrupède miniature arpentant hystériquement mais prudemment chaque recoin et chaque occupant de la pièce. Un Martien est suspendu au plafond, et la chaîne hi-fi, seule rescapée du chambardement, crache les remix métalliques de Björk sous les spots éblouissants, rouges, verts et blancs de Stéphane Sednaoui. Tim et Lisa s'assoient silencieusement devant une télé éteinte; ils se sussurrent des mots doux et se lancent des clins d'œil. La veille, Tim nous avait parlé de son dernier film, né d'une série de cartes à collectionner des années 60, l'occasion pour lui de conjuguer son talent de dessinateur (il a débuté chez Disney) avec sa sympathie pour «le plus mauvais réalisateur du monde» et héros de son film précédent: Ed Wood. ▶

Interview Jacques-André **Bondy**
Photos Stéphane **Sednaoui**

Pendant que Stéphane shoote, Lisa bisque Tim.

54

PREMIERE / Mars 1997

Mar. 1997

PHOTOGRAPHER   *Stéphane Sednaoui*

Woody Allen n'est pas spécialement nain. Pourtant, dans cet immense canapé, sous le tableau gigantesque de ce très grand salon du Ritz, son attitude craintive comme à l'accoutumée lui donne l'air d'un pauvre petit garçon riche qu'on aurait puni et qui attendrait, les jambes pendantes, la fin de son piquet. Surprise: le petit garçon commence par nous engueuler, même si «engueuler» est un mot gros... «Parlez plus fort, s'il vous plaît», murmure-t-il d'une voix à peine audible. Une voix blanche qui, à propos, est l'héroïne du jour puisque, dans son 28ᵉ long métrage, plus aérien que jamais, Woody chante! Ce qui n'est qu'une demi-surprise puisque *Tout le monde dit I love you* est une comédie musicale. Une comédie musicale? ▶

Interview **Diastème & Jean-Yves Katelan**
Photos **Antoine Le Grand**

Tout le monde WOODY I love you

64 PREMIERE / Février 1997

PITT AU TOP

Héros de "Seven", polar déchiqueté et renversant, Brad Pitt est devenu, en moins de cinq ans, l'acteur le mieux coté d'Hollywood. Mais pourquoi lui?

PAR / DIASTEME
PHOTOS / PETER SOREL

Brad Pitt dîne dans un restau indien avec sa compagne Gwyneth Paltrow. New York est sous un mètre de neige, et après quelques jours à Belfast, il tourne *The Devil's Own* sous la direction d'Alan Pakula. Il y interprète un terroriste de l'IRA qui débarque chez un flic newyorkais joué par Harrison Ford. Depuis *Seven*, Brad a fini deux autres films. Le premier est *L'Armée des 12 singes*, de Terry Gilliam (sortie française le 28 février) avec Bruce Willis et Madeleine Stowe, dans lequel il interprète le rôle d'un garçon perturbé, très éloigné de ses précédentes performances. «A priori, ce n'était pas un rôle pour moi. Les gens ne savent pas de quoi vous êtes capable tant que vous ne le leur avez pas montré. J'ai donc voulu rencontrer Terry afin qu'il me donne ma chance. Et il me l'a donnée. Je lui en suis très reconnaissant parce que lui se fout d'avoir des vedettes dans ses films. Ce qu'il veut, c'est travailler avec les meilleurs acteurs possibles.» Le second film est *Sleepers*, de Barry Levinson dans lequel Brad a pour partenaires De Niro, Hoffman, Gassman (il y joue un jeune avocat chargé de défendre quatre enfants martyrs) ▶

William Bradley, dit Brad Pitt.
Né le 18 décembre 1963
à Shawnee, Oklahoma, USA.

top	**Feb. 1997**	*bottom*	**Feb. 1997**
PHOTOGRAPHER	Antoine Le Grand	PHOTOGRAPHER	Peter Sorel

1

PREMIERE (USA)

1	**Feb. 1997**
2	**Apr. 1997**

EDITOR	James B.Meigs
ART DIRECTOR	David Matt
DESIGNER	David Matt
PHOTOGRAPHERS	1 Firooz Zahedi,
	2 George Holz
PUBLISHER	Premiere Publishing Company, LLC

USA

2

Runaway, stripper, drug abuser, rock widow.
With her performance in 'The People Vs. Larry Flynt,' Courtney
Love has become Hollywood's latest infatuation

By Holly Millea   Photographed by Firooz Zahedi

Feb. 1997

EDITOR	James B.Meigs
DESIGNER	David Matt
PHOTOGRAPHER	Firooz Zahedi

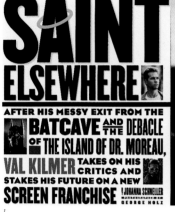

SAINT ELSEWHERE

AFTER HIS MESSY EXIT FROM THE **BATCAVE** AND THE **DEBACLE** OF THE **ISLAND OF DR. MOREAU**, **VAL KILMER** TAKES ON HIS **CRITICS** AND STAKES HIS FUTURE ON A NEW **SCREEN FRANCHISE** by JOHANNA SCHNELLER PHOTO GEORGE HOLZ

1

Hollywoodland

The Naked City

Resident 'Alien'

Stewart Conspires With Gibson

2

A Time to Thrill

PHOTOGRAPHED BY FIROOZ ZAHEDI
by Kristen O'Neill

As she comes to grips with sudden superstardom and sex symbol status, a blooming Sandra Bullock faces life beyond the Girl Next Door

'There she is! There she is!' A gaggle of two dozen backpacked four-year-old tourists stands each other method-ly and jockey for position behind a wooden barricade, staring past the trailers, video monitors, and a tempting catering truck that line a narrow beachside street in Ventura County, about 60 miles north of Los Angeles. Sandra Bullock...

3

Birds of a Feather

Whether it's jobing with Christopher Reeve or sending up Barbara Bush, ROBIN WILLIAMS & NATHAN LANE —the loving couple of The Birdcage— share a willingness to do anything for a laugh by BRUCE BIBBY

4

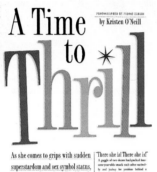

Yearning for KEANU

In which Courtney Love, Cameron Diaz, and your intrepid reporter seek access to the mind of the mercurial heartthrob
BY JOHN H. RICHARDSON

5

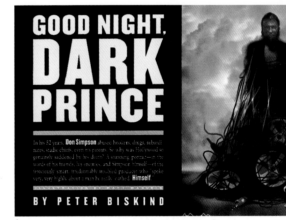

GOOD NIGHT, DARK PRINCE

In his 52 years, Don Simpson abused hookers, drugs, school mates, studio chiefs, even his parents. So why was Hollywood so genuinely saddened by his death? A stunning portrait—in the words of his friends, his enemies, and Simpson himself—of the ferociously smart, irredeemably troubled producer who spoke very, very highly about a man he rarely called Himself

BY PETER BISKIND

6

appetite
Vol. 1 1996

EDITOR   *Sharyn Storrier Lyneham*
ART DIRECTORS   *Stephen Scoble,*
                  Angela Shellshear
PHOTOGRAPHER   *Guy Aroch*
FEATURES EDITOR   *Natalie Filatoff*
FOOD & WINE EDITOR *Sue Fairlie-Cuninghame*
CONSULTING EDITOR *Antonia Williams*
PUBLISHER   *Condé Nast Publications*
                  Pty. Ltd.

Australia

1   **Vol. 1 1996**

EDITOR   *Sharyn Storrier Lyneham*
DESIGNER   *Vanessa Holden*
PHOTOGRAPHER *William Meppem*

2   **Vol. 1 1996**

EDITOR   *Sue Fairlie-Cuninghame*
PHOTOGRAPHER *Petrina Tinslay*
ILLUSTRATOR   *Chris Long*

feeding friendzy

AT THE BEGINNING OF THE WEEK CAMERON PRINCE
GATHERS HIS FRIENDS AROUND FOR AN INFORMAL MEAL,
A FEW DRINKS AND A CATCH-UP ON RECENT EVENTS.

1

dinner
marlin neck curry
yellow fin curry
duck in red curry
steamed jasmine rice
cold beer

listening to the soft 'n' sexy sound
(dave graney and the coral snakes)
highlights from the pluggsd series
(miles davis)

Come Monday or Tuesday you'll find a flock of
friends at Cameron's for dinner. What the flock
depends "on what's available at that time."
Cameron's dog Andre – "he basically
would never call a dog something."
Such a regular guest. A real personality, if
the sign of a culinary mind, left, Cameron's busy
198 putting together the marlin neck curry, above.

2

HOW TO

cutting comments about **lamb**

CARVING A ROASTED LEG OF LAMB
ISN'T AS TRICKY AS YOU MIGHT
THINK. THIS SIMPLE GUIDE WILL HELP
YOU CUT THROUGH THE RED MEAT.

KNIFE POINTS
• Use the correct knife for the job. For a leg of lamb you should use
a carving knife, also known as a slicer. It's long and slender with a
slightly flexible blade up to about 25cm in length, which allows for
controlled slicing around the leg bone.
• Always use a quality, sharp carving knife. Concentrate and keep
your eye on the job.
• After use, hand wash knife in soapy water. The heat from a dish-
washer will retemper the steel and make it brittle and liable to break.
• The best sharpening steels are those with a large, flat surface.

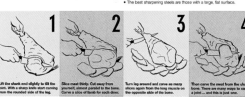

1 Lift the shank end slightly to tilt the
joint. With a sharp knife start carving
from the rounded side of the leg.

2 Slice meat thinly. Cut away from
yourself, almost parallel to the bone.
Carve a slice of lamb for each diner.

3 Turn leg around and carve as many
slices again from the long muscle on
the opposite side of the bone.

4 Then carve the meat from the shank
bone. There are many ways to carve
a joint ... and this is just one.

the best lamb baa none
(serves 8 to 10)
1 whole leg of lamb (chump and shank intact) about 2.75kg
½ cup rosemary sprigs
1 x 50g tin of oil-cured anchovies, drained
3 to 4 cloves garlic, peeled and quartered
50ml olive oil
freshly ground black pepper
1½ tablespoons balsamic vinegar

To cook the lamb: preheat the oven to 200°C. With a small, sharp knife,
cut about 12 small shallow incisions evenly over the surface of the lamb.
Push 1 anchovy fillet, 1 sprig of rosemary and 1 sliver of garlic into each
pocket. Brush the surface of the lamb liberally with olive oil and grind over
some black pepper. Put the lamb in a heavy baking tin and place on the
centre shelf of the oven. Roast the lamb for 1¼-1½ hours depending
on the desired degree of doneness, turning the pan each 20 minutes
and drizzling with the balsamic vinegar after 1 hour. When the lamb is
cooked to your taste, remove from the oven to a warm plate and set
aside to rest for 10 minutes.

To serve the lamb: carve the lamb according to the diagrams (above)
and serve on warm plates, accompanied by sautéed or roasted potatoes
or roasted capsicums, grilled or fried polenta, and mint pesto.
Lamb has a unique, delicious flavour. It is economical and easy to cook
for a family and large numbers, and is very good cold the next day.

appetite for a good carving
knife. Chefs' Warehouse
buyer, David Furley's personal
preferences include slicers
from Sabatier, F. Dick and
Henkels. Pictured from top:
Victorinox 20cm, $42.50,
Sabatier 'Lion'
20cm, $68, F. Dick
20cm, $92, Trident
'Grand Prix' 20cm, $117,
Global 24cm, $165. All knives
from Chefs' Warehouse,
Surry Hills, NSW 2010.

...duce our series on behaviour in the workplace, Appetite
...a look at the big picture of corporate and personal values.

CORPORATE
dilemmas

what a slice

ST KILDA'S CAFE A TAGLIO PUTS AN
AUTHENTIC SLANT ON THE HUMBLE
PIECE OF PIZZA. MELBURNIANS IN
THEIR DROVES ARE ABANDONING
'TROPICANA' AND 'SUPREME' IN
FAVOUR OF THE ORIGINAL FLAVOURS
OF THE MEDITERRANEAN.

leaning towards a pizza?

> "Offices are places
> of pressure, of *stress
> and strain*, of great hopes
> and bitter disappointments.
> They are also places
> where people *fall in love*,
> or think they fall in love,
> where they become jealous,
> sullen, *paranoid, slovenly,*
> *irascible*, irrational and
> apparently irremovable …
> *A code of manners …*
> helps to regulate how
> people behave in an
> office setting."
>
> *Debrett's Guide to Business Etiquette (Headline, $19.95.)*

True or False?

position vacant:

MAKE THE MOST OF AN INTERVIEW TO ENSURE THIS
IS A JOB YOU REALLY WANT.

VOL. 1 1996

EDITOR · Sharyn Storrier Lyneham
DESIGNER · Vanessa Holden
PHOTOGRAPHER · Arthur Elgort / German Vogue

VOL. 1 1996

EDITOR · Sharyn Storrier Lyneham
DESIGNER · Vanessa Holden
PHOTOGRAPHER · Monty Coles
CO-ORDINATOR · Virginia Dowzer

NEW YORK

1 **Jan. 13, 1997**
2 **Feb. 17, 1997**

DESIGN DIRECTOR Robert Newman
DESIGNERS 1 Florian Bachleda,
2 Robert Newman
PHOTOGRAPHERS 1 Ruven Afanador,
2 Danny Clinch
PHOTO EDITORS 1,2 Margery Goldberg,
2 Sabine Meyer
PUBLISHER K-III Magazine Co.

USA

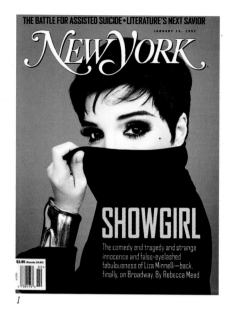

1

2

3

4

5

3 **Feb. 17, 1997**

DESIGNER Robert Newman
PHOTOGRAPHER Danny Clinch
PHOTO EDITORS Margery Goldberg,
Sabine Meyer

4 **Jan. 20, 1997**

DESIGNERS Jennifer Gilman,
Robert Newman
ILLUSTRATOR Owen Smith

5 **Dec. 23-30 1996**

DESIGNER Andrea Dunham
ILLUSTRATOR Istvan Banyai

14 × 2

Fourteenth Street, Manhattan's melting pot and great divide, is also a romantic promenade. Here are ten pairs who happily show the world their love. Photographed by Christian Witkin

movies

Model Behavior

Toy soldiers, pin-up dolls, and cowboys and Indians make serious social commentary in photographer David Levinthal's captivating tableaux at ICP (page 82)

nightlife

1,2,4   Jan. 20, 1997

DESIGNER   Pino Impastato
PHOTOGRAPHER   1 David Levinthal
PHOTO EDITOR   Yvonne Stender

3   Jan. 26, 1997

DESIGNER   Pino Impastato
PHOTOGRAPHERS   Jay Blakesburg, Bernd Avers
PHOTO EDITOR   Yvonne Stender

Dec. 23–30, 1996

DESIGNER   Florian Bachleda
PHOTOGRAPHER   Christian Witkin
PHOTO EDITOR   Margery Goldberg

Esquire

1　Feb. 1997
2　Mar. 1997

EDITORS　　　1 Tim Hulse
　　　　　　　2 Peter Howarth
ART DIRECTOR　Christophe Gowans
DESIGNER　　　Christophe Gowans
PHOTOGRAPHERS　1 Davies & Davies,
　　　　　　　2 Alex Sarginson
PUBLISHER　　National Magazine Co., Ltd.

UK

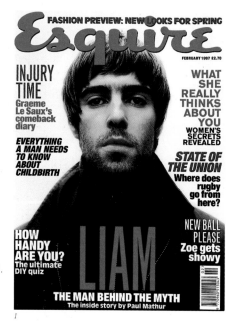

1

2

3

4

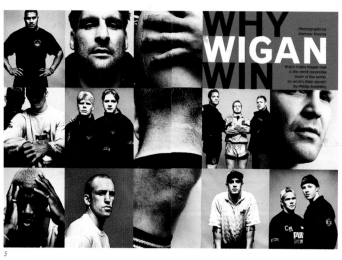

5

6

3　Dec./Jan. 1996-97

EDITOR　　　　Rosie Boycott
DESIGNER　　　Christophe Gowans

5　Dec./Jan. 1996-97

EDITOR　　　　Rosie Boycott
DESIGNER　　　Christophe Gowans
PHOTOGRAPHER　Andrew Shaylor

4　Dec./Jan. 1996-97

EDITOR　　　　Rosie Boycott
DESIGNER　　　Christophe Gowans
PHOTOGRAPHER　Dan Burn Forti

6　Mar. 1997

EDITOR　　　　Peter Howarth
DESIGNER　　　Christophe Gowans
PHOTOGRAPHER　Tom Dobbie

THIS MONTH, TOMMY HILFIGER'S
MENSWEAR BECOMES AVAILABLE IN
BRITAIN FOR THE FIRST TIME

WE COULDN'T HELP BUT NOTICE AT
TOMMY'S SPRING '97 MENSWEAR FASHION
SHOW, HIS FIRST EVER IN LONDON, THAT
ONE MAN IN THE AUDIENCE RECEIVED A
HIGH FIVE FROM AMERICA'S MASTER OF
SPORTSWEAR AS HE TOOK HIS RUNWAY
CALL – OUR VERY OWN MASTER OF
DRUM 'N' BASS, GOLDIE. SO, WHEN WE
WERE LOOKING FOR A MODEL TO PREVIEW
TOMMY'S NEW BRIT-BOUND COLLECTION,
THERE REALLY WAS ONLY ONE OPTION.
HERE, THEN, SHOWING HILFIGER'S NEW
COMMITMENT TO TAILORED CASUALWEAR,
IS BRITAIN'S MOST NOTORIOUS DJ AND
ALL-ROUND 14-CARAT GEEZER

GOLDFIGER

PHOTOGRAPHS BY FABIO CHIZZOLA
FASHION BY OLIVIA POMP

*Opposite page, white
double-breasted
cotton suit, made to
order; white cotton
shirt, £35, both by
Tommy Hilfiger.
This page, grey silk
printed shirt; black
satin trousers,
both to order, by
Tommy Hilfiger*

*This page, James Sleaford, stylist, wears
black herringbone cashmere coat, £1,719, by
Gianfranco Ferré. Black ribbed roll-neck
sweater, £115, by Joseph Homme.
Opposite page, Harland Miller, artist, wears
black cotton trench coat, £398, and black
wool flat-fronted trousers, £170, both by
José Lévy à Paris. Black cashmere roll-neck,
£181, by Pringle of Scotland. Black leather
slip-on boots, £81, by Jones Bootmaker*

Photographs by Ben Ingham. Fashion by Olivia Pomp

PAINT IT BLACK

top	**Mar. 1997**	
EDITOR	Peter Howarth	
ART DIRECTORS	Christophe Gowans,	
	Olivia Pomp	
DESIGNER	Ian Pendleton	
PHOTOGRAPHER	Fabio Chizzola	

bottom	**Nov. 1996**
EDITOR	Rosie Boycott
ART DIRECTORS	Christophe Gowans,
	Olivia Pomp
DESIGNER	Christophe Gowans
PHOTOGRAPHER	Ben Ingham

Men's Journal

1 **Feb. 1997**
2 **Jun./Jul. 1996**

EDITOR	John Rasmus
ART DIRECTOR	David Armario
DESIGNER	David Armario
PHOTOGRAPHER	2 George Holz
PHOTO EDITOR	1 Denise Sfraga
DESIGN FIRM	Men's Journal
PUBLISHER	Wenner Media Inc.

USA

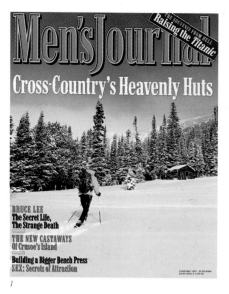

1

2

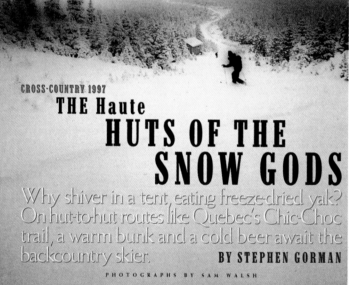

CROSS-COUNTRY 1997

THE Haute
HUTS OF THE
SNOW GODS

Why shiver in a tent, eating freeze-dried yak?
On hut-to-hut routes like Quebec's Chic-Choc
trail, a warm bunk and a cold beer await the
backcountry skier.   BY STEPHEN GORMAN

PHOTOGRAPHS BY SAM WALSH

63
MEN'S JOURNAL, FEBRUARY 1997

hands

FE THEY'VE LED.
THE STORIES THEY KNOW

By Barry Lopez
PHOTOGRAPHS BY KURT MARKUS

ESCAPE

FROM

KASHMIR

In 1995,
two American trekkers were taken hostage by rebels in the Indian high country.
One got away.

By Sebastian Junger
ILLUSTRATIONS BY JOHN COLLIER
PORTRAITS BY DAN WINTERS

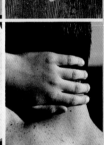

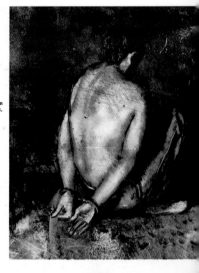

the slow petting
OF THE LOVED DOG IS THE INCREASINGLY
COMPLICATED HEART SPEAKING WITH THE HAND.

**Childs, a chemical engineer,
was used to solving problems. This was just another one: how to escape from
16 men with machine guns.**

i marveled at the hands
R CREATURES, AT THE ELEGANT AND
INCONTROVERTIBLE BEAUTY OF THEIR DESIGN.

AVOIDING DANGER ABROAD

**"It was like a dream where
you run and run and you're not getting anywhere," says Childs. "I thought I was in
cross hairs the whole tim**

Dec./Jan. 1996-97

DESIGNERS — David Armario,
Tom Brown
PHOTOGRAPHER — Kurt Markus

Apr. 1997

ART DIRECTORS — David Armario,
Tom Brown
DESIGNERS — David Armario,
Tom Brown
ILLUSTRATOR — John Collier
PHOTOGRAPHER — Dan Winters
PHOTO EDITOR — Denise Sfraga

opposite page **Feb. 1997**

PHOTOGRAPHER — Sam Walsh
ILLUSTRATOR — Ross Macdonald
PHOTO EDITOR — Denise Sfraga

LIFE
1 Nov. 1996
2 Feb. 1997

EDITORS	1 Dan Okrent, 2 Jay Lovinger
ART DIRECTOR	Tom Bentkowski
DESIGNER	Tom Bentkowski
PHOTOGRAPHERS	1 Lennart Nilsson, 2 Alexander Tsiaris
PUBLISHER	Time Inc.
	USA

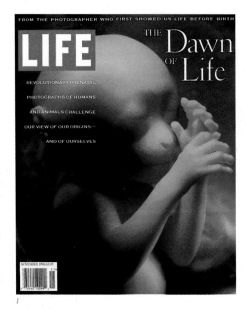

FROM THE PHOTOGRAPHER WHO FIRST SHOWED US LIFE BEFORE BIRTH

LIFE
THE Dawn OF Life

REVOLUTIONARY PRENATAL
PHOTOGRAPHS OF HUMANS
AND ANIMALS CHALLENGE
OUR VIEW OF OUR ORIGINS—
AND OF OURSELVES

1

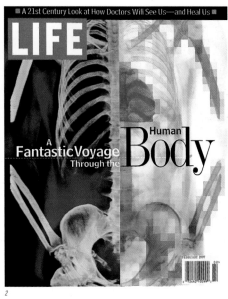

■ A 21st Century Look at How Doctors Will See Us—and Heal Us ■

LIFE

A FantasticVoyage Through the Human Body

2

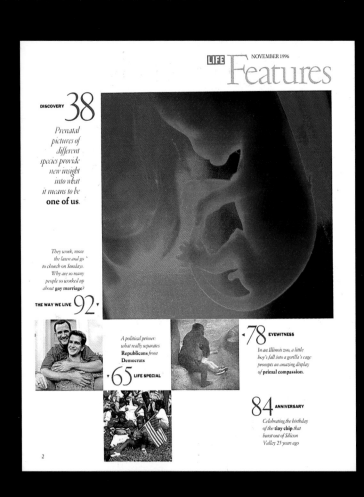

LIFE NOVEMBER 1996
Features

DISCOVERY 38
Prenatal
pictures of
different
species provide
new insight
into what
it means to be
one of us.

They work, mow
the lawn and go
to church on Sundays.
Why are so many
people so worked up
about gay marriage.

THE WAY WE LIVE 92

A political primer:
what really separates
Republicans from
Democrats

65 LIFE SPECIAL

78 EYEWITNESS
In an Illinois zoo, a little
boy's fall into a gorilla's cage
prompts an amazing display
of primal compassion.

84 ANNIVERSARY
Celebrating the birthday
of the tiny chip that
burst out of Silicon
Valley 25 years ago

2

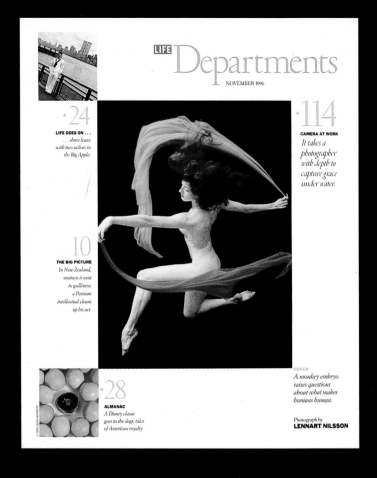

LIFE Departments
NOVEMBER 1996

24
LIFE GOES ON . . .
. . . shore leave
with two sailors in
the Big Apple.

10
THE BIG PICTURE
In New Zealand,
sootness is next
to godliness;
a Parisian
intellectual cleans
up his act.

28
ALMANAC
A Disney classic
goes to the dogs; tales
of American royalty.

114
CAMERA AT WORK
It takes a
photographer
with depth to
capture grace
under water.

COVER:
A monkey embryo
raises questions
about what makes
humans human.

Photograph by
LENNART NILSSON

Nov. 1996

EDITOR	Dan Okrent
DESIGNER	Jean Andreuzzi
PHOTOGRAPHER	Lennart Nilsson (main image)

Nov. 1996

EDITOR	Dan Okrent
DESIGNER	Jean Andreuzzi
PHOTOGRAPHER	Howard Schatz (main image)

Thirty-one years ago, LIFE published Lennart Nilsson's startling photographs of the human embryo—the first-ever images of life before birth. Now Nilsson has created the first prenatal multispecies family album. These pictures pose a fundamental question WHAT DOES IT MEAN TO BE

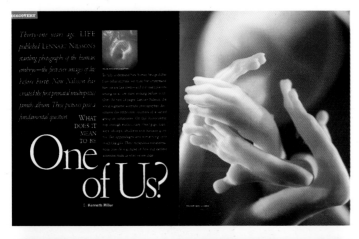

One of Us?

E. Kenneth Miller

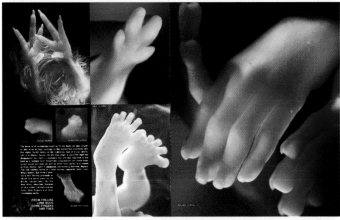

FROM FILM-LIKE LIMB BUDS COME FINGERS AND TOES

Nov. 1996

EDITOR   *Dan Okrent*
DESIGNER   *Tom Bentkowski*
PHOTOGRAPHER   *Lennart Nilsson*

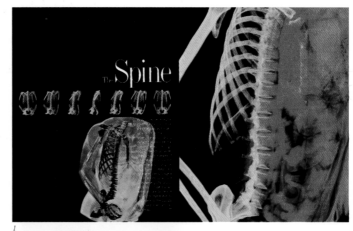

The Spine

1

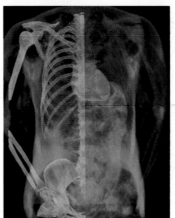

It races with fear, hammers in anger, throbs with love. No wonder the ancient Hebrews believed that this one-pound, fist-size organ was the seat of thought and emotion.

The Heart

2

The Visible Man

The execution and electronic afterlife of Joseph Paul Jernigan

3

Feb. 1997

EDITOR   *Jay Lovinger*
DESIGNERS   *Tom Bentkowski,*
    Sam Serebin
PHOTOGRAPHERS   *1,2,3 Alexander Tsiaris,*
    3 Criminal Justice (left)
ILLUSTRATOR   *3 Steve Walkowiak*

BIBA

1 **No. 204 Feb. 1997**
2 **No. 206 Apr. 1997**

CREATIVE DIRECTOR   *Michel Mallard*
DESIGNER   *Michel Mallard*
PHOTOGRAPHERS   *1 Thiemo Sander,*
                2 Marcel van der Vlugt
STYLIST   *Sandrine Boury-Heyler*
DESIGN FIRM   *Michel Mallard Studio*
PUBLISHER   *Excelsior Publications S.A.*
France

1

2

No. 206 Apr. 1997

DESIGNER   *Michel Mallard*
PHOTOGRAPHER   *Lomographic Society Paris*
STYLIST   *Christine Lerche*

24H
APRÈS UNE RUPTURE...
...ON FAIT QUOI ? ON PLEURE, ON RIT, ON TÉLÉPHONE, ON MANGE, ON DORT. ON S'ARRACHE LES CHEVEUX, ON AIME AILLEURS ? À CHACUN SA THÉRAPIE. PAR ROMAIN BASSOUL.

Joëlle, 31 ans, professeur J'habitais dans le Midi, près de la mer. J'ai filé à la plage et j'ai allumé tous les mecs qui passaient. Je n'étais pas du tout déprimée, j'étais folle de rage. J'ai bien piégé trois ou quatre types : je les ferais, et, au dernier moment, je leur riais au nez. Rétrospectivement, je me dis que j'ai eu de la chance de ne pas tomber sur des brutes...

Lise, 38 ans, relieuse J'ai échafaudé une douzaine de scénarios pour le punir. Tantôt j'épousais un play-boy millionnaire, tantôt je le séquestrais dans une cave où je l'humiliais. Ou alors je retrouvais la chienne qui me l'avait piqué (j'étais sûre qu'il était parti pour une autre) et je la vendais à un proxénète... Je me suis fait des films délirants en les peaufinant dans les moindres détails : la Porsche bleu nuit du play-boy, ma photo dans les magazines, les interviews après le Goncourt que me vaudrait mon premier roman (il racontait notre histoire d'amour et mon incroyable revanche). Heureusement, j'ai fini par m'apercevoir que je devenais folle à lier !

Christophe, 37 ans, banquier J'ai quitté ma première compagne parce qu'elle ne voulait pas de bébé. Elle avait peur de compromettre sa carrière, disait-elle. Quand une fille qui me tournait autour m'a dit qu'elle rêvait d'avoir un enfant de moi, j'ai décidé de rompre. Je me suis tout de suite installé chez la nouvelle. Le premier jour, je l'ai passé à me demander si je n'avais pas fait une grosse bêtise...

Angéline, 37 ans, consultante La veille au soir, au cours d'une engueulade spectaculaire, j'avais jeté dans les toilettes la bague qu'il m'avait offerte. Et tiré la chasse d'une manière théâtrale (du moins, c'est ce qu'il m'a semblé sur le coup !). Inutile de dire qu'il était parti en claquant la porte et sans espoir de retour... Drapée dans mon orgueil, j'ai passé la nuit à me convaincre que c'était ça qui pouvait m'arriver de mieux. J'ai dormi jusqu'à la fin de l'après-midi. Et, au réveil, miracle ! La bague - sans doute trop lourde- était toujours au fond de la cuvette. J'ai interprété ça comme un signe du destin et je l'ai tout de suite rappelé. C'est fou à quoi ça tient une histoire d'amour.

Nathalie, 29 ans, secrétaire Je ne suis pas allée travailler. J'ai passé la journée à lire Le Capitaine Pravasse : je voulais un roman facile, très long, plein de rebondissements. Et surtout pas sentimental.

Marine, 31 ans, comptable Dès que j'ai pu parler sans fondre en larmes, j'ai téléphoné à tous les gens susceptibles de me prêter une oreille compatissante : ma meilleure copine, ma sœur, mon ami d'enfance, l'amie qui nous avait présentés. Ils ont tous été parfaits. Très patients.

Stéphanie, 36 ans, maquettiste Ce que j'ai fait ? Des folies de mon corps. J'ai plaqué mon ex parce que j'avais eu un vrai coup de foudre pour un autre. Hypersensuel. Les premiers jours, on n'a pas arrêté de faire l'amour.

Benoît, 33 ans, informaticien J'ai fait la bringue. Beaucoup bu. Et pris la première (et dernière) cuite de ma vie. Ça m'a rendu malade. Quand j'ai émergé, je me suis trouvé idiot de me détruire pour

cette pouffe. La question était réglée. Je n'ai même pas pensé à chercher le mec avec qui elle était partie pour lui casser la gueule.

Laure, 34 ans, infirmière J'ai fait un grand ménage de printemps. De 8 h du mat' à presque minuit, j'ai astiqué mes deux pièces, tout briqué, avec de l'encaustique et de la lavande, comme ma grand-mère. J'ai aussi changé les meubles de place. Il avait emporté toutes ses affaires, mais j'ai jeté tout ce qui pouvait risquer de me faire penser à lui.

Sandrine, 24 ans, étudiante Je me suis couchée, j'ai débranché le téléphone, j'ai pris un somnifère et j'ai dormi 30 h d'affilée.

François, 38 ans, médecin C'est elle qui est partie. Comme une voleuse, d'ailleurs. Elle a fait ses valises dans mon dos et, le soir, quand je suis rentré, je n'ai rien trouvé, même pas un mot d'explication. Bizarrement, sur le coup, je me suis senti assez euphorique. Beaucoup plus léger. J'ai dû penser "bon débarras" ou quelque chose comme ça. Mais le matin suivant, j'ai eu un gros coup de blues qui a duré plusieurs jours. Là, j'étais très abattu. Surtout à l'idée d'avoir aimé une fille capable de procédés aussi nuls !

Corinne, 36 ans, kiné Je me suis totalement relookée. Nouvelle coupe de cheveux, nouvelle couleur, nouvelles fringues. J'ai claqué presque l'équivalent de deux mois de loyer en une journée !

Hélène, 27 ans, consultante Le grand flash-back. Je voulais comprendre pourquoi il me larguait. Je me suis repassé le film de nos derniers jours ensemble, ce qu'il avait dit, ce que j'avais répondu, ses gestes, les miens. J'ai tout analysé, je me suis demandé s'il avait rencontré une autre femme, si j'avais une chance qu'il revienne, comment je pourrais m'y prendre, etc. Ce rabâchage mental a duré beaucoup plus que 24 h. Et ne m'a rien appris.

Ariane, 32 ans, avocate Je l'ai quitté parce que je m'ennuyais avec lui. Je ne l'aimais plus. Le jour qui a suivi mon départ a été absolument neutre. Je ne me souviens de rien de spécial. J'ai travaillé normalement. Je crois bien que je n'ai même pas pensé à lui.

Anne, 35 ans, médecin C'était ma première année de fac et mon premier vrai chagrin d'amour. Je me suis dit "malheureux en amour". Alors, j'ai illico bouclé mon sac, fermé la porte de mon studio et j'ai débarqué chez mes parents en m'inventant un

méga coup de froid. Il est vrai que je n'arrêtais pas de me moucher. Quoi qu'il en soit, ils ne m'ont pas posé de questions. J'ai réinvesti ma vieille chambre et je me suis fait dorloter par ma mère sans sortir de mon lit. La régression totale. Une semaine plus tard, j'allais beaucoup mieux.

Antoine, 36 ans, comédien Comme c'était ma troisième gamelle de l'année, je me suis dit "malheureux en amour, heureux au jeu". Alors, j'ai joué. J'ai acheté des tickets de Loto, de Morpion, de Tacotac. Je suis même allé au casino pour essayer la roulette. Je n'ai rien gagné. Ça m'a prouvé que je n'étais ni heureux au jeu. Donc, que je devais être heureux en amour malgré les apparences... Je crois dur comme fer aux proverbes !

BIBA 139

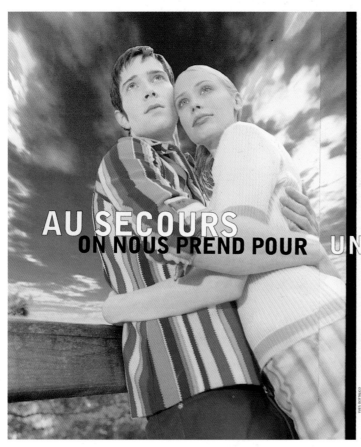

ON A ÉTÉ LES PREMIERS À FAIRE ÉPÉDA COMMUN ET À MÉLANGER NOS CHROMOSOMES. ET DEPUIS, ON TIENT BON. DU COUP, POUR TOUS LES CÉLIBATAIRES, LES DIVORCÉS OU LES MAL-MARIÉS DE LA BANDE, ON EST DEVENU UN "COUPLE-CULTE". QU'ON VISITE EXACTEMENT COMME UN APPART-TÉMOIN, TOUT BEAU, TOUT PROPRE ET BIEN RANGÉ. POUR VOIR COMMENT C'EST UN "VRAI" COUPLE QUI DURE... SAUF QUE NOUS, ON N'ASSUME PAS FORCÉMENT CE RÔLE DE COMMERCIAUX POUR L'AGENCE "AU JOYEUX BONHEUR CONJUGAL"...
PAR PATRICIA CASTET. ENQUÊTE MARIE-CÉCILE PICQUET

AU SECOURS
ON NOUS PREND POUR UN COUPLE-TÉMOIN !

À quelques encablures de la vingtaine, on a joué les pionniers en adhérant les premiers au programme couple-bébé-baraque-à-crédit. Huit ans plus tard, le binôme Bernadette-Jean-Paul est toujours d'actu. Et plutôt en bon état : on ne se lyophilise pas encore d'ennui ; on ne se balance pas de vannes crado devant les potes ni d'assiettes intra-muros ; on ne crise même pas tous les quatre ans malgré les stat'. On ose même arborer quelques signes de richesse amoureuse (petits bisous, mots doux, fleurs impromptues, etc.). Dans les années 50, Monsieur et Madame Pichard seraient un couple banal. En 97, notre histoire sans histoires fait sensation. Car autour de nous, les castings du cœur se succèdent. Steph est passée d'Étienne à Sylvain : un vieil adc, amoureux de son ego, lâché pour un pas libre rencontré la semaine dernière. Babeth, d'un musicos bab' -qui a squatté sa vie six mois- à un GO qui lui a mis le cœur au shaker. Et Luc, depuis quinze jours, un chagrin d'amour pour un quadra Classe Affaires rencontré sur le Paris-Istanbul. Les couples se font, se défont. Un petit tour et puis s'en vont. Pour quelques bagués plan-plan, pas mal qui pratiquent le CDD. S'ins-

tallent ensemble, une main sur la télécommande. Dès que ça ne va plus (panne de cœur, de sexe, de communication, etc.), on zappe pour aller voir ailleurs si l'amour est plus rose.

Couple calme, confortable avec vue sur jardin d'Éden
Du coup, on fait office de référence. De valeur sûre. "Bernadette et Jean-Paul, ça c'est une histoire qui marche !" s'exclame-t-on autour de nous. Et puisqu'on a testé pour eux l'amour longue distance, les ex ou futurs consommateurs de notre entourage nous bombardent couple-témoin : celui qu'on visite comme un appart' pour savoir si c'est si bien que ça. Si ça vaut le coup de signer et d'en prendre pour X ans. Ou, s'ils ont déjà donné sans succès, pour voir comment ça marche quand ça marche. Nous voilà donc, nous, Jean-Paul, le môme dans son parc, l'autre devant son coffre à jouets, la cuisine aménagée et les accessoires (tablier, robot ménager, table à langer, etc.), en vitrine à la grande Galerie du bonheur domestique.

Et nos célibataires de copines (mi-fascinées, mi-ricanantes), d'observer à la loupe ces animaux rares en voie ▶

BIBA 91

---

top	No. 206 Apr. 1997		bottom	No. 206 Apr. 1997
DESIGNER	*Chantal Siri*		**DESIGNER**	*Muriel Illouz*
PHOTOGRAPHER	*Bruno Fournier*		**PHOTOGRAPHER**	*Yves Botallico*

[V I V E M E N T
LE PRINTEMPS !]

OPTION MODE

Sous nos cols roulés et nos pantalons de velours...

1 **Corbeille** à armature, en jersey de coton rebrodé et ajouré, string assorti, Simone Pérèle, 513 F et 187 F. **2 Balconnet** à armature, en soie brodée, string assorti, Anti Flirt, 499 F l'ensemble. **3 Effet drapé** en microfibre Tactel avec armature, slip assorti, Wonderbra, 229 F et 99 F. **4 Corbeille** en tulle brodé et dentelle, string assorti, Lou, 306 F et 249 F. **5 Soutien-gorge** rembourré à armature, en microfibre et dentelle, culotte taille haute assortie, Variance, 111 F et 62 F. **6 Soutien-gorge**, bonnets pleins à armature, en ottoman et dentelle, culotte haute et échancrée assortie, Vanity Fait, 250 F et 180 F. **7 Corbeille** à armature, en dentelle de coton mélangé, culotte taille haute assortie, Barbara, 287 F et 211 F. **8 Corbeille** rembourré en guipure et microfibre, culotte assortie, Chantelle, 255 F et 155 F. **9 Corbeille** à armature en microfibre et bordure de dentelle, string assorti, Lady, 330 F et 199 F.

CUISINE

Manger light sans se priver de pâtes, de hamburger ou de dessert, c'est possible en trichant un peu. Les tagliatelles sont taillées dans des courgettes, le céleri remplace le pain mais le plaisir des yeux reste intact. Par Marie-Caroline Malbec

Trompe- l'œil

RECETTES POUR 4 PERSONNES
◄ Hamburger Mac Biba
Préparation : 10 mn. Cuisson : 40 mn + 12 mn.
4 steaks hachés (150 g chacun), 2 petits céleris-raves, 2 tomates, 2 gros oignon blanc, 4 feuilles de salade, 4 cornichons Malossol, 4 tranches de fromage Sveltesse 20 % de matières grasses, 1 jus de citron, grains de moutarde Albert Ménès, ketchup.
Peler et couper les céleris en 4 dans leur largeur. Le but est d'obtenir 4 tranches pour former les chapeaux des hamburgers et 4 tranches pour former leur base. Faire bouillir une cocotte

d'eau salée et citronnée, y plonger les tranches de céleri et les laisser cuire 40 mn après reprise de l'ébullition. Les égoutter, les sécher et les réserver au four à chaleur douce. Laver et couper les tomates en rondelles. Peler et couper l'oignon en fines tranches, laver et égoutter la salade. Faire cuire les steaks hachés à la poêle dans un filet d'huile d'olive. Retirer les tranches de céleri du four. Poser sur chaque base une feuille de salade, des rondelles de tomate, des tranches d'oignon et de cornichon. Saler et poivrer les steaks, les poser sur leur "buré" de céleri et les couvrir d'une tranche de fromage, les passer sous le gril du four 3 mn. Arroser d'une giclée de ketchup puis coiffer d'un chapeau de céleri saupoudré de grains de moutarde. Servir bien chaud.

Quiche aux foies de volaille
Préparation : 30 mn. Cuisson : 50 mn.
200 g de foies de volaille blonds, 1 tête de brocoli, 3 œufs, 2 cuil. à soupe bien pleines de crème épaisse allégée en matières grasses, 2 échalotes, 2 cuil. à soupe de persil haché, sel, poivre. ►

top **No. 204 Feb. 1997**	*bottom* **No. 206 Apr. 1997**
DESIGNER *Marina Coriasco*	DESIGNER *Valerie Bernier*
PHOTOGRAPHER *Matthias*	PHOTOGRAPHER *Manfred Seelow*
STYLIST *Bernadette Combette*	

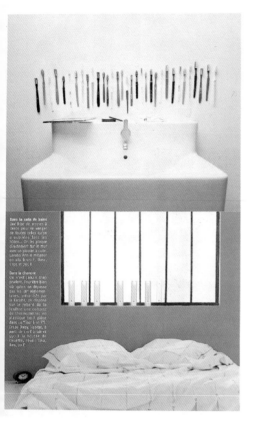

motifs à répétition

UNE BROSSE À DENTS, UNE FOURCHETTE OU UN THERMOMÈTRE,
C'EST UTILE MAIS PAS FORCÉMENT DÉCORATIF,
SAUF SI EN LES ACCUMULANT, LE QUOTIDIEN DEVIENT GAI
ET POÉTIQUE.

Par Catherine Geel
Lumière Claire Rossignol
Photos Michel Bousquet

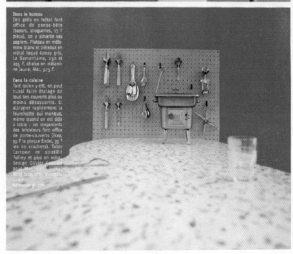

No. 206 Apr. 1997

DESIGNER   Michel Mallard
PHOTOGRAPHER   Michel Bousquet
STYLIST & CONCEPT Catherine Geel

Citizen K

1 **Autumn 1996**
2 **Spring 1996**

ART DIRECTOR *Vincent Bergerat*
DESIGNER *Vincent Bergerat*
PHOTOGRAPHERS *1 Donna Trope,*
2 Guido Mocafico
PUBLISHER *DNA*

France

1

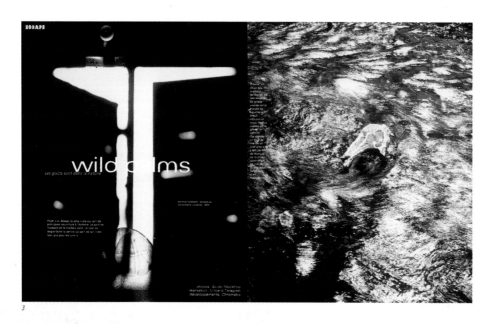

3

4

5

3 **Spring 1996**

DESIGNER *Vincent Bergerat*
PHOTOGRAPHER *Guido Mocafico*

4 **Autumn 1996**

EDITOR *Frédéric Chaubin*
DESIGNERS *Vincent Bergerat,*
Dipesh Pandya
ARTIST *Annette Messager*

5,6 **Autumn 1996**

DESIGNER *Vincent Bergerat*
PHOTOGRAPHERS *5 Jean-Pierre Khazem,*
6 Martina Hoogland Ivanov

INFORMATION
WEAPONS:
GEOMERCURIAL
YELLOW
LIGHT
MISSILES
FOR AN
ULTRA-CLEAN
ENVIRONMENT. NO DUST, NO GERMS, NO FOREIGN BODIES
A SIMULACRUM
FOR
THE BRAIN,
DREAMT-UP
BY MADAME
SEIKO MIKAMI

at worst, they bring it to this world's bustling museums, galleries, and centres of post-contemporary art.
Madame rêve. She is dreaming with the magnificent aloneness of a dream that none other can share. No disciples, no models, no rivals. She cannot help imagining that one day her missiles will give billions of ports like herself something to dream about. Or perhaps she will even succeed, perhaps she will even manage to produce what is ultimately the only possible alternative: the definitive explosion of all the world's ports. Justice at last. All that will be left is the splendid, incisive beauty of the metal missile, its yellow brightness, and the computer babbling at the speed of light. — *Barbara Polla*

THE lady dreams. Slender and magnificent, she dreams of transport. The port, to begin with, is not a dream. She is this port where – huge, tranquil, ephemeral – they lay to in passing, and then are off. She is this haven open to the world, into which they heave, leave their booty and replenish their stock. Heading in, heading out. An unavoidable passage. A through-port. Slender and magnificent, life goes in, life goes out. Versus and trans. But on the seventh day, the lady has a dream. What if she would stop bearing, stop transporting others for once and create her own means of transport. Totally illegitimate. Its only conceivable form: a missile. Shiny, metallic,

fluorescent yellow – the yellow is essential – army green, computer screen. The perfect penis. Detached from man. A computer-controllable, perfectly pliable weapon; chemically clean, habitable, reusable, reproducible *ad infinitum*, but with a variability proper to women and computers. With its inner gardens, miniaturised, asepticised rows of intelligent microchips imparting that feeling of virtual security linked to the inorganic, but also a penetrating, uncertain sense of permanent threat. You can neither undo a missile programme nor destroy it. At best, they transport their explosive charge to other worlds, recently rediscovered by societies adrift;

MADAME RÊVE

Seiko Mikami was born in 1961. She made her public debut on a collaborative project with Nam June Paik, Ryuichi Sakamoto and several other artists. Fascinated by networking systems, she fills space with neuroplants made of cables and music compiled from city noise, creating a Cyberpunk Age landscape. — *Katsuya Anuchi gallery*

Winter 1997

EDITOR
Frédéric Chaubin
DESIGNER
Vincent Bergerat
ARTIST
Seiko Mikami

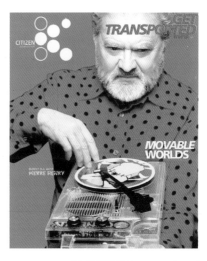

CITIZEN K international
Winter 1997

EDITOR   *Frédéric Chaubin*
DESIGNER   *Vincent Bergerat*
PHOTOGRAPHER *Jean-Pierre Khazem*

UNE RAME NOMMÉE DÉSIR

Winter 1997

DESIGNER   *Vincent Bergerat*
PHOTOGRAPHER *Jean-Pierre Khazem*

Quarterly DUNE
Vol. 10 Summer 1996

EDITOR	*Fumihiro Hayashi*
ART DIRECTOR	*Hideki Nakajima*
DESIGNER	*Yoshinori Ochiai*
PHOTOGRAPHER	*Sofia Coppola*
PUBLISHER	*Art Days Inc.*

Japan

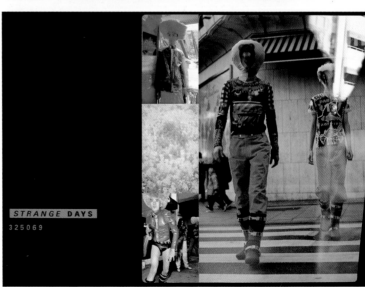

Vol. 11 Autumn 1996

PHOTOGRAPHER   *Naka*

Vol. 10 Summer 1996

PHOTOGRAPHER   *Masashi Ohashi*

top   **Vol. 11 Autumn 1996**
PHOTOGRAPHER   *Kate Orne*

bottom   **Vol. 9 Spring 1996**
PHOTOGRAPHER   *Katsumi Omori*

WIRED

	1	Mar. 1997
	2	Apr. 1997
EDITOR		Hiroto Kobayashi
CREATIVE DIRECTOR		2 Naoki Sato
ART DIRECTOR		Noriyuki Kitsugi
PHOTOGRAPHERS		1 Yoshihiro Nishioka,
		2 Shuichi Maiyama
ILLUSTRATOR		2 Naomi Kusama
HAIR & MAKEUP		2 Koji Kawanishi
PUBLISHER		DDP Digital Publishing Inc.

Japan

1

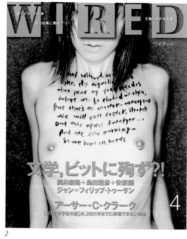

2

Mar. 1997

CREATIVE DIRECTOR	4 Naoki Sato
PHOTOGRAPHER	3 Sogo Ishii
COLLAGE	3 Kiyasu

Apr. 1997

DESIGNERS	5 Fumio Tachibana,
	6 Kazuki Ohashi
PHOTOGRAPHER	6 Hiroshi Tokuda
OBJECT	5 Fumio Tachibana

3

5

4

6

暗号政策の知られざる相貌

川寄稿・石黒一憲（東大法学部教授）

— ster ロボットメガストア Robo Megastore

INVISIBLE WAR OVER ENCRYPTION

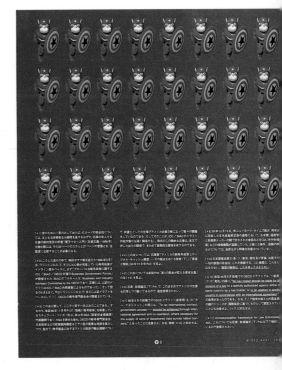

ーターネット・ビジネスを本格化させる起爆剤としての期待が高まる暗号技術。世界中の企業がより安全・確実な「の開発にしのぎを削る一方、各国政府レベルにおいても、その取り扱いについての激しい議論が続いている。しかし、「の「暗号」、単にビジネス・ユースの観点からのみ論じられるべき問題ではなかったのである。「唯一の大国」アメリカ中心とした主権国家同士の安全保障をめぐる暗号政策の「もうひとつの顔」が今、浮き彫りにされる。

マ　ルチメディア、インターネット、そして電子ネットワーク...

（本文中略）

仮に合法的盗聴のための条約が作られ、日本がそれを批准したとしても、条約で憲法の規定を骨抜きにできるのか？

OECD（経済協力開発機構）の暗号政策ガイドライン作成の経緯

OECDは、いわゆるGII（世界情報通信基盤）構想のための実務的検討を、G7情報社会サミット（95年2月ブリュッセル）で開始された...

OECD暗号政策ガイドライン最終案（96年12月）の内容

まず、このガイドラインの位置づけから、各国はいずれも暗号政策を検討する準備として、石炭が導入を図るべきであるとされている...

WIRED APRIL 1997

Apr. 1997

DESIGNER　*Noriyuki Kitsugi*
ILLUSTRATOR　*Robotmegastore*

Mar. 1997

CREATIVE DIRECTOR　*Naoki Sato*
DESIGNER　*Naoki Sato*
PHOTOGRAPHER　*Didier de Fays*

CYBER-PORTFOLIO

モード写真家であるデビ"Catwalk（キャットウォーク）"を自ら立ち上げ、NTTフランスの支援のもと、1996年春夏パリ・コレクションの模様をインターネット上に同時に、フランスモード界に関する初のWebサイト"Catwalk"の閉幕...

フランス・ファッション界から追放されたモード写真家の物語

パリの小さなアパルトマン、艶やかな床の上を滑るように歩く黒猫。暗い体と濃い焦げ色が対照をなしている。短いわげが、台所の方に向かれた疲れたロ元を囲んでいる...

プロジェクト前夜

1995年9月中旬、マスメディアの派手な宣伝にもかかわらず、フランスでのインターネットはひっそりとデビューした。当時インターネットに接続した者は、わずか数千人にとどまっていた...

自分のアイデアの有効性を確信した彼は、さっそくスポンサーを探し始めた。NTTフランスが最も積極的で...

オフラインのスキャンダル

このファクスは、パリ・コレクションの開幕時に全業界人に送付されたもので、「NTTフランスは、キャンセル・デュ・ルーヴルで発表されたプレタポルテコレクションをインターネット上に掲載する」と、意気軒昂と告げていた...

し、オートクチュール連盟のジャック・ムクリエ会長にもコンタクトを取った...

ショーの前日、世界中のモード関係者がパリに押し寄せ、"花の都"は狂乱で沸騰していた...

同時にCatwalkチームの個別なベースでの作業が、2人の元ジャーナリストが記事をひとりのグラフィックデザイナーがHTMLを担当した...

しかし、こうした惜しみない努力の中で、ひとつの問題が持ち上がった。パリ・コレクションの開催さなかに、「フランス・オートクチュール＝プレタポルテ・ファッション連盟」が...

先駆者の苦難

Catwalkは、インターネットにおける著作権という現実的問題のほかに、新しいメディアに対するファッション業界の根強い猜疑心をも明るみに出した...

いくぜ！5000万台

プレイステーションは"次世代機戦争"に終止符を打ったか？

words 山下 卓 *Takashi Yamashita*
image 内藤恭雄 *Yasuhiko Uchihara (p.18,19)*
original photo 徳田 淳 *Hiroshi Tokuda (p.10,41,42,44)*
illustration 楠 伸生 *Nobuo Kusunoki (p.40,41,43,44)*

「次世代機戦争は終わった」。プレイステーションがそう思わせるほどの勢いをともいわれる。最後発でありながら、現在の地位を築き上げた理由は何か。64　みせている。店頭では在庫不足が慢性化し、月産100万台の生産体制に入っているビット機やアーケードの人気ゲームの追撃にも打ち勝ってきた強さの秘密に迫る。

誰もが「次世代機戦争は終わった」。プレイステーションがそう思わせるほどの勢いを

すべてはライバル機の開発から始まった

「当時、デジタル・テクノロジーが発展していくプロセスの中で、コンピュータ技術を使ったエンタテインメントは、ソニーが今後、生活的に関係していく価値のあるものだという認識はありました」

「我々はPSというハードを発売するという意味の次世代機戦争への参戦などというレベルでは考えていない。そして、これから先もメディアとしての意味と機能をも
ち続けるものを提供していきたいという意志があった」

Mar. 1997

CREATIVE DIRECTOR Naoki Sato
DESIGNER Noriyuki Kitsugi
PHOTOGRAPHER 2,3 Hiroshi Tokuda
ILLUSTRATORS 1 Yasuhiko Uchihara,
2,3 Nobuo Kusunoki

期待されない輸出

知りすぎた男

バーチャファイターがくれた贈り物

悪戦し続けるゲーム制作者

「ああ、なんて無謀なことを……」SMEJでSFC用のゲームソフトを制作していた徳川は、32ビットゲーム機の構想が立ち上がったという知らせを聞いたとき、思わずそう呟いた

月産1000万枚のCD-ROM

東京が首都でなくなる日?!

"国家百年の大計"の行方

words 田近伸和 *Nobukazu Tajika*
illustration ロボットメガストア *Robotmegastore*

2010年には新首都で国会を開催するという目標を掲げ,国のプロジェクトとして動き始めた遷都の案件。だが,それを決めた当の国会議員たちでさえ半信半疑のありさまで,世論も一向に盛り上がらない。先行き不透明で,今後,空中分解する可能性もあるが,このままでは,まともな議論がなされないまま"国家百年の大計"が進められてしまう恐れがある。何のための遷都なのか? 遷都は国民にとってプラスなのかマイナスなのか? 議論を国民レベルに引き戻すために,遷都推進派と反対派の論拠を明確にしつつ,その是非を検証する。

「**ま**さか! 冗談だと思っていましたよ」。永田町の国会議員たちから,いまだにこんな他人事のようなつぶやきが聞こえてくる。国会議員たちが「冗談だと思っていた」というのは,"国家百年の大計"であるべきはずの重大案件,遷都の一件だ。90年11月,衆・参両院で「国会等の移転に関する決議」を行い,92年12月には「国会等の移転に関する法律」を超党派で成立させ(共産党のみ反対),遷都を決めたのは,ほかならぬ当の国会議員たちだったにもかかわらず,である。

これでは,気運が盛り上がらないのもムリはない。ジャーナリズムの切り込み不足も大いに問題だ。都市経済学が専門で,遷都反対の立場をとる八田達夫・大阪大学教授(社会経済研究所)はこう指摘する。

「ジャーナリズムはきちんとした分析をやらず,本来の機能を果たしていません。稀に今回,ちょっと異常だと思えるのは日本経済新聞の社説です。『決まったことは粛々とやるしかない』という論調は,遷都よ賛成の立場です。国民の大多数が賛成している状況ならいざしらず,賛成,反対が拮抗している中で,なぜあんな早手回しで賛成するのか,気運を喚起しようという姿勢がまったくみられないのです」

遷都のビジョンは,総理府内に設置された国会等移転調査会(会長:宇野収・関西経済連合会相談役)が,95年12月,当時の村山富市首相に提出した「国会等移転調査会報告」(以下,「報告」)に基づく。もっとも,そこに描かれたビジョンは,国土庁内に設置された「首都機能移転問題に関する懇談会」(座長:八十島義之助・帝京技術科学大学学長(当時))の答申内容を多分に継承している。

後退した「東京一極集中の是正」

「報告」は,遷都の目的として「政経分離」「地方分権型国造りへの改革の契機」「東京一極集中の是正」「災害に強い国土造り」などを挙げ,遷都を「人心一新の好機」と位置づけている。と

移転の対象となるのは,国会などの立法機関,内閣や中央省庁などの行政機関,最高裁判所などの司法機関といった首都機能のみ。新首都の総人口は最大で60万人,合計面積は9000ヘクタール。人口60万人は岡山市や熊本市の規模にほぼ匹敵し,9000ヘクタールは山手線内側の面積の約1.5倍,多摩ニュータウンの約3倍に相当する。人口60万人の内訳は,移転する従業者が10万人(国会議員,国家公務員,特殊法人職員,民間企業の公務部職員等),その家族が20万人,残る30万人は都市の営みに必要なサービス産業従業者など。

街づくりのやりかたは,筑波研究学園都市にみられるようなクラスター方式(クラスターとはブドウの房などを意味する)を採っている。3万〜10万人程度の規模の街が集まり,新首都は構成されることになる。

移転先は東京から鉄道で1〜2時間,おおむね60〜300キロメートルの範囲,空港は正百年用機などが発着可能な滑走路を有する規模であり,空港から40分程度で新首都に到着できることが条件だ。移転に要する費用は総額14兆円,内訳は基盤整備費4兆円,施設整備費7兆円,用地費3兆円。これには,道路・鉄道・空港建設費など公共投資は含まれていない。2000年までに新首都の建設に着手し,2010年には新首都で国会開催を目指すとしている。

ところで,遷都といわず,「国会等移転」や「首都機能移転」という言い方をしているのは,「国民的合意のない中で性急な移転の既成事実化に対しては強く反対する」(青島都知事)と,遷都に異を唱える東京都などをいたずらに刺激しないためだ。遷都推進の事務局の立場にある国土庁が,「新首都」という言葉を使った自前の使用パンフを最近回収した例にはこうした事情がある。

ちなみに,東京都が主張しているのは,東京の周辺都市へ国の出先機関や企業のオフィスを分散させる「展都論」だ。

「中央省庁全体が移転対象になるかどうかは,まだはっきりした回答が出ているわけではありません。一口に中央省庁といっても,政策企画部門と現業部門があります。また,特殊法人などについては現在,行革で取り組んでいる最中ですから,どういう機関が具体的に対象になるのか,正直言って分からない面があります」(大和田哲生・国土庁大都市圏整備局首都機能移転企画課調査官補佐)

国土庁としては「報告」に基づいて着々と業務を遂行する,という構えだが,天野光三・大阪産業大学学長は遷都推進論ながら,この「報告」を「極難薬剤なもの」と断じて批判する。天野学長は東京一甲府一名古屋一大阪をリニアモーターカーで結び,中央省庁を分散配置する「拡都構想」の提唱者として知られる。

「報告」でおかしい点は,第一に遷都の理由づけの曖昧さだ。「報告」の第1章では遷都をつくるニーズとして3つの状況変化を挙げていますが,本来,理由の食べるべきはずの東京一極集中の是正が3番目にやっと登場し,幕に隠されている。しかも,新首都の人口を上限

Mar. 1997

CREATIVE DIRECTOR　*Naoki Sato*
DESIGNER　*Noriyuki Kitsugi*
ILLUSTRATOR　*Robotmegastore*

Apr. 1997

DESIGNER *Mizuki Ishikawa*
ILLUSTRATOR *Yutanpo Shirane (below)*
IMAGE *Koushi Kawachi (above)*

May 1997

DESIGNER *Mizuki Ishikawa*
IMAGE *Koushi Kawachi (below)*

フェニックスは燃えているか？

words ブルース・スターリング Bruce Sterling
translation 野村伸昭 Nobuaki Nomura

アートが戦争になる日——それは、これまで世界各地で数々のパフォーマンス・アートを繰り広げてきたマーク・ポーリン率いるSRL（サバイバル・リサーチ・ラボラトリーズ）の所業によって創造される極めて危険な一日である。サンフランシスコで生まれたパフォーマンス集団SRLの機械による過激な残虐なショー——ようこそ、作家ブルース・スターリングが、あなたをアリゾナ州・フェニックスの危険なステージに招待する。

ブルース・スターリング（bruces@well.com）
テキサス州オースチン在住のSF作家。SF以外に
ノンフィクション誌『ハッカーを追え』（アスキー）や、ウィリ
アム・ギブスンとの共著『ディファレンス・エンジン』
といった著作がある。最新刊は『Holy Fire』。

私 はフェニックスに来ている。といっても、週末にここを訪れているほかの10万人たちのように、スーパーボウル観戦のためにやって来たわけではない。今私は、『アリゾナ・リパブリック』紙の最新版を手にしている。それが配られているコミュニティそのもので、この新聞はとても似ている。体裁は良くて、ばからしいほどに保守的で、奇妙に混乱しているのだ。

1996年2月26日（金）の記事
「石の集中豪雨
チャンドラー警察の捜査進まず」

チャンドラー地区にソフトボールよりも大きな石とコンクリートの塊が降る事件が起きており、民家の屋根や自動車が被害に遭っている。チャンドラー警察は捜査を続け、パトロールの人員も増強したが、石の雨は依然として降り続いている。地元警防団も、石を拾い集めること以外に何の成果も上げられずにいる。火曜日の夜には30個もの塊が降った。これらは何らかの装置を使って投げ飛ばされたものだと住民たちは信じている。

しかし私が本当に探している記事はこれではない。

「凶暴なロボット
近々ダウンタウンを大混乱に」

フェニックスのウエスト・ジャクソン・ストリート429番地にある「アイスハウス」で、土曜日の午後11時に、総重量30トンのロボット的な機械がぶつかり合って火を噴くパフォーマンスが行われる。「百万回の無分別な実験」と名づけられたこの催し

Mar. 1997
DESIGNER   Noriyuki Kitsugi

May 1997
DESIGNER   Noriyuki Kitsugi
PHOTOGRAPHER   UPI / Corbis-Bettman

映画がともに在らんことを——
『スター・ウォーズ』の神話ふたたび

ジョージ・ルーカス インタビュー

文：ケヴィン・ケリー＋ポーラ・パリージ

70年代終わりから、来るべき21世紀を目指し映画を進化させ続けてきた男——ジョージ・ルーカス。彼が創り出す"銀河系おとぎ話"は、SFXの衝撃とともに鮮烈な観客とカメラの結婚という撮影上のテクニックを用いて、観客の心に刻みつけた。「コンピュータと、星間オペラの領域に血肉を通わせた彼は、自分の物語を信じられないほどのものにするためには、「超」がつくほど丹念にしかもかいもいほど目立たないようにすることで、映画の魔術の効果を発揮していったとも言える。新しいテクノロジーとさらに磨きのかかった特撮を盛り込んだ「スター・ウォーズ三部作特別篇」の日本公開に先駆けて行われたロング・インタビューにおいて、進化し続けるテクノロジーと映像の関係、そして完成が待ち遠しい新作「スター・ウォーズ エピソード1」についてルーカス本人が語る。

「スター・ウォーズ三部作 特別篇」と新作「スター・ウォーズ エピソード1」の製作過程を綴る。

199

Axcess

1 **Oct./Nov. 1996**
2 **Mar. 1997**

EDITOR *Rod Dovlin*
ART DIRECTOR *Richard G.Martinez*
DESIGNER *Richard G.Martinez*
PHOTOGRAPHERS *1 Tara,*
1 Bruce W.Talamon,
2 Greg Henry
PUBLISHER *Axcess Ventures, Inc.*
USA

1

2

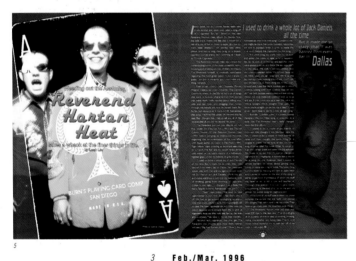

3

4

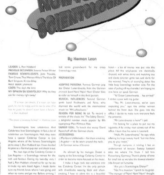

5

6

3 **Feb./Mar. 1996**

EDITOR *Victor M.Vargas*
DESIGNER *Aeon Stanfield*
PHOTOGRAPHER *Aeon Stanfield*

5 **Oct./Nov. 1996**

EDITOR *Leah Jones*
DESIGNER *Richard G.Martinez*
PHOTOGRAPHER *Marina Chavez*

4 **Oct./Nov. 1996**

EDITOR *Richard G.Martinez*
DESIGNERS *Richard G.Martinez,*
Carlos Hernandez
ILLUSTRATOR *Ken Meyer Jr.*

6 **Mar. 1997**

EDITOR *Rod Dovlin*
DESIGNER *Richard G.Martinez*
PHOTOGRAPHER *Janet Vanham*

The Secret Life of Tim Burton

An Exclusive Look at Hollywood's Geek Genius

By Rod Dovlin • Photos by Tara

Oct./Nov. 1996

EDITOR Rod Dovlin

DESIGNER Richard G. Martinez

PHOTOGRAPHERS 1 Tara,
2 Bruce W. Talamon

1

"I worked in restaurants and stuff, but I figured out very early on that I couldn't have a regular job. I figured I'd either do something like what I'm doing now, or I'd be living in a trailer out in Nevada somewhere. A life in the movies or a life of crime."

2

When we first met, I thought to myself, 'Have I met this person before?'

Mars Attacks! Photos by Bruce W. Talamon ©1996 Warner Bros.

alarm? "Not really," he says, "although it felt like a weird *Love Boat* episode after awhile," he confesses. "When you get all of these weird people in a room— here's Jack Nicholson, there's Rod Steiger, there's Pierce, Martin Short, all of these people from all different walks of life. Academy Award winners, comedians, singers— that's the kind of room that makes you go, 'Wow!' It's so surreal that it almost passes you by at the time."

The opportunity to put Jack Nicholson in the White House is a chance that no director would pass up. "It's so great to see Jack acting as the President," he admits, "and then to play his other role as this Vegas real estate guy. A lot of actors are so concerned that they always look good or whatever. I like actors like Jack because they just get in there and do it. They get this look in their eye, they've got this spark. You enjoy it, the crew enjoys it, and it just creates this good energy on the set."

Along with the aforementioned stars, *Mars Attacks!* also features Burton's long-time girlfriend, actress Lisa Marie, as a curvaceous alien babe who attracts the amorous attention of Martin Short. "Lisa Marie is in the film, looking totally fab," Burton says of his companion, who also appeared as Vampira in Burton's *Ed Wood*. "I love working with Lisa Marie because we get to play around. Because we're together, we get to play around and test things out in a way that I couldn't with anyone else."

Burton explains how being a couple has its advantages when doing preproduction research. "Months before the film starts up," he reveals, "we'd go out and test out different looks, different costumes to see what works. We just have fun with it, together. We were in New York and took a trip to Washington DC. We just got some cheap wigs together and went out to sort of get a feeling of what it would look like to have…." Burton again stops himself short, possibly to prevent giving away too much of the film's plot. "You know," he continues, "just testing out some costume ideas that you don't have the luxury of doing with an actress that you're not together with. We just fool around together."

I ask Burton how he and Lisa Marie got together in the first place, not at all expecting the candor of his answer. "We actually met in this now-defunct strip bar in New York called Goldfinger's," he reveals. "I know that strip clubs have become popular lately, but this one was really cool. They had great music, good people. It was just a really cool environment. Not exactly what you might expect. I was there with a group of people. Lisa Marie showed up with some other people. We met and just talked to each other for the whole night. Everybody left and we just stayed there, talking to each other. And that was pretty much it, from then on in."

Burton's world slowly begins to unfold before me, seeming less secretive and more simplified. I could almost see the reclusive Burton emerging from his shell. His entire demeanor seems more relaxed, especially when talking about Lisa Marie. "She was out of it, in her personal life," he continues. "I was out of it in mine, and we just met by chance. It was beautiful, because we both weren't looking for someone. We just sort of connected, you know? It was like something I'd been feeling my whole life and then I just found it. It was great, I felt, and I still feel, as if this is it, this is the one."

I ask Burton how he could be so sure of any relationship. "You just know," he explains. "You just flash on it. When we first met, I thought to myself, 'Have I met this person before?' And then I flashed to having met her long ago, like when I was a child. Then I started flashing on to her, seeing her as a young woman and as an old woman all at the same time. It was weird. It's hard to describe. It was almost like hallucinating. Seeing her change in my mind, from a little girl to an old woman, all in the matter of a few seconds. It wasn't a physical or verbal kind of thing. It was like a deep, visceral response to somebody. It was like a beautiful hallucination of some kind."

Real-life hallucinations are also a hallmark of Burton's films. Did any of the actors on *Mars Attacks!* have a hard time sharing Burton's unique vision, especially when the actual Martians would appear much later in post-production? "I didn't seem to have too many method actors on this film," Burton laughs. "Nobody demanded to see a Martian to play against— which was great, because we'd have been screwed if they did," Burton explains that a sort of youthful exuberance took over the production. "Everybody got into the spirit of acting to nothing. It was like a bunch of kids playing. You know how when you were a kid and you had to pretend that the monsters were there. That's what making this movie was like. To see actors of this caliber playing like that was very surreal. It's kind of funny, in that sense. Nobody will ever get to see that part of the film making process. I've joked about releasing the film with no Martians, just so everyone could get a chance to see this great cast of talent acting to nothing."

The real stars of *Mars Attacks!* could quite possibly turn out to be the bug-eyed, hyperencephalic Martians themselves. What are these little things, anyway? Not surprisingly, Burton is keeping quiet. "They're basically computer animation," he reveals, "but we've gone for a real stop-motion feel because that was the initial inspiration. I've dealt with pretty much all forms of animation— cel, stop-motion and so on— but this is the first time that I've worked so closely with computer animation."

How does an old-school animator deal with the new wave of computer-generated

PLAZM

1	**Vol. 11 Winter 1995**
2	**Vol. 12 Spring 1996**
3	**Vol. 13 Summer 1996**

EDITOR	*Yariv Rabinovitch*
ART DIRECTORS	*1,2 Joshua Berger,*
	1 Niko Courtelis,
	1,3 Pete McCracken
DESIGNERS	*1 Joshua Berger,*
	1 Niko Courtelis,
	1 Pete McCracken,
	2 Modern Dog,
	3 Bruce Licher
PHOTOGRAPHERS	*1 Dxjx @ Studio 3,*
	2 Michelle Rollman
INSTALLATION ARTIST	*2 Michelle Rollman*
DESIGN FIRMS	*1 Plazm Media,*
	2 Modern Dog,
	3 Independent Project Press
PUBLISHER	*Plazm Media*

USA

Vol. 11 Winter 1995

ART DIRECTOR	*Joshua Berger*
DESIGNERS	*Nancy Mazzei,*
	Brian Kelly
DESIGN FIRM	*Smokebomb*

Vol. 13 Summer 1996

ART DIRECTORS	*Joshua Berger,*
	Niko Courtelis
DESIGNER	*John Boiler*
DESIGN FIRM	*Plazm Media*

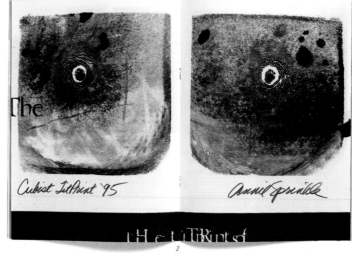

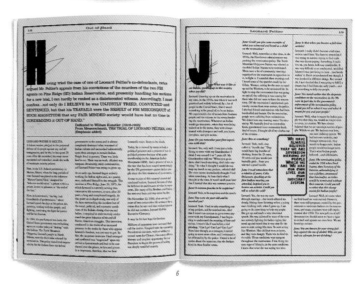

1	**Vol. 12 Spring 1996**	*2*	**Vol. 12 Spring 1996**
ART DIRECTOR	*Joshua Berger*	ART DIRECTOR	*Joshua Berger*
DESIGNER	*Modern Dog*	DESIGNER	*Angus R. Shamal*
DESIGN FIRM	*Modern Dog*	DESIGN FIRM	*Plazm Media*
		TIT PRINT	*Annie Sprinkle*

3	**Vol. 13 Summer 1996**		
ART DIRECTORS	*Joshua Berger,*		
	Niko Courtelis		
DESIGNERS	*Phil Yarnall,*		
	Stan Stanski		
ILLUSTRATORS	*Phil Yarnall, Stan Stanski*		
DESIGN FIRM	*Smay Vision*		

4	**Vol. 11 Winter 1995**	*5*	**Vol. 12 Spring 1996**
ART DIRECTOR	*Joshua Berger*	ART DIRECTOR	*Joshua Berger*
DESIGNERS	*Nancy Mazzei,*	DESIGNER	*Joshua Berger*
	Brian Kelly	DESIGN FIRM	*Plazm Media*
ILLUSTRATORS	*Nancy Mazzei,*		
	Brian Kelly	*6*	**Vol. 11 Winter 1995**
DESIGN FIRM	*Smokebomb*	ART DIRECTOR	*Niko Courtelis*
		DESIGNER	*Niko Courtelis*
		DESIGN FIRM	*Plazm Media*

experiment
1 **Vol. 1 Summer 1995**
2 **Vol. 2 Winter 1996**
3 **Vol. 3 Summer 1996**

EDITOR *Stephanie Talbot*
ART DIRECTORS *Stephanie Talbot,*
Mike Lawrence
DESIGNER *Mike Lawrence*
PUBLISHER *Experiment Magazine*
U K

1   2   3

a t-shirt is a t-shirt a t-shirt is a t-shirt a t-shirt is a t-shirt is a t-shirt a t-shirt is a t-shirt is a t-shirt is a t-shirt is a t-shirt is a t-shirt is a t-shirt ..... Photographer-Jane Mcleish. Stylist - Stephanie Tironelle. Flowerz and Junior. Many thanks to Laurent. Grooming - Tess. Models- Jamie and Michelle at Select, Suzanne, Emma, Aki.

Antoni and Alison T-shirt Dress available
from Way In, Harrods

Vol. 1 Summer 1995

ART DIRECTORS *Stephanie Talbot,*
Mike Lawrence
PHOTOGRAPHER *Jane McLeish*

Photography: Phillip James
Styling: Samson Soboye
Grooming & Hair: Donna Allan
@ The Work for Smiths Salons
Models: Guy & Myron
@ So Dam Tuff

Vol. 2 Winter 1996

ART DIRECTOR *Mike Lawrence*
PHOTOGRAPHER *Phillip James*
STYLIST *Samson Soboye*

1 **Vol. 3 Summer 1996**

ART DIRECTORS *Stephanie Talbot,*
Mike Lawrence
PHOTOGRAPHER *Martin Holtkamp*

2 **Vol. 3 Summer 1996**

ART DIRECTOR *Antoni and Alison*

3 **Vol. 3 Summer 1996**

ART DIRECTORS *Stephanie Talbot,*
Mike Lawrence
PHOTOGRAPHER *John Dawson*

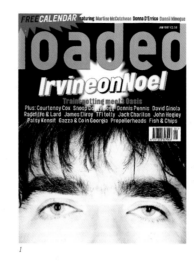

loaded

erection

While others dish up paltry domes and ferris wheels, loaded presents its bold vision for the millennium. Two enormous birds and a fat bloke with a pint glass astride the capital...✈

story by MICHAEL HOLDEN & JON LINK photos by IAN McKELL
architectural drawings by PATRICK McKINNEY

loaded · 157

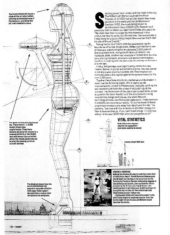

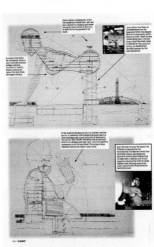

Jan. 1997

ART DIRECTOR   Jon Link
DESIGNER   Jon Link
PHOTOGRAPHER   Iain McKell
TECHNICAL DRAWINGS   Patrick McKinney

SKIN TWO

1 Vol. 18 1996
2 Vol. 20 1996

EDITOR Tim Woodward
ART DIRECTOR Tony Mitchell
DESIGNER Tony Mitchell
PHOTOGRAPHERS 1 Kevin Davies,
2 Nic Marchant
POSTSCRIPT Action Graphics Ltd.
PUBLISHER Tim Woodward Publishing Ltd.

UK

1 2

SOLE POWER

What is it about shoes that makes us go
weak at the knees? MICHELLE OLLEY
extolls the virtues of sexual heeling.
Stiletto life by KEVIN DAVIES

> 'High heels after all
> are slut pumps. Naughty
> boys and girls in high
> heels deserve what they
> get, don't you think?

POOLING TALENT
RUBBER FASHION IN THE SWIM · A SKIN TWO PHOTO SPLASH BY JOLA

A FINE MESH

The rise and fall of hosiery charted by
TONY MITCHELL, a man for whom luxury is
often opaque. Sheer fantasy: KEVIN DAVIES

> They were unbelievably
> sensual to wear and to
> touch. Women would just
> sit there, stroking their
> legs in wonderment

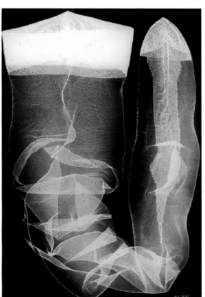

POOLING
TALENT
FROM PREVIOUS PAGE

THE CLOTHES

THE CREDITS

WOMEN MEN

Vol. 15 1994

PHOTOGRAPHER *Kevin Davies*

Vol. 18 1995

PHOTOGRAPHER *Jola*

KEVIN DAVIES

DAVIES & DAVIES

60/SKIN TWO

SKIN TWO/61

1

HOUSK RANDALL

DEREK RIDGERS

TIM WOODWARD

SHINJI YAMAZAKI

2

3

1	**Vol. 20 1996**	2	**Vol. 20 1996**	3	**Vol. 20 1996**
PHOTOGRAPHERS	Kevin Davies, Davies & Davies	PHOTOGRAPHERS	Housk Randall, Derek Ridgers	PHOTOGRAPHERS	Tim Woodward, Shinji Yamazaki

sQueeze

1 Vol. 4 Jun.1996
2 Vol. 5 Aug./Sep. 1996
3 Vol. 6 Oct./Nov. 1996
4 Vol. 1 Dec./Jan. 1996-97
5 Vol. 2 Feb./Mar. 1997

EDITORS   1,3,5 Kees de Kruiff,
                 2 Ruud van der Peijl,
                 4 Hans Blommaert
ART DIRECTORS   1 Anton van Vliet,
                 2,3,4,5 Jacques van Schie
DESIGNERS   1 Jacques van Schie,
                 2,3,4,5 Sylke Bosch
PHOTOGRAPHERS   1,4 Lenny Oosterwijk,
                 2 Maurice Scheltens,
                 3,5 José Costa
PUBLISHER   Maximum Media BV
                 Netherlands

1

2

3

4

5

Arrogantie van ...Cody

De Arrogantie van ...Cody

Vol. 4 Jun. 1996

EDITOR   *Petra Smulders*
ART DIRECTOR *Jacques van Schie*
DESIGNER   *Sylke Bosch*
PHOTOGRAPHER *Cody*

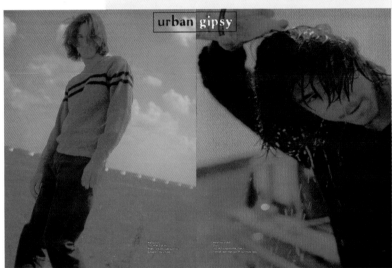

Vol. 6 Oct./Nov. 1996

EDITOR *Kees de Kruiff*
ART DIRECTOR *Jacques van Schie*
DESIGNER *Sylke Bosch*
PHOTOGRAPHER *Paul Posse*

BLUNT

1	**Vol. 8 1996**
2	**Vol. 9 1996**
3	**Vol. 10 1996**
4	**Vol. 11 1996**
5	**Vol. 12 1996**
6	**Vol. 13 1996**

EDITOR   *Marc McKee*
ART DIRECTORS *1,2,3,4 Natas Kaupas,*
              5,6 Jeff Tremaine
DESIGNERS   *1,2,3,4 Natas Kaupas,*
              5,6 Jeff Tremaine
PHOTOGRAPHERS *1,4,6 Rob "Whitey" McConnaughy,*
              2 Justin Hostynek,
              3,5 Jody Morris
PUBLISHER   *Dickhouse Publishing Group, Inc.*
              USA

1

2

issue nine
CONTENTS

blunt

Vol. 9 1996

ART DIRECTOR *Natas Kaupas*
DESIGNER   *Natas Kaupas*
PHOTOGRAPHER *Nico Achtipes*

Vol. 10 1996

ART DIRECTOR *Natas Kaupas*
DESIGNER   *Jeff Tremaine*
PHOTOGRAPHER *Justin Hostynek*
ILLUSTRATOR   *Dave Carnie*

	7	**Vol. 10 1996**
ART DIRECTOR		*Natas Kaupas*
DESIGNER		*Natas Kaupas*
PHOTOGRAPHER		*Jody Morris*

	9	**Vol. 12 1996**
ART DIRECTOR		*Jeff Tremaine*
DESIGNER		*Jeff Tremaine*
PHOTOGRAPHER		*Rick Kosick*

	8	**Vol. 11 1996**
ART DIRECTOR		*Natas Kaupas*
DESIGNER		*Natas Kaupas*
PHOTOGRAPHER		*Rob "Whitey" McConnaughy*

	10	**Vol. 13 1996**
ART DIRECTOR		*Jeff Tremaine*
PHOTOGRAPHER		*Rob "Whitey" McConnaughy*
ILLUSTRATOR		*Sean Cliver*

BIG BROTHER

EDITOR *Marc McKee*
ART DIRECTOR *Jeff Tremaine*
DESIGNERS *Jeff Tremaine,*
5 Marc McKee
TYPOGRAPHER *Jeff Tremaine*
PHOTOGRAPHERS *1 Tobin Yelland,*
2 Rick Kosick,
3 Mike Ballard,
4 Dimitry Elyashkevich,
6 Daniel Sturt
ILLUSTRATOR *5 Marc McKee*
PUBLISHER *Dickhouse Publishing Group, Inc.*
USA

1

7

8

9

7 **Vol. 23 1996**
PHOTOGRAPHER *Dimitry Elyashkevich*

9 **Vol. 22 1996**
PHOTOGRAPHER *Rick Kosick*

8 **Vol. 23 1996**
PHOTOGRAPHER *Mike Ballard*

10 **Vol. 22 1996**
PHOTOGRAPHER *Dave Carnie*

Moses Itkonen

My boy Moses was an underdog from the street. He couldn't quite get the respect he deserved skating, so he turned to alternative means such as destroying limousines, Mercedes, BMWs, and beating up security guards for attention from his peers. Then, once he had everyones attention, he used this new found fame to show everyone exactly what he had to offer. If you've had the chance to see Moses skate you know he is a machine and can do anything he puts his mind to, regardless what he's skating, street or vert. Hes now an irreplaceable member of the Red Dragons and a valuable member of the skateboard world.

–Sluggo

"This whole interview thing is pretty crazy cause I don't even think I'm that crazy of a person to where people would want to read about me. Maybe they would, I don't know. I'm not gonna sit here and think about what I should say to people or whatever. All I'm fuckin doin' right now is skating and partying, that's all my life consists of. I'm not even into doing anything with my life. I don't even care. That's all I've ever done and that's all I plan on doing the rest of my life. I'm not even lookin toward the future, whatsoever. I'm just livin' day by day and doin' my thing and whatever happens, happens.

1 **Vol. 20 1996**
PHOTOGRAPHER *Tobin Yelland*

2 **Vol. 20 1996**
PHOTOGRAPHER *Rick Kosick*

3 **Vol. 24 1997**
PHOTOGRAPHER *Dimitry Elyashkevich*

eternity
1 **Vol. 10 Jan. 1997**
2 **Vol. 11 Feb. 1997**

EDITOR *Eternity Management*
ART DIRECTOR *Eternity Management*
DESIGNER *Eternity Management*
PHOTOGRAPHERS 1 *D. Kingsley*,
1 *Gary Clarke*,
1 *Alex Fisher*
PUBLISHER *Eternity Management Ltd.*

UK

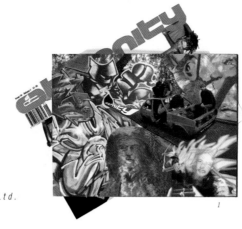

2

Vol. 10 Jan. 1997

PHOTOGRAPHER
Morpheus Productions

Vol. 10 Jan. 1997

Vol. 10 Jan. 1997

Vol. 11 Feb. 1997

PHOTOGRAPHER
Kristin Scott

index of submittors

MAGAZINE TITLE

PUBLISHER / SUBMITTOR

Art Director & Designer
Douglas Gordon

Editors
Kaoru Yamashita / Maya Kishida

Photographer
Kuniharu Fujimoto

Translators
Douglas Allsopp / Setsuko Noguchi

Typesetter
Yutaka Hasegawa

Publisher
Shingo Miyoshi

1997年9月17日初版第1刷発行

発行所　ピエ・ブックス

〒170 東京都豊島区駒込4-14-6 ビラフェニックス301

編集　TEL:03-3949-5010 FAX:03-3949-5650

営業　TEL:03-3940-8302 FAX:03-3576-7361

e-mail: piebooks@bekkoame.or.jp

©1997 P・I・E BOOKS

Printed in Singapore

本書の収録内容の無断転載、複写、引用等を禁じます。

落丁、乱丁はお取り替え致します。

ISBN4-89444-046-6 C3070

CORPORATE IMAGE DESIGN
世界の業種別ＣＩ・ロゴマーク
Pages: 336 (272 in Color) ￥16,000
An effective logo is the key to brand or company recognition. This sourcebook of total CI design introduces pieces created for a wide range of businesses - from boutiques to multinationals - and features hundreds of design concepts and applications.

POSTER GRAPHICS Vol. 2
好評！業種別世界のポスター集大成、第２弾
Pages: 256 (192 in Color) ￥17,000
700 posters from the top creators in Japan and abroad are showcased in this book - classified by business. This invaluable reference makes it easy to compare design trends among various industries and corporations.

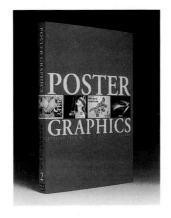

BROCHURE & PAMPHLET COLLECTION Vol. 4
好評！業種別カタログ・コレクション、第４弾
Pages: 224 (Full Color) ￥16,000
The fourth volume in our popular "Brochure & Pamphlet" series. Twelve types of businesses are represented through artwork that really sells. This book conveys a sense of what's happening right now in the catalog design scene. A must for all creators.

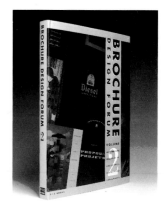

BROCHURE DESIGN FORUM Vol. 2
世界の最新カタログ・コレクション
Pages: 224 (176 in Color) ￥16,000
A special edition of our "Brochure & Pamphlet Collection" featuring 250 choice pieces that represent 70 types of businesses and are classified by business for handy reference. A compendium of the design scene at a glance.

A CATALOGUE AND PAMPHLET COLLECTION
業種別商品カタログ特集／ソフトカバー
Pages: 224 (Full Color) ￥3,800
A collection of the world's most outstanding brochures,catalogs and leaflets classified by industry such as fashion, restaurants, music, interiors and sports goods.Presenting each piece in detail from cover to inside. This title is an indispensable sourcebook for all graphic designers and CI professionals.

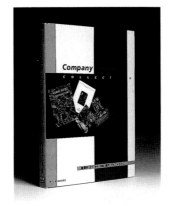

COMPANY BROCHURE COLLECTION
業種別（会社・学校・施設）案内グラフィックス
Pages: 224 (192 in Color) ￥16,000
A rare selection of brochures and catalogs ranging from admission manuals for colleges and universities, to amusement facility and hotel guidebooks, to corporate and organization profiles. The entries are classified by industry for easy reference.

COMPANY BROCHURE COLLECTION Vol. 2
業種別会社案内グラフィックス　第２弾！
Pages: 224 (Full Color) ￥16,000
Showing imaginative layouts that present information clearly in limited space,and design that effectively enhances corporate identity,this volume will prove to be an essential source book for graphic design work of the future.

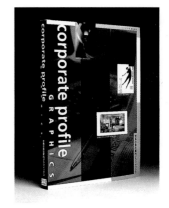

CORPORATE PROFILE GRAPHICS
世界の会社案内グラフィックス
Pages: 224 (Full Color) ￥16,000
A new version of our popular "Brochure and Pamphlet Collection" series featuring 200 carefully selected catalogs from around the world. A substantial variety of school brochures, company profiles and facility information is offered.

CREATIVE FLYER GRAPHICS Vol. 2
世界のフライヤーデザイン傑作選
Pages: 224 (Full Color) ￥16,000
A pack of some 600 flyers and leaflets incorporating information from a variety of events including exhibitions, movies, plays, concerts, live entertainment and club events, as well as foods, cosmetics, electrical merchandise and travel packages.

EVENT FLYER GRAPHICS
世界のイベントフライヤー・コレクション
Pages: 224 (Full Color) ￥16,000
Here's a special selection zooming in on flyers promoting events. This upbeat selection covers wide-ranging music events,as well as movies,exhibitions and the performing arts.

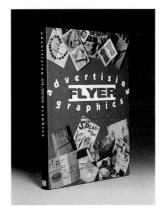

ADVERTISING FLYER GRAPHICS
衣・食・住・遊の商品チラシ特集
Pages: 224 (Full Color) ￥16,000
The eye-catching flyers selected for this new collection represent a broad spectrum of businesses,and are presented in a loose classification covering four essential areas of modern lifestyles: fashion,dining,home and leisure.

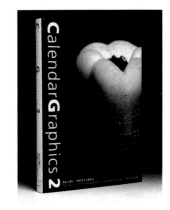

CALENDAR GRAPHICS Vol. 2
好評カレンダー・デザイン集の決定版、第２弾
Pages: 224 (192 in Color) ￥16,000
The second volume of our popular "Calendar Graphics" features designs from about 250 1994 and 1995 calendars from around the world. A rare collection including those on the market as well as exclusive corporate PR calendars.

DIAGRAM GRAPHICS Vol. 2
世界のダイアグラム・デザインの集大成
Pages: 224 (192 in Color)　￥16,000
The unsurpassed second volume in our "Diagram Graphics" series is now complete, thanks to cooperation from artists around the world. It features graphs, charts and maps created for various media.

NEW TYPO GRAPHICS
世界の最新タイポグラフィ・コレクション
Pages: 224 (192 in Color)　￥16,000
Uncompromising in its approach to typographic design, this collection includes 350 samples of only the very finest works available. This special collection is a compendium of all that is exciting along the leading edge of typographic creativity today.

1, 2 & 3 COLOR GRAPHICS
1·2·3 色グラフィックス
Pages: 208 (Full Color)　￥16,000
Featured here are outstanding graphics in limited colors. See about 300 samples of 1,2 & 3-color artwork that are so expressive they often surpass the impact of full four-color reproductions. This is a very important book that will expand the possibilities of your design work in the future.

1, 2 & 3 COLOR GRAPHICS Vol. 2
1·2·3 色グラフィックス、第 2 弾
Pages: 224 (Full Color)　￥16,000
Even more ambitious in scale than the first volume, this second collection of graphics displays the unique talents of graphic designers who work with limited colors. An essential reference guide to effective, low-cost designing.

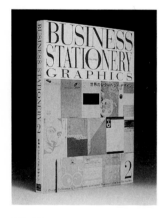

BUSINESS STATIONERY GRAPHICS Vol. 2
世界のレターヘッド・コレクション、第2弾
Pages: 224 (176 in Color)　￥16,000
The second volume in our popular "Business Stationery Graphics" series. This publication focuses on letterheads, envelopes and business cards, all classified by business. Our collection will serve artists and business people well.

BUSINESS CARD GRAPHICS Vol. 1 / Soft Jacket
世界の名刺コレクション／ソフトカバー
Pages: 224 (160 in Color)　￥3,800
First impressions of an individual or company are often shaped by their business cards. The 1,200 corporate and personal-use business cards shown here illustrate the design strategies of 500 top Japanese, American and European designers. PIE's most popular book.

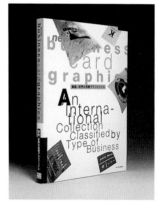

NEW BUSINESS CARD GRAPHICS
最新版！ビジネスカード グラフィックス
Pages: 224(Full Color　￥16,000
A selection of 900 samples representing the works of top designers worldwide. Covering the broadest spectrum of business categories, this selection of the world's best business cards ranges from the trendiest to the most classy and includes highly original examples along the way.

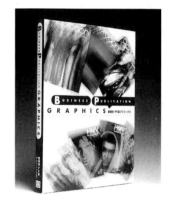

BUSINESS PUBLICATION GRAPHICS
業種別企業ＰＲ誌・フリーペーパーの集大成！
Pages: 224 (Full Color)　￥16,000
This comprehensive graphic book introduces business publications created for a variety of business needs, including promotions from boutiques and department stores, exclusive clubs, local communities and company newsletters.

POSTCARD GRAPHICS Vol. 4
世界の業種別ポストカード・コレクション
Pages: 224 (192 in Color)　￥16,000
Our popular "Postcard Graphics" series has been revamped for "Postcard Graphics Vol. 4." This first volume of the new version showcases approximately 1,000 pieces ranging from direct mailers to private greeting cards, selected from the best around the world.

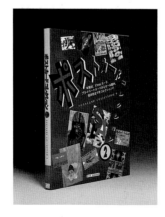

POSTCARD COLLECTION Vol. 2
ポストカードコレクション／ソフトカバー
Pages: 230 (Full Color)　￥3,800
Welcome to the colorful world of postcards with 1200 postcards created by artists from all over the world classified according to the business of the client.

TRAVEL & LEISURE GRAPHICS
ホテル＆旅行 案内 グラフィックス
Pages: 224 (Full Color)　￥16,000
A giant collection of some 400 pamphlets, posters and direct mailings exclusively delivered for hotels, inns, resort tours and amusement facilities.

SPECIAL EVENT GRAPHICS
世界のイベント・グラフィックス
Pages: 224 (192 in Color)　￥16,000
A showcase for event graphics, introducing leaflets for exhibitions, fashion shows, all sorts of sales promotional campaigns, posters, premiums and actual installation scenes from events around the world. An invaluable and inspirational resource book, unique in the world of graphic publishing.

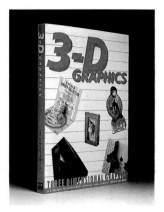

3-D GRAPHICS
3Dグラフィックスの大百科
Pages: 224 (192 in Color) ￥16,000
350 works that demonstrate some of the finest examples of 3-D graphic methods, including DMs, catalogs, posters, POPs and more. The volume is a virtual encyclopedia of 3-D graphics.

PROMOTIONAL GREETING CARDS
ADVERTISING GREETING CARDS Vol. 4
(English Title)
厳選された世界の案内状＆DM
Pages: 224 (Full Color) ￥16,000
A total of 500 examples of cards from designers around the world. A whole spectrum of stylish and inspirational cards, are classified by function for easy reference.

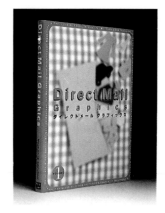

DIRECT MAIL GRAPHICS Vol. 1
衣・食・住のセールスDM特集
Pages: 224 (Full Color) ￥16,000
The long-awaited design collection featuring direct mailers with outstanding sales impact and quality design. 350 of the best pieces, classified into 100 business categories. A veritable textbook of current direct-marketing design.

DIRECT MAIL GRAPHICS Vol. 2
好評！衣・食・住のセールスDM特集！ 第2弾
Pages: 224 (Full Color) ￥16,000
The second volume in our extremely popular "Direct Mail Graphics" series features a whole range of direct mailers for various purposes; from commercial announcements to seasonal greetings and are also classified by industry.

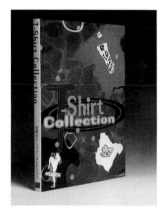

T-SHIRT GRAPHICS / Soft Jacket
世界のTシャツ・コレクション／ソフトカバー
Pages: 224 (192 in Color) ￥3,800
This stunning showcase publication features about 700 T-shirts collected from the major international design centers. Includes various promotional shirts and fabulous designs from the fashion world and sporting-goods manufacturers as well. This eagerly awaited publication has arrived at just the right time.

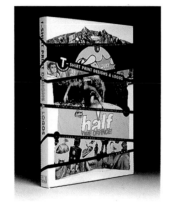

T-SHIRT PRINT DESIGNS & LOGOS
世界のTシャツ・プリント デザイン＆ロゴ
Pages: 224 (192 in Color) ￥16,000
Second volume of our popular "T-shirt Graphics" series. In this publication, 800 designs for T-shirt graphics, including many trademarks and logotypes are showcased. The world's top designers in the field are featured.

The Paris Collections / INVITATION CARDS
パリ・コレクションの招待状グラフィックス
Pages: 176 (Full Color) ￥13,800
This book features 400 announcements for and invitations to the Paris Collections, produced by the world's top names in fashion over the past 10 years. A treasure trove of ideas and pure fun to browse through.

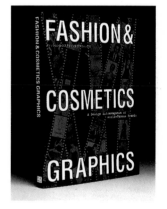

FASHION & COSMETICS GRAPHICS
ファッション＆コスメティック・グラフィックス
Pages: 208 (Full Color) ￥16,000
A collection of promotional graphics from around the world produced for apparel, accessory and cosmetic brands at the avant-garde of the fashion industry. 40 brands featured in this book point the way toward future trends in advertising.

SPORTS GRAPHICS / Soft Jacket
世界のスポーツグッズ・コレクション／ソフトカバー
Pages: 224 (192 in Color) ￥3,800
A collection of 1,000 bold sporting-goods graphic works from all over the world. A wide variety of goods are shown, including uniforms, bags, shoes and other gear. Covers all sorts of sports: basketball, skiing, surfing and many, many more.

LABELS AND TAGS COLLECTION Vol. 1 / Soft Jacket
ラベル＆タグ・コレクション／ソフトカバー
Pages: 224 (192 in Color) ￥3,800
Nowhere is brand recognition more important than in Japan. Here is a collection of 1,600 labels and tags from Japan's 450 top fashion names with page after page of women's and men's clothing and sportswear designs.

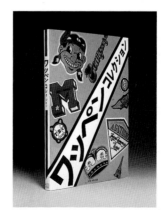

INSIGNIA COLLECTION
ワッペン＆エンブレム・コレクション／ソフトカバー
Pages: 224 (Full Color) ￥3,800
Over 3000 designs were scrutinized for this collection of 1000 outstanding emblems and embroidered motifs that are visually exciting, make innovative use of materials and compliment the fashions with which they are worn.

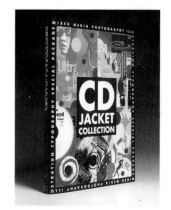

CD JACKET COLLECTION
世界のCDジャケット・コレクション／ソフトカバー
Pages: 224 (192 in Color) ￥3,800
Featuring 700 of the world's most imaginative CD and LP covers from all musical genres, this is a must-have book for all design and music professionals.

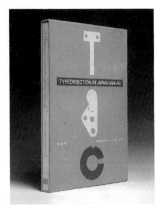

TYPO-DIRECTION IN JAPAN Vol. 6
年鑑 日本のタイポディレクション '94-'95
Pages: 250 (Full Color) ¥17,000
This book features the finest work from the international competition of graphic design in Japan. The sixth volume of our popular yearbook series is edited by the TOKYO TYPE DIRECTORS CLUB with the participation of master designers worldwide.

THE TOKYO TYPEDIRECTORS CLUB ANNUAL 1995-96
TDC 年鑑95-96
Pages: 250 (Full Color) ¥17,000
A follow-up publication to Japan's only international graphic design competition. Featuring 650 typographic artworks selected by THE TOKYO TYPEDIRECTORS CLUB, this book provides a window on the latest typographic design concepts worldwide.

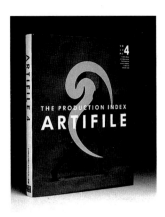

The Production Index ARTIFILE Vol. 4
活躍中！広告プロダクション年鑑、第4弾
Pages: 224 (Full Color) ¥12,500
The fourth volume in our "Production Index Artifile" series features vigorously selected yearly artworks from 107 outstanding production companies and artists in Japan. An invaluable source book of the current design forefronts portraying their policies and backgrounds.

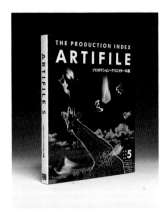

The Production Index ARTIFILE Vol.5
最新版プロダクション・クリエーター年鑑
Pages: 224(Full Color) ¥12,500
ARTIFILE 5 features artwork from a total of 100 top Japanese production companies and designers, along with company data and messages from the creators. An invaluable information source for anyone who needs to keep up with the latest developments in the graphic scene.

SEASONAL CAMPAIGN GRAPHICS
デパート・ショップのキャンペーン広告特集
Pages: 224 (Full Color) ¥16,000
A spirited collection of quality graphics for sales campaigns planned around the four seasons and Christmas, St. Valentines Day and the Japanese gift-giving seasons, as well as for store openings, anniversaries, and similar events.

SHOPPING BAG GRAPHICS
世界の最新ショッピング・バッグデザイン集
Pages: 224 (Full Color) ¥16,000
Over 500 samples of the latest and best of the world's shopping bag design from a wide selection of retail businesses! This volume features a selection of shopping bags originating in Tokyo, NY, LA, London, Paris, Milan and other major cities worldwide, and presented here in a useful business classification.

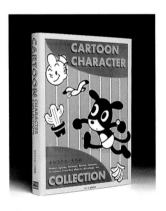

CARTOON CHARACTER COLLECTION
5500種のキャラクターデザイン大百科
Pages: 480 (B&W) ¥9,800
A total of 5,500 cartoons and illustrations from some of the most successful illustrations in the industry have been carefully selected for this giant, new collection. The illustrations included are classified by animals, figures, vehicles, etc, for easy reference.

カタログ・新刊のご案内について
総合カタログ、新刊案内をご希望の方は、はさみ込みのアンケートはがきを
ご返送いただくか、90円切手同封の上、ピエ・ブックス宛お申し込み下さい。

CATALOGUES ET INFORMATIONS SUR LES NOUVELLES PUBLICATIONS
Si vous désirez recevoir un exemplaire gratuit de notre catalogue général ou des détails sur nos nouvelles publications, veuillez compléter la carte réponse incluse et nous la retourner par courrierou par fax.

CATALOGS and INFORMATION ON NEW PUBLICATIONS
If you would like to receive a free copy of our general catalog or details of our new publications, please fill out the enclosed postcard and return it to us by mail or fax.

CATALOGE und INFORMATIONEN ÜBER NEUE TITLE
Wenn Sie unseren Gesamtkatalog oder Detailinformationen über unsere neuen Titel wünschen, fullen Sie bitte die beigefügte Postkarte aus und schicken Sie sie uns per Post oder Fax.

ピエ・ブックス
〒170 東京都豊島区駒込 4-14-6-301
TEL: 03-3940-8302 FAX: 03-3576-7361

P·I·E BOOKS
#301, 4-14-6, Komagome, Toshima-ku, Tokyo 170 JAPAN
TEL: 813-3940-8302 FAX: 813-3576-7361